W9-BWD-141

An Introduction to the Poetry of YVOR WINTERS

An Introduction to the Poetry of YVOR WINTERS

Elizabeth Isaacs

SWALLOW PRESS
OHIO UNIVERSITY PRESS
Chicago Athens, Ohio London

Library of Congress Cataloging in Publication Data

Isaacs, Elizabeth, 1917-
An introduction to the poetry of Yvor Winters.
Bibliography: p.
1. Winters, Yvor, 1900-1968—Poetic works.
I. Title.
PS3545.1765Z73 811′.52 80-17013
ISBN 0-8040-0353-X

Printed in the United States of America

For Alan Swallow
and Janet Lewis

Table of Contents

PREFACE

"The Brink of Darkness"

This book was suggested to me by Alan Swallow in the spring of 1965. He had come as visiting lecturer and consultant for the English Department of Cornell College, and we were sitting around my fireside relaxing after a long day of formal appearances. The talk turned to young unknown writers and Swallow's constant willingness over the years to give them a chance through his press. He recounted several anecdotes from his teaching and publishing career, and Cornell's young poet Robert Dana and I listened with great interest. Suddenly Swallow turned to me and said, "I want a book on Yvor Winters. He's one of the most important writers I've ever published. His poetry's been neglected too long. Why not write this book for me—something like your Frost book?" Affectionately calling Winters by his first name, Swallow then added, "Whoever does do it will have to be brave enough to interview Arthur. Don't be put off by him when you go!"

Alan Swallow's assumption that I would ever go seemed farfetched to me that spring night. But I was more and more conscious of this necessity as I read Winters at the Newberry Library the next summer. When I talked to his Stanford colleagues at the winter MLA, they told me he was dying of a throat malignancy and that my interview—if it were ever to take place—would have to be soon. Still feeling presumptuous, I risked a request for such an interview in the summer of 1967 through Robert Dana, who called on Winters while studying in California. (After all, Dana was a young poet then about the age Winters had been when Swallow first published him; he couldn't refuse *him*.) His visit resulted in Winters writing me a characteristically blunt note, which read, in irregular typescript:

> Dear Miss Isaacs,
> Last December I underwent radical surgery for cancer on the side of my neck. I am severely and painfully crippled. It causes me a great deal of pain to type this note. You cannot expect me to correspond with you about your book. If you care to call on me for 30 minutes or less, I shall be glad to see you, but I will not explain my work to you. Please phone before calling; do not phone after 8:00 PM.
>
> Best wishes,
> Yvor Winters

I was naturally put off by the tone of the note, and except for the "Best Wishes" at the end, I would have retired from the scene at that point. But somehow a combination of curiosity, naïveté, and a sudden sense of direction from the recent reading I had done led me across country to his door within a month. I telephoned from San Francisco on the appointed day and was told by the very cordial Janet Lewis Winters how to reach their home in Los Altos. She had remembered my name, offered to pick me up at the bus stop, and, before we reached the house, she had briefed me about her husband's condition, warning me that he could not speak aloud. We drove up to a small Spanish-style house set off to itself behind a high wood fence which bore on its gate the formidable sign, "Keep Out: BULLDOG!" In a state of trepidation I entered behind her, trying to recall my carefully-prepared interview questions.

She led me to a small, dim bed-sitting room where Mr. Winters reclined on a couch. He was very thin, dressed in grey slacks and a dark plaid shirt, with his massive grey head held rigid in pain on the pillow. But even thus incapacitated he reflected immediately a sense of calm strength and control. There seemed the stability and permanence of stone about him; before one word was spoken he looked at me for a long time, and I suddenly understood why I had come and what I must do. The grey stone shadow of a man waved me to a chair beside the bed and without wasting time for introductions whispered hoarsely to me, "How do you see me?"

For precisely twenty-five minutes it was I who talked. He listened carefully, painfully, politely, and at the end of my recital gave me a few random suggestions about his associates who might be helpful with added material. His wife, ever attentive to his unspoken need, supplied words and voice when his failed. Then there was another long silence. Never once had he registered approval or disapproval of my project or my plans for developing it. I imagined he had smiled a bit awkwardly when I said I'd admired him for "promulgating heresies." Most of the time his bearded face had been completely impassive, grey and permanent in my memory. I had no opportunity to ask *my* carefully formulated thirty questions. At the end of the half-hour he rose painfully from the couch, retired to the next room, and returned with an autographed copy of his *Early Poems*, which had just come out. He bowed, presented it, shook my hand formally, said "Good luck," and ordered Mrs. Winters to take me back to the bus stop. Then he lay down, folded his hands, and closed his eyes.

We went out a rear door into the warm desert garden. There was the scent of decayed and drying fruit in the heavy, still air. Nothing was green; nothing moved.

"Would it amuse you to see our dog and orchard?" Janet Lewis Winters asked cordially. I was suddenly grateful for her understanding of the tension of that half-hour and her assistance in helping me break it. She told me of her husband's lifelong interest in breeding and training Airedales; showed me their "old-age dog, Rocksy," the huge English bulldog whose great vitality was an ironic contrast to the frailty of his shadowy master within; and led me through their grove, which Winters had delighted in filling with "classical trees." "He liked to sit out here to rest or write," she said quietly. Here was an exotic variety admired by their friend Marianne Moore. "The leaves look like little mice," she said, as she led me from fig, to persimmon, to loquat, to fevola. I felt as though I were absorbing with the heat that powerful personality withering within who had lived so completely here in "Time and the Garden." This thin woman in the blue dress was calmly facing the "dead living and the living dead."

As she drove me back past Stanford, where Winters had been mentor for so many young writers, we talked of books and writing. She told me of his devotion to his students and their faithfulness to him in his illness. She asked if Robert Frost had ever seen my book about him before his death, and I was glad to be able to say that he had received it in the final weeks of his life. Her last words to me as I got out of the little car into the sunshine were, "That must have given him a touch of immortality." As I closed the car door, I sensed her commission to complete this book; and I knew that she knew that I knew.

If Yvor Winters stood on the final "brink of darkness" in 1967, it was not the first time he had looked over the edge of the abyss. His short story of that title carries this prefatory comment: "The story is a study of the hypothetical possibility of a hostile, supernatural world and of the effect on the perceptions of a consideration of this possibility."[1]

The story relates in the first person an experience Winters had during his stay in the Western mountains, where he had gone to teach and recuperate from tuberculosis in the early twenties. He lived alone in a cold, bare, upstairs room in which his dogs and his glowing stove were his only live companions. As the cold descended, he was aware of disturbing, uncentered feelings, as though he were possessed by some demon. Finally even his trained dogs ran away, and he was left alone with a heightened perception of imminent death all around him. For days he fought hallucinations of stepping over the brink of the rational universe into an immoral, inimical, and irrational eternity. His dogs finally returned, injured in their battle with the wild animals they had gone to join. Winters nursed them back to health almost against their will, and at the same time returned to his own sanity. "I had begun to recover the limits of my old identity . . . The invading power I could not identify. I felt it near to me still, but slowly receding." He vowed never to return to that place of terror and moved away.

In the last dark days of his fatal illness, he may again have seen all too clearly the unleashed forces of wilderness that had almost stolen those trained dogs from his control. He had recently edited his early free-verse Imagist poems; he had just completed the last volume of his formalist criticism; and he faced the final brink with the dogs snapping at his heels. The personal and professional struggle of his life may be clearly identified in the metaphor of this allegorical tale.

Yvor Winters spent most of his professional life trying to put the world "in order." In his famous essay called "The Function of Criticism," he wrote, "The professor of poetry must be a poet first ideally. It is not enough to be merely a scholar of the history of poetry."[2] He might then become eventually the professional critic. When Winters died on January 25, 1968, the *New York Times* obituary headlined him as poet-professor-critic. The final irony of this particular sequence would probably have amused and pleased the wry Winters, for the world in general had recognized him in reverse order. That Winters was finally posthumously recognized in the former order is a fitting summary of his hopes for his own career. For him, poetry was the most important of his three pursuits; criticism, the least. "The mind's immortal, but the man is dead," he had written in one of his finest poems.

* * *

This book is primarily concerned with Yvor Winters' poetry. He has been well known for his controversial literary criticism for close to a half-century, but no critic has yet commented on his poetry. Since Winters was poet first and critic second, and since his theory actually grew from his practice, such a volume seems long overdue. The two are actually inseparable, and Winters himself explains their interrelationship in the autobiographical remarks that open *The Early Poems of Yvor Winters*. So it is necessary to include at least a survey of his career as critic insofar as it relates to his poetry.

Like Thomas Hardy, Winters would probably have preferred to be better known for his poetry than his prose. But also like Hardy, he suffered the accidents of history and fate that perversely gave his prose more attention. Literary tempers of both centuries caused this problem for the two writers, and they wrote their poetry for a small, esoteric contemporary audience. Only in recent years has the poetry of Yvor Winters begun to appear in anthologies, and this high literary irony must have given him bitter satisfaction after his own criticism had made a reputation for many a lesser poet. It now seems appropriate to correct the imbalance between minor explications of his poetry and major definitions of his criticism.

Anyone presuming to write on Winters' poetry faces two nearly insurmountable obstacles: Winters' personality, which discouraged amateurs in any field; and Winters' critical finesse, which was indeed professional to the highest degree. However, such a book did need to be written, and he knew it.

He knew it so well that he wrote a set of directives that no critic could miss. He also organized his poems before the end of his life in the careful collation of *The Early Poems* (". . . an authorized edition of my early and experimental work," 1966) and *The Collected Poems* (". . . all I wish to keep," 1952 and 1960). And he warned his future critic, "Any other uncollected material is rubbish." One has the feeling that he wished he could have written this book himself. Whatever his painful visions of this work must have been, he did provide, in an essay called "Problems of Criticism" in *The Anatomy of Nonsense*, a workable plan for it—a plan I have attempted to follow in this book.

Critics today recognize the need for a work on Winters' poetry to supplement the many short assessments in periodicals. From his earliest poems in *Poetry Magazine* in 1920 to his last critical volume—*Forms of Discovery*—in 1967, he has evoked an interested and highly controversial critical following. He was a tough man to tangle with in the press, and his own critical voice—loud and clear when necessary—made more enemies than friends for his writing. But after the personal aspects of these battles have died away, there are still critics and poets who respect him in both capacities and who see him steady and whole. Guy Cardwell: "He was one of the more influential, controversial, and versatile writers of his generation."[3] Denis Donoghue: "Winters is a major critic, one of the few who make the difference."[4] Howard Nemerov: "His is the kind of poetry that is relatively timeless and unaffected by fashion . . . an ancient and continuing art that belongs to life and serves it."[5] Allen Tate: "He is a poet whose moral imagination takes, without didacticism, the didactic mode, striving for precision in language and in verse, for formal elegance."[6] Such accolades indicate the quality and interrelationship of Winters' poetry and criticism.

One feels a certain sense of satisfaction in adding to the overdue recognition of a poet who discovered so many others. Donald Justice has called Winters "a master obscured by history,"[7] and surely he was. As a critic he sought always to exhibit the best poetry; if this meant the work of neglected writers, Winters never hesitated to promote the unrecognized talent for the small, receptive audience. Harriet Monroe had "found" him first in *Poetry*, and it was to her credit that she encouraged him for years with personal assistance. Marianne Moore "mothered" him through many crises with the help of books and advice. He never forgot their early support. He wrote much later of one author's fine poem: "Whether or not it ever *does* acquire its deserved popularity, it is too fine a piece of work to be ignored by the sophisticated adult, whether now or in the future." It is a statement which might as easily have been made of his own poetry. His audacious independence and his impeccable taste made popular acclaim beside the point. In the pure priesthood of his art, he practiced, confident that it would eventually reach its appropriate audience.

Acknowledgments for this book include my thanks to Dean Howard Troyer, Cornell College, for a sabbatical year and a Ford Foundation research grant; to Alan Swallow, Gus Blaisdell, Janet Lewis and Yvor Winters for instigation and encouragement; to Robert Dana and Winifred Van Etten for invaluable criticism of the manuscript, and to Shari Schartman, Production Manager of the Ohio University Press.

PART ONE

"The Badger Diogenes"

To Yvor Winters —

something of a badger Diogenes—
we are indebted technically; and
attached personally, those of us who know him;
are proud of his hostility to falsity;
of his verse reduced to essence;
of a tenacity unintimidated by circumstance,
He does not hesitate to call others foolish,
and we do not shrink from imputations
of folly—at annoying a man to whom
compliments may be uncongenial;
—wise to be foolish when a sense of indebtedness
is too strong to suppress.

—Marianne Moore

Biographical and Critical Backgrounds

The Private Personality of the Poet

Yvor Winters was born October 17, 1900, in Chicago, the son of Harry and Faith Ahnfeldt Winters. He spent a part of his childhood in California and first became interested in poetry at age fourteen in high school. Back in Chicago by the age of nineteen, he used to frequent McClurg's Bookstore for bargains in contemporary poets and issues of *Poetry Magazine*, *Others* and *The Little Review*. In 1917–18, he studied at the University of Chicago where he formed many lasting friendships with other young writers through its Poetry Club: Glenway Westcott, Elizabeth Maddox Ford, and Harriet Monroe. Miss Monroe, as editor of *Poetry Magazine*, took an interest in the talented young student, let him browse in the wide collection of poetry in her office, and published some of his earliest poetry in her columns. Her editorial influence continued through many years of Winters' life. He has written happily of these formative years, and it was from this group that his future wife was to come, though he did not know her there—Janet Lewis, a promising young novelist and poet.

At the end of the autumn quarter 1918, he discovered he had tuberculosis and moved to Santa Fe, where he remained in a sanitarium until late October, 1921. Here he spent his time reading widely and corresponding with Miss Monroe, who found in his poetry "something of a mystic—with that feeling *below* the main feeling that persists in many of his poems. . . "[8] He studied in an indirect way and continued to build the fine collection of poetry he had started in Chicago. He fell into correspondence at this same time with another young poet, Marianne Moore, who was then a librarian at the New York Public Library. She exchanged poems and loaned him books "illegally by mail." At her recommendation, he became an avid student of modern poetry as well as the classics.

After his release from the sanitarium, he taught school for two years: one at a grammar school in Madrid, New Mexico, and one at a high school in Los Cerillos. His subjects ranged from English and French literature through zoology, boxing, and basketball. (He even served as constable for the weekend dances.) He writes movingly in his introduction to *Early Poems* of these lonely years, "I was alway treated with great deference. The miners tipped their hats to me on the streets, the Mexicans addressed me as Maestro, and students as Professor."[9] Here he learned respect for a life of primitive simplicity from which he absorbed both physical and psychic stamina as he recuperated from his critical illness.

By the time he did this first teaching he was already an experienced poet, and many of his early poems show his youthful catholic tastes. He particularly admired Hardy, Bridges, Dickenson, the French Symbolists, the classics, translations from Romance languages, Japanese, and American Indian poets; he later became interested in Valery, Stevens, and W. C. Williams. (These influences are evident in his first two volumes, *The Immobile Wind*, 1921, and the *The Magpie's Shadow*, 1922.) But there was also an original tone that came from his loneliness as he fought a mortal illness in a remote, strange country. His autobiographical sketches tell how he fought this loneliness by writing very personal poetry that made use of every nuance of this barren dry landscape, its primitive strengths and beauties, and its forbidding dangers. The young poet experimented here with the form that seemed most natural for him—free verse with varied cadences and images that he picked up from the lonely sights and sounds of his enforced exile.

In this desert country he felt himself often in a frenzy of self-awareness in a strange universe whose every atom seemed to sensitize his nerves to a pitch of hallucination. The early poetry poignantly dramatizes this self-sense silhouetted against the horizon of the universe's impassivity; he was determined to record every moment in the face of its fatality. Later he described these years in a letter to an old friend as a time ". . . when I was young with no literary friends beyond two or three of my own age and state of ignorance, and when I was forced by ill health and various other circumstances to live in a desert country, remote from books and much of the time from anything approaching civilized society."[10] This early poetry shows a young man clinging to life with a terrified, defiant stare; a sense of its wonder and its perils; a determination not to lose one moment of its sensations and its experiences. Even then he seemed full of the horror of death and the pain of history; he began the long struggle that lasted for a half century to fight them and to gain a permanent foothold for himself and other deserving young poets. Determined to endure and to prevail, he developed an intense concentration of his sense impressions and a thick protective shield.

He sent many of his original poems from these years to his old friend and editor Harriet Monroe, and she introduced them in *Poetry* magazine in 1920:

> Mr. Yvor Winters of Chicago was for a time a member of The Poetry Club of The University of Chicago. At present he is sojourning in Santa Fe . . . These poems show the discipline of deserts and mountains, the art of primitive races. They work with studious insistence, their closely packed thoughts in rhythms of original and delicate beauty. Their effect has an ardor of youth in a new and personal tone.[11]

(Twenty-five years later she wrote proudly in those same editorial columns: "Yvor Winters of Los Altos has earned a high reputation as poet and critic since his first appearance here in 1920.")

He continued graduate study along with his teaching in the West and finally received a B.A. and an M.A. in Romance languages with a minor in Latin from the University of Colorado in 1925. Here he became interested in Old French, Old Spanish, and Italian and worked on many translations from these languages. From 1925 to 1927, he taught as instructor in French and Spanish at the University of Idaho in Moscow, where he also learned Old Portuguese, studied the poetry of the English Renaissance and the French Symbolists, and began to read the prose of Flaubert and Proust. When he later decided to enroll as a graduate student at Stanford, classical and modern foreign literatures were actually more familiar to him than the English-American tradition; their influences are apparent in his early poems. He had already developed the westerner's mistrust of eastern universities, and in retrospect he remarked rather proudly that he had spent his formative years not in Paris or on the east coast, but in the western wilderness with books rather than travel. As a graduate student he began a systematic study of the history of English-American literatures and began to develop the appreciation of Renaissance poetry that was to influence his writing for years to come.

In June of 1926 he married Janet Lewis in Santa Fe, where they had met when she, too, came from Chicago for her health. The following summer they went to California and Winters entered Stanford in the autumn of 1927. The influence of his wife on his life and poetry was immeasurable. She is herself a fine poet and novelist, and her personality seems to have been the ideal complement to his throughout the forty years of their married life. Ever patient, calm, sensitive, and reserved, she provided the necessary counterbalance for his own extremes of temperament. His deep love for her is evident in many of his poems: "Earthbound," "Love Poem," "The Marriage," and "Before Disaster." At the conclusion of his last book of criticism he pays her high professional praise as fellow poet: ". . . if I may be forgiven for saying so," he writes with characteristic reserve and formality.[12] In this same article he explicates her fine poem "The Gift of Herbs," and his remarks attest to the satisfaction and comfort that their domestic life brought to him. She seems to have been one of the few sources of real peace in his turbulent inner life.

This high sensitivity that developed early in his youth shows in all of his family relationships and is reflected in his poetry. He writes of these personal ties sparingly and somewhat obliquely but with the intensity and control of great passion and devotion. He was always one to sense the underlying drama of a moment of inconsequence and to spin it into a fine mystic permanence. In all of his family poems there is often the frustration of broken ends and incompleteness, but a constant dedication to the few people close to him. Only in his poetry about his wife is there any sense of continuing fulfillment. ("For My Father's Grace," "To My Infant Daughter," "Prayer for My Son," "Before Disaster," "The Cremation," "At the San Francisco Airport," etc.)

Winters became a full-time instructor at Stanford in 1928, completed his doctorate there in 1934, and continued as both poet and professor for over forty years. His advancement from student to professor was matched at the same time by a shift in his poetic method: from free-verse Imagist style to more traditional forms and meters. He changed his method, explored more formal patterns, and developed certain principles resulting from practice. "At this time I found myself unable to write as I wished, and I therefore changed my method,"[13] he says candidly. More sure of himself psychically, or at least more controlled, he started the long progression of poetic and critical writings that was to grow between the years of 1928 to 1968 to some twenty books and innumerable essays in periodicals. Although best known for his eight volumes of criticism, he actually wrote and published ten volumes of poetry during this interval and edited two anthologies in a series called *Poets of the Pacific*.

When he became a professor at Stanford, he quite naturally gathered around him a group of young student writers similar to his old Chicago Poetry Club. They met informally with Winters as their leader and called themselves "The Gyroscope Group," after the magazine which Winters founded and edited from 1929 to 1931. It boasted among its subscribers many of the leading literary figures of the day and became one of the most prominent little magazines since the *Transatlantic Review* and *Transition*. The Gyroscope Group was a small but devoted scholarly clique; members were evangelical in their fervent desire to improve their craft according to the *dicta* of their mentor. By this time Winters had turned away from all varieties of "romanticism" and scorned his former Imagist tradition. The group's manifesto was stated in the first issue as that of a cult which had moved toward neoclassicism, approving control and form as opposed to all doctrines of emotional and religious expression. It emphasized moral and intellectual responsibilities, but it attached a particular meaning to "moral"—moral in craft, not in soul. It opposed the "emotional receptiveness" of the modern school whose members, he wrote, "employed despair as a drug and a luxury and therefore may be justly suspected of never having actually experienced it."[14] It denounced the critical obscurantism in contemporary vogue and proposed that the *forms* of art *are* a method, perhaps the only satisfying one, of ordering and evaluating experience. Though the Gyroscope lasted only two years, its effect was germinal in the development of Winters' own poetry and criticism. From this original youthful instructorship at Stanford, Winters developed into a mature, respected literary leader with an international reputation.

His teaching career lasted until his retirement in 1966 from the coveted Albert Guerard Professorship. During those years he managed the Gyroscope Press, on which he printed a volume of his own poetry in 1940 with the proud inscription: "I have printed these poems by hand with my own press. . . " He also edited two volumes of the work of friends and students entitled *Twelve Poets of the Pacific* (1937) and *Poets of the Pacific* (Second Series, 1949). Of this first volume he said, "This group of poets is in no sense an accidental one; they have all been at one time or another my students." He summarized the general common aims of his "school" in the introduction: clarity of expression as opposed to obscurantism, purity and freedom from mannerism in style. The first volume included Howard Baker, J. V. Cunningham, Janet Lewis, and some of his own poems. The second is a sequel including some later students. With typical confidence, he predicts that "some of them will make distinguished names for themselves in the literary field; and at least two of them have already done so."[15] From this "school"—sometimes labelled "cult" by his critics—there eventually emerged a group of young scholars, poets, and teachers who went to other universities and other publishers to promote the cause of clarity and precision.

His students all report that he was a brilliant, incisive teacher with a dry wit and a great sense of fair play in the classroom and in his critical comments on their manuscripts. They were all careful to rise to his defense in later years whenever they felt that any criticism in the press of his own books was unfair. A fine portrait of Professor Winters is painted by his student Judith Roscoe in *Sequoia*, Winter, 1961. She remembered him as "grave, sadly frowning . . . his appearance in general, striking only because it suggests determination, a little impatience, stolidity. His face, though seldom in motion, sometimes breaks into the most arresting of smiles. . . The student eventually comes to see that here is a rational man, a craftsman intent upon morality."[16] One of his most successful student-poets, Ann Stanford, spoke of him at the Academy of American Poets' tribute after Winters' death. She stressed that, contrary to many people's impression of him as a too-severe critic, he was always warm-hearted and kind to his deserving students, always extremely helpful and generous in the criticism of their manuscripts, and meticulous in his pride as lecturer in classes. Several of the poems in his collected volumes are dedicated to his students. He was extremely proud of their successes and very fair in his relationships with them. When he published his special monograph on "The Poetry of J. V. Cunningham"—after his student had been recognized as one of America's leading poets—he was careful to point out that Cunningham had gone beyond his original master, that he had taken new and important steps on his own, and that he should not suffer any guilt by association from Winters' enemies. "He has repeatedly suffered from my label, since I have long been an unpopular critic and poet." And yet at the end of his last volume he said candidly: "I think I have been an excellent teacher; six or seven of my former students are among the best poets of this century; some of these and a few others are distinguished scholars."[17] From another less sensitive man, this might sound like consummate ego. From Winters it is simply a typically direct statement of one of the most important achievements of his lifetime.

His relationships with his academic colleagues at Stanford seem to have been frequently controversial, though he respected the university and most of his department. In characteristic fashion, he took his profession *so* seriously that he felt his achievements gave him license to criticize those who did not come up to his standards of excellence. And he was constantly critical of the "Establishment" whenever it seemed to stifle creativity. At one point in his career when his department chairman told Winters that his reactionary writings were "a disgrace to the department," Winters countered with a magnificent defense of what it means to be *truly* "reactionary."[18] He mistrusted the "yes-men" in academic bureaucracy, and in at least two of his poems he laments the necessary battles that he felt morally bound to wage. "An Ode on the Despoilers of Learning in an American University" criticizes nearsighted administrators ". . . desiring trivial power/ And terror struck within / At their own emptiness." His last poem in the *Collected Poems* speaks wistfully and courageously of his academic stand. He wrote "What was all the talk about?" as he recalled some of the many controversies that arose from his extremely high standards for his department and university.

Yet he was as eager to praise as to blame academe, and he dedicated two fine poems to a respected member of his department whom he considered a truly great teacher: "For the Opening of the William Dinsmore Briggs Room," and "To William Dinsmore Briggs Conducting His Seminar." In the *Function of Criticism* he writes with pride that the university is the intellectual and spiritual center of our world today. "It offers a concrete embodiment, an institutional representation of the most important ideals of humanity; of the belief in absolute truth and the effort to approximate it; of intellectual freedom; of the dignity of man. (I speak of principles, not persons since great men are rare!)" After providing a list of the few really great teachers whom he had known, he concludes: "After a lifetime of teaching, I am convinced that teaching is possible . . . but it must be done by men competent in *all* areas of criticism and poetry."[19] He did not hesitate to call a man a fool in public when he felt an article in the *American Scholar* was a disgrace both to this profession and to Phi Beta Kappa. And he lamented that some men were "merely professors"; for he hoped to claim several important careers. ("Poets perceive at twenty what mere professors may manage to perceive at sixty!")[20]

His training and constant self-education for his profession were indeed awesome and enviable. He could summon examples from the most esoteric ancient languages and literature or from the most contemporary "little magazines" to prove his points, and he seemed actually to savor the sheer mass of his scholarship. He made a minute study of all the genres in literary history and evaluated one against the other. In the last of his many books of criticism he concludes that the poems most congenial to him are the short ones of the English Renaissance and the Post-Symbolist moderns. This book, like all of his previous critical volumes, is a veritable compendium of individual references to obscure *and* well-known poets of *all* periods, as well as to the best-known classics. His was indeed a rare systematic study of literature that laid the fine foundation for his own poetry, his teaching, and his critical essays.

His high standard demanded that "the true teacher must be both aware of poetry *and* criticism." He believed that the ideal university should be the one place where the poet and scholar might cooperate and interchange professions: "I would not go so far as to say that training is a substitute for talent, but I am convinced that the teaching of poets is possible, and that if a man is brilliant it is usually possible to improve him."[21] He had a great respect for general courses such as the history of ideas and literary history, but he cautioned the poet-student against going too far into "mere" scholarship. He found a degree of sophistication among the younger scholars of his time that he had not found in his own contemporaries or in his elders; he was extremely optimistic about the future of the American university and its contribution to the development of poetry. He closed his last book, *Forms of Discovery*, with a tribute to "these university poets who mark a new kind of poetry . . . and deserve very special attention."

There were many who were not included among his fit-though-few students who saw him as a caustic, dour, unfashionable curiosity. For the happy few who were themselves potential poet-scholars, he was more than an eccentric "maestro"; he seemed to have a unique sense of being a patriarchal figure among them. This is reflected in the *ex cathedra* tone of his lectures and his critical writings. Of his second anthology of student writing, he said proudly: "This book seems to me a good one, or I would not trouble myself with it. I believe that it contains a certain few poets who will make distinguished names for themselves."[22]

There is evidence that the teacher-Winters often crept into the writing style of the critic-Winters, and sometimes these intrusions make uncomfortable reading. Having lectured for so many years to note-taking students, he occasionally tends to write with his outline showing. In fact, he sometimes repeats its structure so often that the reader is embarrassed to be led as obviously as though he were a freshman.

"Before examining these poems, one should recall briefly the main outline of English poetry. . ."—and then the teacher-critic gives a thumbnail course in it. Or, "I will now write of the chief Victorians. . ." or, "In conclusion, I have tried to. . . ." The teacher here exacts what he must in an over-pedantic fashion. And yet he may be forgiven these directives when he summarizes his attitude toward the academic world which he respected all of his life:

> It is only, I believe, in the combination of the talents of the poet with the discipline of scholarship that one can hope to produce a really finished critic.[23]

Winters found the posture of the professor a successful stance for this production.

In his essay, "The Poet and the University," he claims that the university man is no more disassociated from real life than the barber or the salesman, and maintains that the materials and activities of the professor-poet are intrinsically more civilized than theirs are. He represented in his own extracurricular life a wide variety of interests, both general and specific, public and private. He served as the municipal chief of civilian defense for Los Altos during the Second World War, with some four hundred men from all walks of life working directly under him in this patriotic effort; he was an active member of groups combatting racial, social, and religious discrimination; and he often used his own poetry to express his feelings in this regard ("White Spiritual," "This is Why the South is Dead"). He called himself a liberal in politics, disavowed the Modern Language Society and Phi Beta Kappa on principle, and considered himself 'an old-fashioned American.' In one of his most outspoken controversies in the press, he wrote several letters concerning his liberal beliefs to answer a reviewer who had accused him of literary fascism, vowing that his highest allegiance was 'only to Absolute Truth.' He went on to defend himself as a man of many secular tastes, interested in dog breeding and gardening, with a wife who worked in the Girl Scouts of America!

One of Winters' most significant public-spirited demonstrations was his two year defense in the public press and in courts of a university workman who had been persecuted by the academic and civic community and prosecuted by a corrupt county political organization. In an article entitled scornfully "*More* Santa Clara Justice," Winters remarked that the attorney general of their state had "the mind of a prune picker." This essay in the *New Republic* was a finely wrought polemic against a negligent society about to condone the death of a "gentle, amiable, innocent man"; Winters took up the cudgels in his behalf with biting poetry and prose. He was always willing to continue a controversy—"Reply with Rejoinder." He did not believe that poets and professors should live in ivory towers. "If one's blessed little immortal soul cannot take a certain amount of roughing around, it is probably not worth preserving anyway! . . . University life is varied, active, serious, and conducive to intellectual growth. It wears one out, but so does life in general!"[24] It was certainly neither escape nor sanctuary for this active spirit who could never let a controversy die without a good fight.

He was devoted to Stanford though he often criticized its "Establishment" in his poetry and his criticism. He recognized the fact that academic life could be the salvation or the suicide of any literary man. He paid tribute to the first possibility in his introductory essay to *The Function of Criticism:*

> The first problem with which the scholar of literature is confronted is to find a mode of living which will enable him to develop his mind, practice his art, and support his family . . . The university offers him the obvious solution . . . the traditional place for poets and professors to scorn each other and develop each other.[25]

In this same essay he relates some instances in which the scholarly attitude of his department hurt him as a poet, but he summarized gratefully the advantages which a university career and locale offered to him and felt that progress was being made in understanding. "The scholars, in brief, have become more literary; the literary men more scholarly; and in America, both are generally in the universities, which is of the utmost importance." Near the end of his academic career, as he was departing for a sabbatical to work on his last volume in 1961, the Stanford magazine *Sequoia* (Winter, 1961) printed a Winters issue which contained essays about him, and poems by him and his students. The issue opens with a poem by Marianne Moore dedicated to him, an essay entitled "Homage to Yvor Winters" by Allen Tate, "A Publisher's Comment" by Alan Swallow, then various essays and poems by students such as Thom Gunn, J. V. Cunningham, Don Stanford, Alan Stephens, and Donald Hall. A fine essay by Albert Guerard is included as well as poems and one essay by Winters himself. The issue attests to the impact that he had on Stanford and its English Department.

His long association with this university included full-time teaching, editing, writing, translating, and lecturing for over forty years. As his literary reputation grew to international proportions, he continued to live simply with his wife and family at Los Altos and to take part in various civic and community affairs. But most important always was the poetry that he created with such rigorous self-criticism in his quiet little garden study. It was his first cause. By the end of his life he had culled it and announced with characteristic austerity that which he considered "the best of it." In a note at the end of *The Collected Poems*, 1961, he remarked: "This volume contains everything which I wish to keep and represents in addition a kind of definition by example of the style which I have been trying to achieve for a matter of thirty years. The poems omitted seem to me inferior in quality and they would certainly obscure the issue which for me is the principal issue." By the end of his career, his poetry and criticism had been published not only in the most distinguished American and English periodicals, but had also been translated into Japanese, French, German, and Italian journals as well.

He owed his wide reputation, in part, to his faithful friend and publisher, Alan Swallow of Denver. Their association was one of the most poignant and practical influences of Winters' life. A mutual interest in young writers and the promotion of western publishing originally brought them together for many years of significant collaboration. Though some of Winters' earliest experimental poems had come out in *New Directions*, it was Swallow who first collected them. He also brought out Winters' three most important critical volumes, as well as a revision of *The Early Poems* (1966) and *The Collected Poems* (1952 and 1960). Their letters witness their long friendship and abiding literary respect. Winters always returned to the Swallow Press with all of his manuscripts, even after his fame brought invitations from larger and more prominent houses. Swallow wrote three pieces in proud tribute to his successful writer in *An Editor's Essays of Two Decades:* "He has lived to fulfill to the greatest degree the potential that he had; his criticism performs uniquely in our time the function of 'the whole critic,' and his poetry has developed in the last thirty years to become one of the greatest bodies of poetry that we can offer the future."[26] And when Swallow died suddenly, as Winters' *Forms of Discovery* was at his press, the old poet wrote a moving tribute to his friend and editor of so many years. (He turned this remaining manuscript over to their mutual associate G. Blaisdell, editor of the University of New Mexico Press, for completion, and he invited another of his former students, Kenneth Fields, to help with its sequel, *The Quest for Reality*.) The unique mutual loyalty of Winters and Swallow resulted in a lifetime's author-publisher relationship that discovered and developed many unknown young poets. The new Swallow Press in Chicago continues to list Winters as one of its "stars."

Winters' strict selectivity won for him some of his country's most prestigious awards: teaching fellowships at the Kenyon School of English, a grant from the National Institute of Arts and Letters in 1952, Brandeis University's creative arts award in 1960, Yale's Bollingen Poetry Prize in 1961, and Guggenheim Fellowships in 1961 and 1962. The year before his death he was one of five American writers to receive a $10,000 award from the National Endowment for the Arts "to honor writers who have hitherto not received all recognition due them."

By 1966, when Winters retired from the department of English at Stanford, he had developed a throat malignancy. Working against time, he finished correcting the proof sheets for his volume *Forms of Discovery*, to be published by the Swallow Press. There is in this book a tone of finality; he summarizes his career in its introduction:

> . . . I have devoted my life to the study of poetry. I have taught English and American poetry for well over thirty years and have tried to understand what has happened, why it has happened, and how to distinguish the better from the worse. I have tried to understand this for my own improvement and for the improvement of my students.[27]

He died on January 25, 1968, two months after the publication of this book, survived by his widow and two children, Joanna and Daniel.

The chairman of his department at Stanford wrote of him: "He was not only a poet and critic of immense distinction; he also was one of Stanford's great teachers. He can never be replaced."[28] The Academy of American Poets arranged a memorial tribute at the Guggenheim Museum in New York, and two of his former students, now important poets, were asked to participate. Ann Stanford spoke movingly of his sympathy and help to young creative writers; Thom Gunn read some of Winters' poetry. The tributes in the press came from all corners of the literary world, from the *London Times* to the *Des Moines Register*. But perhaps the respectful accolade of fellow poet-critic Allen Tate is the one which Winters might have appreciated most of all. It was written in 1953, fifteen years before his death, and he was always one to prefer criticism while the living could still profit from it. It sums up all Winters aspired to and claimed to be:

In his own generation he has the eminence of isolation. He has conducted a poetic revolution all his own. His writing has clarity, elegance, and power. I have not been able to find another living American poet so much life centralized in language. He has a few mistakes to live down as any poet in our century.[29]

The Public Character of the Critic

To understand the writings of Yvor Winters it is necessary to observe his public character as critic as well as his private personality as poet. One may imagine that his insistence on order might well have evolved from his early sensitivity and instability. Winters himself said that he changed from free verse to formal poetry because it actually offered him *more* variation in its final effect. Perhaps the shift in character from lonely sensitive poet to public aggressive critic may all have been part of the same purposeful metamorphosis in person as well as in print. Certainly there was beneath the eventual austerity of the mature Winters an early delicacy which remained all of his life, well protected from the crass public eye. Hints of it show in all the many aspects of this complex character.

His classic question, "How do you see me?" seems to have been a constant preoccupation. He insisted that the public "see him" and all other deserving poets and critics with meticulous precision, and these efforts sometimes border on persecution. He was determined to identify "greatness" even in a single poem, and for this he was often labelled "perverse" by his enemies. The key to his public critical character may be found in this finely attuned demand for perfection that he imposed upon himself and other artists. He was not an amiable man in print; he was never satisfied with himself, and his discontent made him a romantic in private and a neoclassicist in public.

A similar schism shows in his religious attitudes, which seem to have been based in a sort of practical humanism. He claimed no formal denominational ties. Though he often writes of his respect for the basic Christian position, he calls himself "one of the unregenerate . . . not a Christian in the formal sense." An early poem—one of three published in a small Cummington Press private pamphlet modestly entitled "Fragment"—says, "I cannot find my way to Nazareth. . . ." and sets the tone for a lifetime of soul-searching; he seemed always more impelled toward a private mystical religion than a public one. The self-awareness that he had experienced as a young poet living in the mountains is constantly reflected in his later poetry. Though he often lamented man's inhumanity to man, he concluded that only the meditative life of contemplation can finally satisfy the poet. In spite of his temporary transient rages against the world, he believed that original order could prevail if the willing poet-philosopher would only seek it in his art. The frustrations of the here and now might thus be forgotten in the creative process of poetry:

> While those whose minds are living
> grow hard and cool and gray,
> Elude the unforgiving,
> And somehow have their say
> In words no fool can touch
> Because they mean so much.

This was religion enough for Yvor Winters, "moral" poet.

It is as a literary critic that Winters' "hard, cool, gray" character has met the most adverse publicity, and some of that has unfortunately reflected on the criticism itself. As critic he was as tenacious as the bulldog who guarded his door to his death; a sign on his front fence warned "Beware of Dog!" But behind that fence was a tender man sitting in his garden, playing with that dog, and thinking about the verities of life. And behind the high fence of his criticism there was also a softer personality than the literary world ever knew because the critic barked so loudly.

It is true that his private personality had a direct influence on his style of criticism. His own search for personal order that came after his early, passionate, hallucinatory poetry is directly related to his search for rational pattern in poetic theory. As a young man he had been shy, lonely, and withdrawn into his literary studies when his illness forced a change of pace and locale. Moving from the scholarly world of the University of Chicago to the primitive society of the Southwest mining camps, he became preoccupied with his basic search for identity and survival. Every sense impression in this new clear world became infinitely important as he struggled against the ever-present imminence of destruction. This desperate crisis seemed to call for an early poetic practice and principle that celebrated a reckless passion and intense concentration with a free imagistic style of writing. When he recovered from the worst of his physical illnesses and felt more assured of his future, he seemed to draw in his resources, tighten his style of writing, and restrict himself to the critical dogma that was to become his hallmark.

He had always been a perfectionist and a devotee of detail. The precision that he now demanded of his new poetry and criticism was reflected in his personality as he set out to learn all there was to know about literature during his graduate years and early teaching at Stanford. The timidity of earlier days became hidden behind his pride in his poetry; his assurance that his theories were correct developed eventually into a dictatorial and defensive attitude against the developing critical style in the early century. The more the literary world evolved techniques of obscurantism and free form, the more dogmatic and contentious the Winters personality became "in defense of reason." And the crusty mien that these critical controversies demanded seemed to develop into an image of a dour, perverse pedagogue seeking an audience. (Winters' critical theories will be examined in detail with examples from his writing in the next chapter.)

Winters admired Samuel Johnson as the great critic of all time, and perhaps he began to see himself in a similar position as a corrective for his own century. Yet his personality as critic had little of the relaxed, genial Johnsonian ease and humor. He seemed always to give the impression that he was carrying on a nervous battle for causes that must not be lost. Even in some of his lighter attempts at social and literary criticism—as in "Letter to a Social Muse"—he becomes scathing where the object of his scorn scarcely deserves to be treated so seriously.

A solitary prophet, lonely in his unpopular critical theory, he adopted an armor of defense in style; he anticipated controversy. He seemed to welcome the label "reactionary" and wrote of himself, "I am one of the unregenerate." Fellow critics have observed that he was a bitter and dangerous man to combat in print. His wide erudition and insatiable reading led him to quarrel—at one time or another—with most of the prominent critics and reviewers of his time; he could usually outwrite them because he had out-read them. He would reply to reviews with counter-reviews; to books with counter-books; to letters to editors attacking him with more letters in self-defense. His appetite for controversy was insatiable, and his patience and energy for argument were immense. One critic has called Winters a "Baroque Personality" in tribute to this complexity.

The great complexity of his personality as critic is reflected in the varied techniques of his flashing mind: comparisons, *dicta*, evaluations, cross references, invective, lament, and prophecy. When the criticism is read in quantity, the effect of this intense personality so close to the surface is often overbearing and tedious. As a critic Winters is hard on his readers; he demands in return the strength he gives to his manuscript. He was a close, imaginative reader himself, and he wanted *his* reader to be able to concentrate with an equal stamina. That he doubted his gentle reader's ability in this regard is all too obvious in the attitude he takes toward him. Thus readers were often put off by the compulsive, blunt manner and missed the brilliance of the method and materials there.

It is true that some of his criticism is prejudiced; the candid observer of the Winters personality must admit that this is all a part of the whole. But the constant uphill battle that he had to maintain for even a toe-hold in the mountain of "new criticism"—which he considered so dangerous—caused him to over-emphasize his own prejudices by isolating single authors, poems, lines, or even images with a microscopic technique. This "baroque" style leaves the unscholarly reader in a welter of detail that often confuses him. Only such an erudite personality could evoke this feeling of scholarly suffocation as he flashes through the full corpus of English and Continental literature for examples both major and minor. The dedication of Winters' personality shows in the fact that he took the artistic process to be one of constant moral evaluation of the human condition. "The human average has never been admirable," he writes from the depths of his long, candid look at it.

As a critic he was aware that his position was often in jeopardy since his *dicta* represented such a deviation from the popular norm of his time; he developed a bravado in facing the repercussions which he knew were bound to come. "I am about to promulgate a heresy"; or "I am fully aware that these remarks are heretical"; or "I mention my enemies lest someone think I am unaware of them."[30] At the end of his final volume he takes the trouble to list the major poets on whom he has *not* written to assure the reader that he *does* know they exist. (He concludes magnanimously, "The learned scholar who wishes to devote a history to these poets has my blessing.") It seems unfortunate that years of such defensive tactics sometimes drove him to bitter and cruel comments. It took a great deal of stamina for him to hold out, and he gave to his craft and art of criticism all the tremendous self-discipline of which his personality was capable. If it sometimes broke out in invective against his own critics, it is not surprising, though indefensible.

He speaks in one essay of the cleansing power of hatred ("It sometimes gives me a very clear view of the ugly.") A less committed critic might cringe from such a brutal catharsis. He seemed often unwilling to allow his combatants their fair share of time in the field; he resented their meanderings, which to him seemed a waste of time. Accusations of poor sportsmanship toward his "great corrective" occurred from time to time; but Winters had what Swallow observed in him: "That most admired of all Western virtues—the ability to stick to your guns."[31] And when he was labelled narrow, dogmatic, or parochial, he merely replied with another well-aimed blast about critics whose erudition and methods were limited or scattered; he was a hard man to fight because his own supply of ammunition was boundless and he took precise aim.

Yvor Winters' critical writings show little sense of humor or whimsy, though his searing dry wit made him a master of scathing sarcasm. His family, his garden, his dogs, and his reading and writing may have given him serious pleasure but he seems to have had no taste for humor in the world in general. His was a desperate search for the best in himself and others, and the man must have felt he could not afford to be whimsical about failure. He was even careful to note with candid eye and vitriolic tongue what he considered flaws in a list of "greats" which included Shakespeare, Spenser, Milton, Blake, Wordsworth, Shelley, Keats, Poe, Yeats, Eliot, Pound, James, Hemingway, and Faulkner.

He was a patient and farsighted worker, a close reader and a constant reviser; for example, he worked for seventeen years on the five essays in *Primitivism and Decadence* and was a constant practitioner of Flaubert's dictum of "*le mot juste.*" He cautions the unworthy and unwilling: "To master an art one has to labor with all of one's mind and with at least a part of one's body."[32] In spite of all his years of perverse negation in private and public defense of his critical theories, Winters seemed to get a certain gloomy satisfaction out of his own accomplishments. He was certainly aware of the perils of his great quest; but however petulant he might be in his criticism of others, he was always humble and patient before his own craft—a real perfectionist who savored the private pleasure of accomplishment. He wrote somewhat grudgingly of this: "As to scholarship and criticism—one has to look for it wherever it happens to lie concealed. One tracks it down year by year; one reads and reads and does one's best to remember. It is a messy business, anyway one takes it; but it is also fascinating."[33]

This stern man of principle wrote of particular authors with whom he seemed to find a personal rapport, though he could not praise their writing in any unqualified way. Of Nathaniel Hawthorne in "Maule's Curse," he says: "There can scarcely be virtue without a comprehension of sin, and the wider and more careful the comprehension, the richer the virtue." Winters seems here to be looking into the Hawthorne mirror, aware of the boundless sins of humanity in his own dark soul, yet ever searching to widen the possible field of virtue with his own writing. He speaks knowingly and poignantly of Hawthorne's battle against "the smooth impassive surface of the intense inane." All through his own lifetime Winters seemed to be seeking a way out of this intense inane, as he strove to respond to it and to have it respond to him. If it would not respond, then how could he rise above it, or plough through it, or go around it ?

He understood the loneliness of genius, and he wanted to be remembered or recreated as he had recreated so many others who were lost in the "intense inane." He had written with particular insight about certain writers who also struggled against an introspective obsession: Hawthorne, Melville, Robinson, Crane, and Stevens. They were all men who sustained themselves in loneliness with an inner integrity, a disciplined order which they made for themselves in their writing. Preoccupied with the lonely terror of the human spirit, each sought a pattern in defense of some reason against the void of chaos. Winters traced in each of their writings a frightening insecurity; his writings about them seem always to be particularly focused on the same obsession that he recognized in himself: the loss of identity and the loneliness of isolation.

Certain of his comments on the writings of these five authors are relevant to understanding his own personality. For instance, he notes the constant struggle that Hawthorne endured for moral understanding: "Only a few scattered individuals, at the cost of inordinate labor have achieved the permeation of human experience by a consistent moral understanding which results in wisdom and great art. If art is to be measured by the greatness of difficulties overcome—and the measure is not wholly unreasonable—then these few writers are very great indeed.[34] Certainly Winters could match any other contemporary writer in that measure, and his quasi approval of it is an interesting psychological insight.

Preoccupied with this same theme of struggle against isolation, Winters writes of Herman Melville's art: "His symbolism is based on . . . the antithesis of sea and land: the land represents the known, the mastered, the human experience; the sea, the half-known, the obscure instincts, uncritical feelings, dangers, terror . . . where the monsters are."[35] Like Melville's reasonable and heroic Mr. Starbuck, Winters seems constantly to be saying: "Push off not from that isle; thou cans't ne'er return." Yet also like the passionate Ahab, he knows too well the attraction of the great dark search through the lonely sea, and he finds himself constantly on its brink in his own artistic motivations. It is significant that Winters wrote an occasional poem, "To a Portrait of Melville in My Library," and that he allowed it to stand in the severely edited *Collected Poems.* In it he speaks directly to *his* "Maestro":

> O face reserved, unmoved by praise or scorn!
> O dreadful heart that won Socratic peace!
> What was the purchase price for thy release?

He observed when he named this series of essays "Maule's Curse" that these particular authors were all cut off from the popular traditions of their times; and he seemed to feel himself lost to his own heritage in a painful isolation of this century.

His rapport with the writings of E. A. Robinson is partially based on a similar affinity: "Many of his characters were very like himself—weak and insignificant in the eyes of the world, but who sustain themselves in loneliness on some kind of inner integrity. His personal greatness of style is seldom achieved in our century. It is unfortunate that he published so voluminously. No poet can publish in this manner with impunity."[36] Winters' standards demanded a greater selectivity; yet he acknowledged the same sort of misjudgment by much of the critical world.

The poetry of Hart Crane appealed to him because, "he had the courage of his convictions and the virtue of integrity. He embodies concepts which for a century have been generating the most cherished principles of our literature, education, politics, and personal morals."[37] Winters concluded his Crane essay with a plea that his own generation of writers might maintain these same principles he espoused.

Another example from Winters' criticism that seems relevant to an understanding of his personality comes in his last book's essay on Wallace Stevens. He finds Stevens' hedonism insufficient as a philosophy and finds Stevens himself eventually bored with it, therefore declining in poetic excellence in the later poems. Yet he feels a certain identity with Stevens' philosophical position:

> Stevens appeared to have one central theme: the situation of the isolated man in a meaningless universe . . . The universe is beautiful but appalling . . . The only mitigation comes from speech, poetry . . . I do not object to his refusing to offer any consolation to the reader; I myself can offer none. But the confrontation of this universe, the almost pure confrontation, confrontation without human complications, is a very limited theme; there is more to be said about life, even in Stevens' universe, than he has suspected.[38]

Such a purely aesthetic position would never suffice for Winters; though he might enjoy imagery with full sense impression, he would always add his own particular brand of "moralism" in the expression of it.

And, finally, in his essay on Henry James he discussed what he considered the fatal flaw that he recognized latent in himself—"His conscientious concentration upon obscurity—almost to hallucination—of the moral problem, the development of the feeling in excess of the motive."[39] Winters sought always to avoid this division in his poetry and to combine the best of both elements in its order. Though he felt the lure of the powers of darkness, he propelled himself away from their implacable wilderness with a compulsive singleness of motive.

In a candid appraisal of his own or any artist's life, Winters writes:

> The fact remains . . . that the artist, if he is really an artist is really isolated, and his personal life in this respect is a hard one. There are few people with whom he can converse freely without giving offense or becoming angry. It is no accident that so many great writers have sooner or later retreated from society; they retreat because they are excluded. A first-rate poet differs from his contemporaries not in being eccentric or less human, but in being more central, more human, more intelligent . . . , but to the world at large the poet seems wrong-headed and eccentric . . . and he may become neurotic under such pressure.[40]

Winters was willing to accept this gulf between poet and reader—even between poet and scholar—and he made no effort to build any false camaraderie. He was willing to accept the necessary loneliness of living among what he called "the dead living, who according to their own natures, hate the small number of living on sight with intensity . . . The distinguished poet is always a member of the smallest of all "minority groups," and during most of his life and often for all of it, is regarded as everyone's inferior and as a fair object for contempt."[41] (Winters used this phrase "the dead living" in an early poem on this theme; shortly after his death, one of his students used it again in a commemorative poem in tribute to his lost teacher-poet.) By the end of *Forms of Discovery*, which was published shortly before his death, Winters seemed almost desperate in his attempt to save certain poets from the brink of isolation; to the end, his *cause célèbre* was to salvage "great" poets with "great" poems.

Yet Winters himself was able to look straight into the face of the reality of oblivion without hiding behind any romantic illusions. This is evident in an essay where he is comparing Coleridge to Stevens; in a favorite passage he admires the latter for his ability to "test the reality":

> . . . . . . where then is paradise?
> There is not any haunt of prophecy,
> Nor any old chimera of the grave
> . . . . that has endured
> As April's green endures . . . .

Winters writes significantly that he has known these Stevens lines "by heart for fifty years or more and they have seldom been far from my mind."[42] Like another of his favorite poets, Rimbaud, he felt the necessity to fight constantly against hallucination with an enduring grip on reality.

One of Winters' favorite epithets for successful poetry was "mature." His admiration for mature poets depended not on age, but wisdom: that wisdom which realized the potential destruction of the physical and the necessary salvage of the spiritual. He mistrusted the merely sensory flow of experience and put his faith in rational "maturity" of theme and style. He dismissed most of the Romantics, as well as the "Fugitive School" of the twentieth century, by claiming their loud immaturity; yet he claimed quiet maturity for Christina Rosetti for one particular image which he felt was evidenced in most of her poetry. . . . "a *stillness* that is almost Paradise." His own poetry of his late years frequently includes a progressive metaphor based on a similar imagery: "stone, stillness, maturity, eternity" (see Part III: section on imagery, and Part IV: final explication).

In spite of his claims concerning the artist's necessary isolation, he never felt, as critic, that he could completely allow himself this luxury.

So he spent a lifetime alternating between his public critic-teacher performances and his private poetic withdrawal into his garden or study. Unwilling to remain long in artistic isolation, he sought what he wanted for his own poetry and that of his peers in the world of reality and the columns of the public press. He set about to establish an ambitious, realistic life-style for his selective school. How should the artist live in today's world so as to avoid oblivion? He must first of all write with the highest personal artistry to deserve fame; he must then be found and saved by some sensitive rational critic; but he must always be wary of this world and shun its fickle, cavalier qualities. The twentieth century, Winters felt, held for its artists certain irreducible difficulties. In *In Defense of Reason*, he defines the only viable procedure for the contemporary poet:

> . . . to define the various possible mysteries, and where choice is possible to choose those which eliminate the greatest possible number of the remainder; and to keep as scientific, as Aristotelian an eye as possible under the conditions of our life as we actually find ourselves forced to live it, so that we may not make the mistake of choosing a mystery which shall, in proportion as it influences our actions, violate those conditions and lead to disaster.[43]

He recognized that ours was not a "high" civilization and that the human race was probably not capable of ever reaching a high one again; but he was pragmatist enough to offer certain improvements for poets and critics. In this position he often made himself obnoxious in his earnest evangelism. (One of Winters' most severe critics berates him for this: "Convinced of his important investment in the life of culture and ideas, he hugs his mythological examples of individual heroism with lordly boasts of immortality."[44])

At least Winters took precautions against ever writing critically about his *own* poetry. (He chastized one of his successful student poets for doing this. When J. V. Cunningham wrote an essay explaining some of his own poetry, Winters called him "rash.") He hoped, nevertheless, for some other careful critic—with standards to match his own—who would someday evaluate the Winters poetic canon. "Certain particular things need to be done in the near future to preserve the poetry of some of our best current writers," he wrote months before his death. "We need an exhaustive study of certain minor poets of this century by men of professional competence."[45] Though he was too delicate to list himself among them, he does indicate a careful history of his own development (both in *Forms* and in the introduction to *Early Poems*) for the aid of "some future critic" who might want to make such a study of his work. He wished that other poets would be as self-critical as he had been so that their total output in anthologies and collections would be selective and small. "The taste which enables a reader to recognize a good poem among fifteen hundred or more pages of bad is very rare." His favorite admonition was "Write little; do it well."[46] He practiced what he preached by cutting his own *Collected Poems* to what he considered the bare minimum. And he gives a final and very specific directive to any future scholars of his own material as to where they may be found. He held it against the Stanford University Library and English Department for years that they did not follow his suggestions for collecting and preserving the manuscripts of all the Stanford writers of his own group, and he doubtless hoped for his own preservation there as well.

This fond hope should not be interpreted as mere desire for self-aggrandizement but understood as one more step in the general scholarship which Winters thought was due all good poets. He believed in this study as a therapeutic process in the world "where artistic process is one of moral evaluation of human experience by means of a technique which renders possible an evaluation more precise than any other."[47] Whenever Winters does use his own work as critical example, he always accompanies it by an apologetic note: "If I may be pardoned for insisting on my views on these matters. . . ," or, "I offer the following none-too-sympathetic observations for what they may be worth from my own work, not through vanity but merely by way of precaution." He detested what he called "excessive self-dramatization" such as he found in the poetry of W. B. Yeats. In one small moment of self-dramatization—when he praised a dissertation which he had supervised—he chastized himself in a footnote: "It is vanity that impels me to mention the fact. . . ," yet he left it in the manuscript! His meticulous scholarship sometimes drove him to ridiculously long footnotes explaining how and where certain of his manuscripts were preserved; and his pride was often hurt—as shown by letters to editors—if he was not mentioned in bibliographies. One might interpret such protest as sheer ego, but it seems rather to have been a righteous wrath for *all* poets not properly recognized. It was a part of his scholarly nature to provide everything for any future critic of his writing except an evaluation. In a late footnote in the final volume of his criticism published in his lifetime, he sighs hopelessly, "This footnote will have to be completed by posterity." The stark fact of incurable illness caught up with him before he could add the final meticulous last fact. Haunted by this throughout the preparation of this final manuscript, he felt obliged to leave directions in its introduction for any scholar who might take up this project; his warning, "Good writers of good poems do not survive automatically," echoes throughout every line of his own careful scholarship.

His final ambition was to be a creative poet and a corrective critic. This apostle of discipline, after he had stepped over the brink of those first passionate, imagistic poems, turned to rigorous self-correction. He remarked in the introduction to *Twelve Poets of the Pacific*, "Life is difficult to understand and the irrelevancies of personality are insistent and are but imperfectly amenable to discipline."[48] He warned his young poets against their own weak natures, and he knew better than anyone else his own fatal flaws and what he must do about them. Assessing his school's achievement under his tutelage, he commented, "Let us say that we have sought to correct our weaknesses instead of to cultivate them."

Driven throughout his lifetime in his battle with the "intense inane," he held to his doctrine of moral rationality with frantic strength, often alone in the isolation of his critical theories. Two images of his poetry often reflect this preoccupation with permanence. Obscured by the accidental history and the literary fads of his time, he expected his writing to lie quietly buried among his "stones" of eternal timelessness or to lie fallow in his "gardens" of the living present. Hopefully some critical renaissance might eventually bring him to life; in which case, he wanted to have his books set in order with every document and footnote ready. He had saved many obscure writers, and he must have been aware of the ironic position of his own poetry—so little known and read in his time—and so carefully perfected. He hoped that his writing might eventually be identified in the great traditional tide of English poetry, rather than becalmed in the sloughs of insignificant tributaries.

Though his art was the constant master of his life, in the end he is still Winters the Man, as well as Winters the Poet: "I would rather abandon my art than my self-respect." If his renaissance did not come, it could never be said that he had compromised his beliefs for his preservation. Some of his happiest literary associations had to be sacrificed: his student J. V. Cunningham, whose poetry had meant more to him than any writer of this century, was disavowed when he could no longer condone the younger writer's style. Marianne Moore's visits came less often; and Allen Tate wrote:

> I don't know when our correspondence ceased. I was still learning a great deal from my unseen friend, but I suppose he lost interest, since it became obvious that he could learn nothing more from me . . . Arthur is one of the most 'intellectual' men I have ever

known; and his human relations are kept well in check by his critical views.[49]

Near the end of his life he wrote: "I am pessimistic about the human race. Few men are born with sufficient intelligence to profit by more than a small part of the tradition available to them."[50] Yet the basis for his critical stance seems always to lie in his belief that life was a process of revision in the interest of greater understanding. He would have been very proud of the tribute from Donald Justice, a poet of the next generation, who wrote of him: "His volumes will become handbooks for more than one poet of the future. We need him."[51]

PART TWO

"Write little; do it well"

Winters' Critical Theory as it is Related to His Practice of Poetry

History of His Reputation as Critic

"Those writers of my own generation whose stated ideals seem to me most definitely related to my own repel me in their verse . . . by various species of hit-or-miss awkwardness, cuteness, or sweetness." In 1927, when Winters was just beginning to formulate his first prose essays on his theory of poetry, he wrote this significant commentary in *Poetry Magazine*. It set the focus for his own position as literary critic in the twentieth century. To understand this position it is necessary to survey the history of Winters' career as a literary critic and then take up his poetic theories as a background for the explication of his poetry in subsequent sections. These theories include his ideas on the philosophical purpose of poetry, the aesthetic process of poetry, and the practical management of the various elements of poetry—theme, content, form, imagery, diction, and tone—as they are interrelated in the final creative product. From these theories, his absolutist ideal for criticism evolved.

Winters began to publish criticism almost as early as he began to publish poetry. His first poems appeared in 1920 in *Poetry Magazine*, and his first critical reviews were printed there in the early years of that same decade. As early as 1922 another critic, reviewing Winters' second book of verse, *The Magpie's Shadow*, wrote:

> Yvor Winters is one of those rare American poets who are active critically and whose theories are not laid by in the creative process. With him, art is sacrosanct; therefore, he says, let us discover the nature of this art. His is a disillusionment which knows science and discounts reality universalized through the emotions. He lifts above universals and plunges into particulars—forcing the first into coherence by means of the second.[1]

His career as critic continued to coincide with his career as poet. However, his idiosyncratic, unorthodox criticism, propelled by an aggressive public personality, made bigger news in the contemporary literary scene than did his quiet poetry, even though their publication dates often coincided. At the end of almost a half-century of writing in both fields, he saw his reputation as poet known only to the esoteric world of other poets, though his controversial criticism was known to every college English major.

His early critical essays appeared in the most important "little magazines" of the literary world: *Hound and Horn, Poetry Magazine, American Literature*, the *American Review*, the *Kenyon Review*. These were later collected in small volumes published by a variety of houses between 1937 and 1947. Finally, in 1947, Alan Swallow gathered them all together in an impressive collection significantly entitled *In Defense of Reason*. It is divided into three sections: "Primitivism and Decadence: A Study of American Experimental Poetry" (1937); "Maule's Curse: Seven Studies in the History of American Obscurantism" (1938); and "The Anatomy of Nonsense: Problems in Criticism of the Works of Henry Adams, Wallace Stevens, T. S. Eliot, John Crowe Ransom, and Hart Crane" (1943). The book was acclaimed by Swallow as "undoubtedly the most impressive volume of criticism in our time." This controversial collection made Winters famous as a critic. In his foreword to *In Defense of Reason*, Yvor Winters wrote:

> Although this collection, like any collection of essays, suffers from its miscellaneous character, there is a single theory of literature developed throughout and a single theory of the history of literature since the Renaissance. I call it moralistic . . . It has not been adequately defined in the past . . . but is loosely implicit in the inexact theorizing which has led to the most durable literary judgments in the history of criticism.[2]

It was Winters' own "moralistic" theory of literature that rose to plague all other modern theorizers: didactic, hedonistic, romantic, deterministic, relativistic. Winters defended it as absolutist and measured what he concluded to be the "great" poetry of the world by its standard. The tenets of this volume were to him a deadly serious business; his was a necessarily therapeutic calling. He believed that our literary culture had been disintegrating ever since the seventeenth century and that he was the self-appointed catalyst to reconstruct it at this critical moment in literary history. With complete and candid confidence, he says, "My critical and moral notions are derived from my observations of literature and of life; I did not proceed in the opposite direction." Thus, the inductive critic here summarized his views and his methods in over six hundred pages, backed by half a lifetime of scholarly erudition, poetic creativity, and appropriate literary quotation.

His next important collection of essays appeared in a smaller volume in 1957, entitled *The Function of Criticism*. By this time, all "modern" critics and poets knew his name and his isolated position against what he considered to be the indefensible world of unreason: "associational obscurantism," as he called it. The introductory essay entitled "Problems for the Modern Critic of Literature" summarized his own critical *raison d'être*. It was followed by various essays on unrelated subjects: "The Audible Reading of Poetry," "The Poetry of Gerard Manley Hopkins," "Robert Frost, or The Spiritual Drifter as Poet," and "English Literature of the Sixteenth Century." All had appeared before in such reputable literary journals as the *Hudson Review*, the *Sewanee Review*, and the *Kenyon Review*.

Exactly one decade later—almost as though on schedule—the final volume of Winters' criticism was published. Several of the essays had previously appeared in various periodicals, anthologies, and collections, but they were carefully re-edited, revised, enlarged, and logically arranged within the larger framework. This volume was released to the public just two months before Winters' death in January, 1968. It is a great irony that he did not live to see it reviewed by other critics. In *Forms of Discovery* he brought his full powers as distinguished poet-critic to bear in all of their maturity. The tone of the book shows great critical acumen, but also great perversity. This may be understood, if not excused, by the fact that he was constantly struggling against the imminence of death during its preparation and revision.

Since this study is mainly concerned with Winters as poet, his critical theory will be summarized only as it relates to poetry. When Winters collected his poetry in 1952 and again in 1960, he was ruthlessly selective, including none of it that denied his developed critical principles. The 1966 volume entitled *Early Poems of Yvor Winters, 1920–28* seems to have represented an afterthought for any critic who might want to study his poetry's development; although he finally rejected much of his early Imagist free verse, he is a critic careful enough to include that which actually exhibits the line of development in his eventual critical theory. It is this simultaneity of development of theory just after practice—of criticism just after poetry—that is most interesting to students of Winters: the unconscious act of creativity and the subsequent conscious understanding of it. Few contemporary poets have been so willing to re-study their own works, and it is this negligence that Winters deplores when he writes of them. As a professional critic, he sought to develop from his own poetic experience a critical system—an *ars poetica*—that would be practical. He believed that a good poem should combine a clear understanding of motive and an evaluation of feeling. The intensity and success of the work of art would lie in the combination of the value of its subject and the precision of the artist's judgment and artistic technique. From his earliest one-line perception poems to his last formal odes he sought rules for the degree of emotion proper and reasonable to each subject. In this search he developed a critical theory that interrelated the philosophical purpose of poetry with the aesthetic process. The result, he hoped, would be a skillful management of all of the elements of poetry with taste and perception. Thus, the eventual poem would be essentially a "moral" evaluation of experience conveyed through the proper choice of all the details and variations of content, form, imagery, and tone.

As his own elaborate study of literature developed, he seemed to find his requirements best achieved in the sixteenth-century short lyric and in certain short poems of the twentieth century which he labeled "Post-Symbolist." Too many cursory readers of Winters' criticism and poetry dismiss him as a perverse antiquarian without realizing that he arrived at his conclusions after years of personal experience with the Symbolist and Imagist movements in his own creative development. In his zealous singling out of individual unknown "great" poems, he is simply cutting away the dross of tradition that makes so many anthologies "standard" rather than "poetic." His tone of authority equals his power of controlled discernment in choosing the truly great poems for consideration. His wide knowledge and his narrow taste eventually settled on the pattern of the short lyric as having the greatest possible poetic potential. He began to build an entirely new body of poetic commentary—both creative and critical—and he drew his own conclusions from his wide reading and his constant writing experience.

When the eventual decline of the Imagist-Symbolist tradition began to affect his own verse, he turned to the severities of seventeenth century "plain style," using the lyrics of Jonson, Gascoigne, and Fulke-Greville as masters. At the same time, he was reading and translating Spanish, French, and American Indian poetry. He became convinced that he must capture and control the perceptions of his early Imagist verse and perpetuate its chaotic emotional reverie in a more ordered form. He developed a cool power to appraise the "immorality" of his own early poetry, and a critical theory based on his particular "moralism" evolved: a poetry in which motive evoked the proper emotion but was not overshadowed by it. By the time the Gyroscope Group at Stanford had developed, he was ready to issue a credo in *Twelve Poets of the Pacific*: "In the matter of conception, clarity as opposed to contemporary obscurantistic tendencies; the expression of feeling in terms of motive; in the matter of style, purity and freedom from mannerism, as distinct from the contemporary tendency to substitute mannerism for true originality." These tenets remained the basis of all of Winters' criticism through the rest of his career.

The final goal of this criticism was always evaluative, as was that of his master, Dr. Johnson. He listed in detail the processes, culminating in evaluation, that constitute the process of literary criticism as he saw it: (1) historical and biographical information necessary to understand the poet; (2) analysis of his theories to evaluate what he has done; (3) rational critique of the paraphrasable content (motive) of the poem; (4) rational critique of the feeling motivated (details of style: language, imagery, tone, etc.); (5) and the unique, final act of judgment.[3] On these bases Winters accepted, rejected, and urged correction. By these tenets he finally acclaimed certain poets of the mid-twentieth century whom he labelled Post-Symbolists.

The Basis of His Poetic Theory

Winters' definition of a poem is a good touchstone for his particular type of literary criticism: "A poem is a statement in language about a human experience." He develops this further, explaining that, "since language is conceptual by nature, this statement will be more or less rational or at least apprehensible in rational terms or else the medium will be violated."[4] Insofar as the rational statement is understandable and in so far as the feeling is properly motivated by the rational statement, the poem will be "good." The great poet of natural talent must have wide and excellent training in order to succeed in this. His knowledge must not bind him; it must eventually set him free. As a critic, he saw himself living in a period which seemed convinced that reason and poetry were mutually destructive; that any rational structure was the defeat of the poem; that poetry was primarily sensual depending for strength on its imagery alone. He saw no reason in an objective correlative; rather the breakdown of order and the celebration of the absurd.

He identified the sources for what he considered the error of contemporary poetry in two earlier, anti-intellectual traditions which supported and supplemented each other: the sentimentalism of Shaftesbury (in which impulse is treated with respect, and reason with suspicion) and the doctrine of association derived from Hobbes and Locke (in which juxtaposition of disparate objects is accepted, and from which Freudian concepts evolved). Winters felt that these two roots had adversely affected the content and structure of most twentieth century poetry. His three major critical volumes are all based on this approach to literary history, and he evaluates the best of his own poetry and that of others by these principles. He believed that the two best periods in English poetry were "from Wyatt to Dryden inclusive" and "from Jones Very to the present." The limit of these periods is in itself characteristic of Winters' catholic taste and tremendous scope.

Having defined his critical position early in this century, Winters proceeded in 1957 to summarize *The Function of Criticism.* He supported the university as the place where the critic might best live and write with the impetus of the academic world. He saw himself as poet-critic-teacher guiding young writers to understand "the potentialities of different kinds of subject matter and various literary forms." He espoused a method whose final job was one of judgment—rational and emotional—of experience. "We will regard as greatest those works which deal with experiences which affect human life most profoundly."[5] He believed that poetry could do this better than prose, that the short poem could do it best of all, and that such a poem as Valery's *Ébauche d'un Serpent* does do it best of all. He concludes at the end of this volume: "If I seem to be attempting to instigate a revolution, it is merely in critical thinking and not in the practice of literature."[6] He gave himself twenty years to be a winner by default if his arguments should be merely brushed aside. If wrong, he said he would have to be so persuaded by reasonable argument. In this autobiographical tone, he set his own specific problem and function as twentieth century critic of poetry.

Though Winters' criticism has been condemned by other critics as stubborn and dogmatic, he is actually extremely flexible within the structure of his rational theory. In a famous essay on Robert Frost, he wrote:

> It is not foolish to change one's mind; one learns by changing one's mind. . . Life is a process of revision in the interest of greater understanding, and it is by means of this process that men came down from the trees and out of the caves; and although civilization is very far from what it should be, nevertheless mankind has shown a marked improvement over the past thousand years. This improvement is the result of the fact that man is a rational animal.[7]

Winters has been willing to change his mind about both his own poetry and that of others (Hart Crane, Archibald MacLeish, Wallace Stevens, Allen Tate, etc.) through the years of his development. (He has even written a monograph to acknowledge his revised opinion about his own protégé, J. V. Cunningham.) On the other hand, when he feels justified, he clings dogmatically to favorable opinions concerning the poems of friends, students, and disciples and to unfavorable opinions of poets who do not fall within his rational framework (particularly Yeats, Pound, and Eliot). He thinks that too many critics of today have no real structure for criticism—for judging a poem good or bad. They merely ask, "Is it of our century? Does it follow the mannerisms of our time?" As such, they are mainly helpless to identify honest writing in the best of the plain style, clinging to associational techniques long after they had lost their originality. He sees his function to cut away from schools and movements and to speak out his own heretical opinions. His personal growth—first as poet and second as critic—gave him the right to his convictions, and in the last analysis he feels that poets always know more than critics about their art. Yet they must be widely educated poets to be able to find themselves in the "tradition."

> There is likely to be over-long periods of what one might call an underground, or unpublicized, tradition of the best writing which one can discover only if one has the perception to trace the tradition from poem to poem. I am fully aware that these remarks are heretical.[8]

It is interesting to note that Winters as a very young man practiced what he preached. In a 1927 *Poetry Magazine* review, he proclaimed that Hart Crane was "one of the five or six 'great' poets writing in English today." The magazine's cautious editor, Harriet Monroe, felt constrained to remark in a tolerant footnote, "Mr. Winters strikes this editor as somewhat over-decisive. It is hazardous to hurl 'great' at any contemporary. However, the left wing has always flown with conviction, and it has seemed best not to attempt any clipping in this instance but to admit an analysis of Mr. Crane's artistic motive and style as offered by a poet in complete and enthusiastic sympathy with his art."

Winters could be so sure of himself because he had developed early a structure for his critical theory. He called it "moralistic" and "absolutist." It is best elucidated in the essays of *In Defense of Reason*, which he collected at the peak of his critical power in 1947. They represent a full fifteen years of writing and revision. He summarizes his theory thus:

> It behooves us to discover the nature of artistic literature, what it does, how it does it, and how to evaluate it. . . . The theory of literature which I defend in these essays is absolutist. I believe that the work of literature in so far as it is valuable, approximates a real apprehension and communication of a particular kind of objective truth. . . . The short poem exhausts the inherent possibilities of language more fully than any other form.[9]

Winters continues to identify a poem as "great" insofar as it makes a defensible rational statement about a given human experience and at the same time communicates the emotion which ought to be motivated by that rational understanding of that experience. The rest of the book appraises the literary production in his favorite period—the sixteenth and seventeenth centuries—and the gradual deterioration of poetry since the opening of the eighteenth century through the early twentieth century. His hopeful projection for the future came in 1967 in *Forms of Discovery*, in which he forecasts the success of what he calls the Post-Symbolist movement. He concludes *In Defense of Reason* by acknowledging his own delicate position with characteristic determination: "Our literary culture (to mention nothing more) appears to me to be breaking up . . . I hope that my efforts may in some small way contribute to the alteration of these tendencies; the rescue of it appears to me to be a matter of greater moment than the private feelings of any minor poet or scholar."[10]

The nucleus of this important volume is contained in the section called "Preliminary Problems"—problems which present themselves constantly to practicing poets and critics. They establish the basis for his "defense of reason" in his famous theory of motivation: can one assume that constant principles govern the poetic experience? ("Yes! Experience tells us so!") Can poems be rationally judged good or bad by these principles? ("Of course, by their structural patterns and their motivation.") Is this judgment a matter of intuition or rational elucidation? ("The latter, always.") What is a poem? ("A statement in words in which special pains are taken with the experience of feeling.") Thus he reduces the basic experience of poetry to bare essentials and goes on from there to develop a highly complex theory of criticism.

This critical theory is based on certain specific principles. Words are audible sounds, or their verbal symbols, which communicate by conceptual content and vague association of meaning. Rational content is essential to poetry and interrelated with feeling in any good poem; it is a relationship of motive to emotion. The exact motivation of feeling by concept is not inherent in any rational statement; any rational statement will govern the general possibilities of feeling derivable from it, but the task of the good poet is to adjust feeling to motive precisely by selecting words containing not only the right relationship within themselves, but the right relationship to each other. The good poet cannot escape the relationship of motive to emotion by confining himself to words which denote only emotion, for these words also represent concepts. One cannot extinguish the rational content of language while retaining the control of association. A good poet-critic will determine the satisfactory relationship of motive to emotion by an act of moral judgment . . . "the theory of morality deriving from reality because it guides us toward the greatest happiness which the accidents of life permit." In any "moral" situation, there is a "right" judgment as an ultimate possibility; the closeness of any judge's approximation will depend upon the accuracy of his rational understanding and his intuition and their interaction upon one another. There is, then, according to Winters, a definite moral relationship between art and human action since art gives us a better way of judging representative human action than we should otherwise have. It is thus a civilizing influence and affects the quality of daily judgment and action. Hence, the great "moral" responsibility in the aesthetic choices of the poet-critic.

Winters concludes that the nature of the critical process includes five steps: (1) the statement of such historical and biographical knowledge as may be necessary to understand the mind and method of the writer; (2) the statement of such analysis of his literary theories as may be needed to understand and evaluate his process; (3) the statement of a rational critique of the paraphrasable content—"roughly, the motive"—of the poem; (4) the statement of the rational critique of the feeling motivated—the details of style as seen in language techniques; and (5) the final act of judgment, a *unique* act, the general nature of which can be indicated, but which cannot be communicated precisely. This summary of the critical process concludes with a tactful warning from Winters-critic to Winters-poet: "It should be noted that the purpose of the first four processes is to limit as narrowly as possible the region in which the final unique act is to occur!"[11]

All of the subsequent volumes of Winters' criticism were based on exemplification and reiteration of these principles. Discerning professional critics had long since recognized their worth. They knew that he had the temerity to trust his own judgment because he had a wealth of erudition that could not be disputed; they respected this background because it came from a poet-critic with philosophical and technical finesse. They recognized that his insistence upon the term "moral" was a highly specialized use of language. It did not mean didactic in the usual sense; it meant "moral" in a technical, aesthetic sense; it was the morality of a craftsman-artist combining the best of his elements in the best possible manner so that the unique product would be rationally perfect. A poem could be considered "moral" when its "balance between feelings and perception" was achieved exactly. Winters was one of the few contemporary critics who devised a complete system of standards against which to measure works for this balance. Throughout the entire Winters canon one sees this unique act of judgment—fitting artistic sense with critical acumen—which was the final evaluation.

Two distinguished poet-critics—of whom Winters himself approved—have written enthusiastically of his prowess in both poetic and critical act. Their careful, experienced assessments are the sort of unique praise that he respected. Robert Lowell's "Tribute" in *Poetry Magazine* says: "I have been reading Winters continually since 1937. His best poems have compassion and are made of iron. His *Collected Poems* is a marvelous book. . . . He has a Malherbe-like integrity. No literary critic has a greater flair than he for making the right quotation. Ben Jonson might have written of him: 'He who casts a living line, must sweat / For a good poet's made as well as born'."[12]

Allen Tate assessed Winters' reputation with a similar commendation: "He has conducted a revolution all his own that owes little or nothing to the earlier revolutions of Pound and Eliot, and goes back to certain great, likewise neglected Tudor poets for material and stylistic models. . . . He is of the company of Gascoigne, Jonson, Greville, Raleigh, Donne. . . . He has clarity, elegance, power: qualities seldom, in our age, found together."[13]

The Philosophical Purpose of Poetry

The survey of Winters' reputation as critic logically evokes an analytical summary of his critical principles as they relate to the development of his poetry. It is significant that these principles were always propounded as a theory resulting from his active practice as a poet after he had shifted from his early experimental verse to his later traditional forms. His convictions and conclusions resulting from that shift include his ideas as to the philosophical purpose of poetry, the aesthetic process of poetry, and the management and interrelationship of its elements: theme, content, form, image, diction, and tone.

Winters' critical doctrine stems historically from his mistrust of the Romantics' dependence upon the expression of emotion for effect, and it results in his attack upon experimentalism in modern authors. For him, a poem is "moral" only if its concept motivates its emotion, and he felt that most poetry from Shaftesbury through Pound and Eliot failed in this because it separated ideas and perceptions. He believed that it was the duty of the poet to begin with content which is rationally apprehensible and then to endeavour to communicate the emotion which is approximate to the rational apprehension of that subject: "The work is thus a judgment, rational and emotional, of the experience—that is complete and moral judgment insofar as the work is successful. We regard as greatest those works which deal with experiences which affect human life most profoundly and whose execution is most successful."[14] It is thus the first business of the poet to make a statement about a *worthy* experience that must be in some sense and in fair measure acceptable rationally. All additional elements of poetry must serve this master, reason. And yet his own judgment of "moral" involves a further structural analysis. To be pronounced truly "moral," a poem's elements must work together; it is in this final act of balance that the critic recognizes the poet. John Crowe Ransom recognized Winters thus: "He is a poet first, not an illiterate moralist breaking into literary criticism. He is a master moral ideologist with a special and exotic principle of his own, far from ordinary, hard-hearted moralism—a saintliness of religious recognition—or more likely a Stoicism, saintliness's secular counterpart."[15]

Allen Tate used a Winters metaphor to describe this same "moral" test:

> The test of morality in his poetry is a profoundly understood concept motivating emotion in which the poet stands perpetually at the edge of an abyss [as at the "brink of darkness"] which he knows

> will be an abyss in spite of the fact that everybody else is eagerly trying to fall into it; the sense of unremitting crisis so heightens his awareness that his perceptual particulars become immensely vivid; but the powerful disorder of this situation is counteracted by an equally powerful mastery of language. The abyss is not denied; it is assimilated and affirmed. Winters rejects nothing; he brings his experience to order and form, and then order and form are then themselves part of the experience.[16]

These two poet-critics are the only two of Winters' own generation who seem to have realized the centrality of his concept of criticism: that the poetic elements are all aesthetically balanced around the original moral, rational concept that holds them together. Winters develops from this basic concept a structural analysis of poetic composition; when he discovers in any poem a lack of concepts adequate to the emotions expressed, he declares that poetry to be incoherent, merely qualitative, and "pseudo-referential."

As Winters developed in the thirties from his near-hysterical, perceptual free verse to the highly controlled formal poetry of his later years, he looked back from this "brink of darkness" to assess in theory what he had felt compelled to do in practice. In a key passage in a set of lectures delivered in 1957 at the Johns Hopkins Poetry Festival, he analyzed this problem to which he had set himself as poet-critic: "It ought to be possible to embody our sensory experience in our poetry in an effective way, not as ornament, and with no sacrifice of rational intelligence." Anything less than rational intelligence, he alway felt, was an insult to man's dignity, and he demanded it for what he believed to be man's highest art form. Mere coherence of feeling was not enough; he scorned "pseudo-referential" poets who retained only the syntactical form and vocabulary of reason while they reduced rational coherence to an absurd minimum. His critical test for the "great" poem was always whether or not it embodied sensory experience *rationally* and was thus logically constructed to express theories of universal, serious experience.

Too many cursory critics of Winters' criticism have attacked him for what they denounce as traditional "moralism" because they do not read the genesis of his critical development. As early as 1922, he wrote his first formal criticism of E. A. Robinson and called him significantly "The Cool Master." He digressed in his analysis of Robinson to state his germinal criteria for good poetry and eliminated once and for all the purely didactic concept with which he has been erroneously charged by amateurs:

As long as a man gives us his perceptions as they arise in the milieu of his own social and spiritual environment, he is an artist. When he becomes more interested in the possible effects of his beliefs on his reader, he becomes a philosopher, a preacher, or a mere pedlar. . . . It is not the material that makes the poem great, but the perception and organization of that material . . . in its perfect balance . . . its infallible precision.[17]

This first critical statement disabuses the notion of mere moralism of subject and includes the more subtle, complex moralism of artistry. But he was generally misinterpreted by his peers who were steeped in the twentieth century tradition of antididactic sensory emphasis. Against the grain, he settled stoically into his lonely isolation in a critical milieu suggesting to him that thought and poetry were mutually destructive, that rational structure was a defect in a poem rather than a virtue, and that sensory images should be all. He lived to see many of his critical theories vindicated in some of the best young poets of the middle of the century. Among those successes, he was proud to point out some of his own students, who in his last volume of criticism achieved this accolade from the old master: "They write with the exact adjustment of feeling to motive which results on certain occasions in poetry of extremely great value."[18]

Because he was poet first and critic second, his analysis of his art begins and ends with the artist's experience with his medium and its control in his hands. If a poem "says something in language about a human experience," then the process by which it gets said can only be second to that "something" said. The relationship of process to materials preoccupies him as poet-critic. He summarized his lifelong experience as a language artist in his last volume:

He [the artist] writes in language; it is conceptual in nature. The realm which we perceive with our unaided senses *may* be an illusion; but in that illusion we pass our daily lives, including our moral lives; the illusion is quite obviously governed by principles which it is dangerous, often fatal, to violate; this illusion is our reality. But our perceptions of this reality are inseparable from our conceptions; and one person's perceptions are sharper than another's. . . . One improves one's understanding of the general by examining the particular; one improves the particular by referring it to the general. . . . To write about human experience with distinction, one must know the relevant universals; to manage poetic form with distinction, or to perceive it clearly when managed by others, one must know the relevant universals. Language then is

> essentially conceptual *or* denotative. Philosophers and scientists employ only the denotative aspect of language, the poet employs the total context.[19]

It was this awareness of totality of concept that made the rational motive of any poem its basic element for Winters.

Two samples of Winters' "moralistic" criticism may serve here as examples of the entire body of his work. In an early essay on the poetry of Marianne Moore (*Poetry*, 1925), he writes of this poet's art:

> This exacting moralist who enforces with such intricate resonance the profound convictions of her ethical and emotional fastidiousness, has dumbfounded most of those readers whom she has not completely subjugated. Transference of the metaphysical into physical terms is her most noteworthy achievement. She is one of whose genius one feels sure.[20]

In a much later essay on Emily Dickinson, he praises the earlier poet for her work that is "based on known limits yet deals with the inexplicable facts of change. Her best poetry represents a moral adjustment to certain major problems which are carefully defined. She is one of the greatest lyric poets of all time."[21] His standards of intrinsic "morality" allowed him to make statements of finality as to the "great" poetry of any century; his final judgments were the results of what he called "certain feelings of rightness and completeness," formed and refined through his exhaustive studies of literary masterpieces. And as a result of this survey, he formed certain conclusions about the resulting poetry of this century.

He found most contemporary poetry mainly divided into two types, neither of which he found attractive: the "primitive" and the "decadent." A much smaller and more select school he termed "Post-Symbolist," in which he held great hope for the future. The "primitive" he defined as those poets who utilized all of the means necessary to the most vigorous forms, but whose range of materials was limited; "the decadent," as those who displayed a fine sensitivity to language and had wide scope, but whose work was incomplete formally or was weakened by "a vice of feeling." Experimentalism that indulged in extremes in either direction appalled him and led to the ultimate failure which he considered unconscious or conscious "obscurantism," which was for him the final morass of "the intense inane."

He found both Pound and Eliot guilty of this sin against poetry's "morality." Pound's influence and career he saw mainly as an act of reverie, his work primarily as a matter of remembered impressions of violence or sentimentality—"a sensibility without a mind." He had even less use for Eliot, who, he felt, carried the error into conscious, purposeful obscurantism. "He suffers from the delusion that he is judging when he is merely exhibiting."[22] Their common basic error, according to Winters, was to believe that they had to bend their poetry to conform to the *Zeitgeist*. "Art need not be chaotic because it is born in a time of chaos," he admonished. So this corrective absolutist sought a poetry that was "moral" in a theoretical organic manner, not just in a didactic effect. It was a poetry that would have its *own* ethic because it was aesthetically complete from motive to statement.

The Aesthetic Process of Poetry

Winters' critical theory concerns itself in a very practical way with the aesthetically "rational" process of the poetic art. This includes the "moral" choice of exact sensory details of meter, diction, and image that combine to make up tone. He knew from his own poetic experience that these did not come to the artist in any particular or sequential order. "We do not have theoretic statement followed by ornamental sensory detail, but intellectual and sensory material are so intimately related that they exist as one and the same simultaneously." Whenever he found sensory perception and philosophical concept in a carefully controlled balance, he called the poem "great," but where one outstripped or overshadowed the other, he considered the poem a failure. ("Sunday Morning" by Wallace Stevens, "The Cricket" by F. G. Tuckermann, "*Ébauche d'un Serpent*" and "*Le Cimetière Marin*" by Valery represent the wide catholicity of his favorites. He says of them, "They are sophisticated poems in every way.")[23]

The poetic process for all such sophisticated poets seemed to him to be one in which a moral evaluation of an important human experience was conveyed through all details and variations of rhythm, versification, and literary form. The poet in action was an artist creating at the highest point of intensity. Whether his material was consciously digested before that point, then simply organized and set down, or the point of intensity reached first and the material set down out of the subconscious, would depend on poet and poem. Winters believed that the latter sequence was the more usual and the more valid, since form and matter would have then come simultaneously into being, interdependently fused without loose ends. Unfortunately, this happy coincidence could not always be counted on in the poetic mind, as Winters knew all too well: "The man who comes to a form with a definitely outlined matter will more than likely have to cram or fill before he is finished; the result is broken, and rhyme as an absolute may force the issue." The more successful artist would spin images and meters out of his storehouse of combined sense and thought; his basic philosophy and emotional tone would provide the necessary unity; his rational concept would evoke the proper aesthetic emotion; and a "moral" poem would evolve from this happy focus of the artist's mind on the subject at hand. All of his individual self-consciousness would thus be eliminated, and the "great" poem would stand alone.

How then to bring about this happy process? How to encourage it and record its passage? Winters speaks autobiographically as poet in all of his critical essays on this subject. The happiest condition of all seems for him to be the one in which the poet speaks with certitude and finality. His distrust of pure process itself came after long years of experiment. He admits the fortuitous blend in the master poet's artistic moment; but he knows that its pure fluidity is dangerous. Good poets must do more than simply record their emotional processes. They must shape their material from the moment of its genesis. They must maintain the abstraction from the experience "at the brink," then reactivate the concept "recollected in tranquillity," and state it with certitude and finality as the elements are artistically blended together after the fact. The sequence of the making must always be observed again in the perspective of time—not recorded as it is being played out—for certitude. Chance art of all sorts is simply not art for Winters, because process is not enough. His aesthetic mode is neither dramatic, whimsical, occasional, or associational. After his early experiments in free verse drove him to a near hysteria of perceptual chaos, he learned to trust control and formalism. So his defense of reason comes from his own experience; in the process of poetry he finds rationality a relief after passion. He does not disown passion's necessity, but for him the finished poem is the after-word, the revised product—never the recorded flux.

It should be noted historically that, while Winters was developing his theories from his early critical essays to his last volumes, his statement of mistrust of pure process was unfortunately overexaggerated by his enemies. Winters the poet acknowledged always the ecstasy of the moment when the artistic process fused; but Winters the critic knew that correction was equally inevitable and important. The "process" of poetry for him had always been a triple experience: the ephemeral moment of the emotional present when perception takes place; the contemplative recapitulation of its abstraction in the immediate past where conception is added; and the eventual formal shaping of the material into a "moral" poem for the future.

In one of his reviews for *Poetry Magazine*, Winters digressed in a philosophical summary recording one of his most succinct statements on "process." "As long as a man gives us his own perceptions as they arise in the milieu of his own environment, he is an artist . . . however, it is not just the material that makes the poem great, but the perception and organization of that material."[24] Ever the teacher, Winters echoes himself as poet-critic in these *dicta*: "To write about human experience, to manage poetic form with distinction, or to perceive it closely when managed by others, one must know the relevant universals." His poet-philosophers must thus express these relevant universals in words which are both denotative and connotative and which evoke the proper feeling for the proper subject matter. The successful poem will first have a "moral" concept that is purely theoretical and intrinsically artistic, not just didactic; its style and content must match properly to make it more "moral" as the process evolves; finally, the "moral" attitude of the poet toward his subject matter will be unerringly communicated in the completed poem if the process has been successful at all stages. Winters' remarks on "process" conclude with his awesome self-commission: "The spiritual control in any poem, then, is simply a manifestation of the spiritual control within the poet."[25]

Winters starts from this one premise in all discussions about any of the elements of poetry; their success depends upon this first requirement. For instance, "Limp versification is inseparable from spiritual limpness . . . the greatest freedom is where the greatest clarity of form exists; free verse is not really free." Or: "Sensory perception for its own sake or even in traditional simile or metaphor is not enough; it must be charged with perfectly explicit meaning by the total concept."[26] He was confident that each poem's new perceptions—well executed and controlled—would sharpen and train the sensibilities of the poet for his next experiment; thus the developing poet could strive toward the eventual perfection of poetic form which he sought for himself. Whenever Winters was criticized by his contemporaries for such didactic pomposity, he replied that they were merely lazy about the burdensome responsibility for "moral" poetic practice.

Winters used these principles of "morality" of concept and style to criticize poets from all periods and of all persuasions. His great range of literary erudition could catch in its wide net the smallest or largest aberration from his norm. For example: "Poe's aesthetic of observation grows out of his uncertainty regarding the nature of moral truth: a willful dislocation of feeling from understanding."[27] "The catastrophe of Hart Crane results from his blind faith in his moment-to-moment inspiration so that he becomes a kind of stylistic automaton."[28] "John Berryman needs to learn to think more and feel less."[29] "Thomas Hardy seems somehow to involve the tragedy and wisdom of the whole of human experience; in Louise Bogan, the poem is only a sharply defined segment of experience."[30] "J. V. Cunningham draws abstractions from the experience and discards the experience itself."[31] In all of his criticism he demanded that "moral" totality that he tried to achieve in his own poetry, and he admitted that it was no easy task:

> A poet today, in order to free himself from the philosophical misconceptions of the age, has to turn metaphysician in a profound and serious way if he is not to be victimized by false emotions as most contemporaries are. Very few are aware of the difficulty or make the effort to justify and make possible with a measure of ease, a normal and more or less classical dignity of attitude toward human destiny and human experience.[32]

The Interrelationships of Elements

In Winters' final analysis, the "morality" of a poem depends not only upon philosophical purpose and aesthetic process but upon a more inclusive third concept: the poetic balance of the elements of the medium. The poet literally works with content, form, and image. Out of these basic elements, theme and tone are evoked through the choice of diction and the arrangement of syntax. Purpose and process concern morality of concept and evocation of experience; the balance of elements concerns the literal poem. Winters' criticism usually combines a discussion of the first two, which are theoretical, and then proceeds to analyze the third, which is purely practical. In it lies the final proof of prowess. "The two main marks by which we most readily recognize a poet, I presume, are *first* an ability to grasp and objectify a particular subject so that it is rendered comprehensible both as an individual thing and as a symbol of general experience, and *second* a command of the potentialities. The second is even more important than the first."[33]

Any survey of Winters' critical comments on poetic prowess is, of course, best exemplified as he analyzes and explicates specific poems.

His range is so catholic that it is difficult to be fair in isolating a few remarks to stand for all of his principles. However, since the purpose here is to trace his theory as it refers to his practice, it seems wise to use an historical sampling from various periods of his criticism to exemplify the whole. As a poetic analyst, he is extremely skillful in his minute examination of elements. As a synthesist he has less to say, and he leaves the final re-examination of the entire texture to the sensitive reader's own reactions. What he does demand is a careful, painstaking reading which brings complete erudition line-by-line to its explication. He has ultimate scorn for readers, critics, or teachers who offer less.

He usually comments first on content as he explicates poetry, often beginning with a general statement reiterating his famous definition of a poem, the necessity for its "moral" concept, and then some specific discourse as to why the content under examination may or may not be in accord with these principles. Unworthy, shallow subject matter cannot evoke the true poetic experience; the motive will dictate the proper content. The choice and management of content in any good poem should offer a new perception not only of the exterior universe, but of human experience as well; in other words, it should add to what we have already seen. Again Winters is willing to apply his *dicta* from one end of the poetic range to the other. He suggests for instance, that Yeats' content is "pseudo-referential" and not worthy of truly great poetry because "it is based on his own private fairy-tale—a homemade mythology and a loose assortment of untenable social attitudes."[34] (At the same time he is careful to praise Yeats for his sonority, excellent rhythm, and exciting symbol.) On another occasion he chastizes a completely unknown poet for his insipid content ". . . rather too much of peacocks, moonlight, and gardens here, though his best poems may be with us for a long time."[35] He criticizes sternly the content of J. V. Cunningham's poetry, even though Cunningham was his own protégé. He deplored its doctrine of "haecceity," the evil of nonselective choice of content. "It is lacking in all the being in the universe rather than in its own particularity."[36] Winters rejected its content as "the mysticism of pure passivity" which drew abstractions from the experience but discarded experience itself. For him choice was constant and necessary for morality. But while questioning the content of Cunningham's poetry—which he felt was "chosen" with a Stoic indifference—he admired his plain style and dedicated one of his own books to him as "the poet who has meant the most to me in this century."[37] Such examples indicate a fairness of spirit and an unlimited vision which never condemns a poet completely for the failure of one element.

His critical judgments of form are, of course, the direct result of the dramatic shift in his own practice of poetry reported in the autobiographical introduction to his *Early Poems*. Having sensed, as a young practicing poet, the necessity to move from the chaos of free verse to the controlled—and thereby greater—freedom of traditional patterns, he based his critical theories on form. He sees many modern poets making bad use of old forms or attempting new ones that will not work, thus leaving them in structural confusion. Always he returns to his initial position that a formal structure is necessary if the poem is to be a truly "moral" one worthy of its rational motivation. He created a vast and elaborate rationale of his theory of metrics in *Primitivism and Decadence* and concluded that "good free verse" is not really free at all, but actually scannable in terms of a long foot containing one heavy syllable plus any number of light accents and unaccented syllables: in other words, not really "free" but accentually cadenced. He felt the need for external form to support his own free verse before he discarded it for stricter traditions. He was disgusted with what he considered the modern, lazy assumption of many contemporary poets: that a chaotic age must result in formless poetry. In *Primitivism and Decadence* he evaluated the "new" structural methods (of repetition, logic, narrative, pseudo-reference, transference of values, qualitative progression, alternation, or of "double mood") and showed them all misguided as poet after poet was examined.

He was an extremely precise metrical analyst who heard well and read well with a professional eye, ear, and voice. For him, no verse could be truly "free" unless there were some metrical system introduced to free it *from*. Occasional variations, he felt, were more interesting when they were highlighted against a regular metrical pattern, a definitive scheme. Traditional meter was for him the frame of reference from which a skillful poet may free a phrase for the sake of texture and tone; but Winters would insist that poems that are *all* tone and texture—with no metrical form or "moral" structure—are pointless, hardly poetry at all. He saw a sad relationship between those poets who avoided the issue of rational content and those who avoided the discipline of traditional metrics; he felt that they were evading both "moral" and aesthetic issues by avoiding life's realistic pattern in their art forms. He blamed such poets as Yeats, Crane, and Jeffers for flight from form (which he found infinitely variable) with a uniformity of chaotic results. He spoke scornfully of poets whose content is nothing *but* texture (the "post-Celtic twilight" of Poe and Aiken) and those whose form is nothing but freedom (the "plasmordial delirium" of Whitman and Sandburg). The interrelationship of rational content and strict form was for Winters evidence of mature culture and honest workmanship.

As early as 1928, reviewing the "Fugitives" in *Poetry*, he predicted that these young writers—"raised on the thin modern atmosphere"—would not be able to stand the strain of building vigorous new forms for energetic poetry. He thought they were, moreover, using old forms badly if at all.

> The formlessness of younger poets seems to have taken two directions: the Eliotic breakdown of dramatic lines or those imitators of Whitman and Sandburg who throw themselves about the world and the printed page in an annihilation of meaningless exhaustion and waste.[38]

He believed that the twentieth century's increasing concentration on sensory detail and random progression had been harmful to the evolution of strong poetry, and that no sharp perception had resulted to make up for the loss of form and "morality."

Winters' major essays on form are contained in his *Primitivism and Decadence: A Study in American Experimental Poetry*. These five essays abound with precise example; all espouse traditional rather than experimental forms, and support the short lyric (which he thought was "unfortunately named") as the best form for structural principles of logic and reason. For him, it is the one form most essentially poetic because it uses the raw material of generalization and compresses it most effectively into form through rational and emotional means. Stanzaic patterns, rhyme, rhythm, and all other devices of poetic form assist in this compression, with meter being the most important element of all. His essay entitled "The Influence of Meter on Poetic Convention" makes this basic distinction.

Here he first states his theories about the relation of form to the norm of feeling—that which helps create the aesthetic "morality" of poetry. This particular essay draws some general conclusions regarding the poetic effectiveness of various types of meter and studies the influence of free verse on poetic convention. It encompasses four centuries of English literary history showing the relationship of experimental and traditional meters; it analyzes quantitative, accentual, and syllabic verse and concludes with Winters' own principles for the scansion of the best English "free" verse (using two of his own poems as examples!). When he scans his own free verse ("Quod Tegit Omnia" and "No Bitter

Moon") to illustrate his theory, he remarks that the best of his verse is always "balanced on a tightrope" between free verse and an iambic in a kind of counterpointed effect. This entire series of essays on meter finally asserts that "to depart from *any* given movement is to abandon it." Therefore he dogmatically concludes that free and traditional verse have mainly encouraged "careless substitution" in the older meters. His own total abandonment of it shows his conviction.

The determination of a poem's form, Winters believed, was as much a part of the poem's "morality" as the choice of its content. It is also involved in the evolution of what he calls the poem's "attitude." He regarded as fallacious the modern notion that the attitude necessarily preceded the form; he stated on the authority of his own experience that form *may* precede, but that attitude is never definite until the form is achieved. Having mastered form and control of emotion successfully, a poet became a stronger, more "moral" artist. This did not mean that he set up art as a substitute for religion or ethics, but simply that he found the discipline of poetic form good for the poetic soul. And best of all, it made poet and product more "mature," always a welcome transition for Winters. "If a poem constitutes a moral success in the face of certain experience, then that poem will be most valuable which, granted it achieves formal perfection, represents the most complex and difficult victory. Too many modern poets avoid mastering the more complex forms of experience."[39]

Winters' critical insights regarding imagery are widely scattered throughout his reviews and essays on other poets. He speaks of "images" in the most comprehensive sense to include the pure image, the metaphor, and the symbol as they are developed through appropriate diction and clear syntax. He believes that their purpose in poetry is, again, more than merely decorative or emotional, but in the larger sense, aesthetically "moral" because they help provide the final tone for the poem. He speaks critically of this matter in two of his essays: "The Anatomy of Nonsense" and "The Function of Criticism." These theoretical remarks serve his practical analysis of many well-known and unknown poets.

The evocation of the proper feeling for the exact content of any poem is the real test of poetic prowess for Winters. The tools are both objective (rhythm, meter, form, etc.) and subjective (imagery, diction, syntax, etc.) Skillfully blended, they balance to interweave a texture, tone, or mood—that most ineffable and personal element of all. This mixture will succeed if the poet has been skillful enough to evoke just the right sensory perceptions through image, diction, and syntax. Since language is so delicate in its varying levels of denotation and connotation, this exercise in the poetic art is one of the most difficult.

The "Seventh Problem" in Winters' "Anatomy of Nonsense" introduces this difficult task of word management. He warns that any statement—prose or poetry—may be loose or exact depending on the relationships of the words to each other, since the precision and connotation of any word depends to some extent upon its surroundings. After many examples of well-known and unknown poets of various periods, he concludes: "Concepts may be affected by connotations due to various and curious accidents . . . the exact motivation of feeling by concept is not inherent in any rational statement . . . the task of the poet is to adjust feeling to motive precisely. He has to select words containing not only the right relationships within themselves, but the right relationships to each other. The task is very difficult, and this is no doubt the reason why the great poetry of a great poet is likely to be so small in bulk."[40]

The Winters theory of language choice and management is all derived from this original insistence upon the right relationship of motive to content and style—and thereby to the evocation of the proper emotion. Images, symbols, diction, syntax will all fall into harmony of true perception if this relationship is achieved. His reviews and essays on a variety of poets illustrate his practical criticism from this basic premise. Characteristically, the positive aspects of his theory often have to be inferred from the negative statements!

As a rational authoritarian, Winters has often been too easily accused of being "anti-image." His essays denouncing Romanticism's sensibility have led to the mistaken impression that he disavows *all* sensory impressions. This is not true. He does support the necessity for appropriate sensory detail in poetry, and he counts on its effect for that proper synthesis. For instance, he criticizes J. V. Cunningham for not allowing enough romantic sensory detail, for writing poetry that is "a kind of mysticism of absolute passivity" without sufficient image, symbol, or connotative diction to evoke any emotion whatsoever. Winters' critique of a particular Cunningham poem ends with the phrase: ". . . beautifully written *if* one could imagine the experience," noting that its dearth of imagery and symbol, its choice of arid diction and stony syntax prevents any emotional experience from sensory detail. "There is nothing Romantic about the employment of sensory perception *per se*; though such perception is often used irresponsibly."[41]

In writing of Hart Crane, he again approaches the management of image, symbol, diction, and syntax from a negative perspective. He criticizes Crane for his "boundless catalogues when listing is the only effect"; he suggests that Crane lacks ". . . fluid expression bathing the perceptions and giving them a significant relation. When this hypnosis is achieved, lines of pure electricity occur!" The best poet, he concludes here, is the one whose motivation of emotion is "sound and inevitable." His problem is to give order to that emotion so that the feeling is thereby "implicated" in the pure perception. Crane, Winters felt, disintegrated early because he did *not* achieve such a synthesis due to his "Whitmanian inspiration." As a result his images were meaningless for any philosophical extension.[42]

His criticism of Yeats clarifies by negative example his ideal for the use of symbol. Yeats' symbols, Winters says, do not give us *real* meaning, but only the feeling of meaning—what Winters calls "pseudo-reference," full of the "sickness of ambiguity." The symbols go wrong, Winters states, because the ideas are wrong, and he cites several of Yeats' "wrong" ideas that for him evoke false symbols: "All good comes from emotions"; "even madness is good"; "wisdom is a pejorative term, while ignorance is the reverse"; "lust and rage are virtues"; "sex is mystic," etc. For Winters, the complexity of Yeats' symbols falls short of greatness because they are not motivated "morally" with the proper relationship of content to style, and hence, they are unreasonable.

The proper relationship of diction and syntax in Winters' poetic synthesis is emphasized in an essay on Randall Jarrell and John Berryman. Here he calls for a "command of the potentialities of language, phrase by phrase, including the rhythmic potentialities." He concludes that without the choice of proper language the best subject in the world will fall stillborn, and that Jarrell did not manage this choice. "He sounds like a female genius in a country newspaper . . . trite, banal, no sense of grace; dead passages; worse than prose freshman composition at Stanford!" While he commends Berryman for his more facile use of language, he finds him unable to define his themes clearly, disinclined to understand and discipline his emotions. "He needs to mitigate his infinite passion for himself and the universe!" He finds in neither poet the exact combination of language management, sensory detail, and morality of motive that makes for pure poetry.[43]

Having revolted against the expiring Symbolist tradition, Winters promoted what he calls the "Post-Symbolists" in *Forms of Discovery*: "Those moderns who are not interested in 'the word' only but who seek the organic perfection of the 'composition' with fine metrics, right rhyme, stanzaic integrity," all of which he aspires to in his own poetry. As he examined contemporary poets in this analytical fashion, he usually found one or more elements out of perfect balance. For instance, he would even object to a diction that did not reveal the poet's philosophical or religious attitude. Single word choice—the manipulation of that most basic element of all—was still tied in with theme and morality of motivation. The "great" poet was one who could command the abstract language of precise ethical and metaphysical thought and still not be reduced to mere sensory detail or reverie. He sought in the best Post-Symbolists and in his own poetry the use of abstract words in a descriptive context so that sensory vividness was not just decorative and illustrative, but actually organically involved with the ideas. Such words, well-chosen for both purposes, would then build and support the vitality of the perceptions.

The most ephemeral and most personal of all the poetic elements is tone. Properly synthesized, all other elements create and support it. Winters believed that the "tone" or attitude of any great poet would come from the fortuitous combination of sensory perception charged with perfectly explicit meaning by the total context. ". . . mind and matter: the two are inseparable, complex and profound. Their aim is mastery, not eccentricity or obscurity."[44] One of Winters' most dramatic pieces of criticism, his famous essay on Gerard Manley Hopkins, speaks most conclusively on this subject of tone: how the poet takes himself. Winters always preferred to have the world criticize the poem rather than the poet; but in the case of Hopkins, he thought, this could not be done because the tone was not objectified. "In my terms it is the business of the poet, not to communicate his own inscape, but to arrive at a true judgment of his subject—whatever that may be. We all have individuality, but few of us have intelligence; good poets try to exhibit the truth, not themselves."[45] Winters' basic objectivity and insistence upon controlled emotion is often mistaken for lack of "tone" in his own poetry; conversely, it is the essence of an explosive power that is all the more effective when released.

When Winters applied the five steps of his theory of criticism to a particular poem, he was completely candid and thorough. One interesting example of this technique is his analysis of a poem by his wife, Janet Lewis. He opens his remarks by saying that she is mainly a fiction writer, "one of distinguished professional standards," and that she was also "an occasional poet." His introductory comments concerning her *Poems: 1924–44* are forthright in an assessment of her specific strengths and weaknesses.

> Her themes are for the most part domestic, but the domestic theme can be as good as any other. She is a stylist of remarkable native gift and possesses an unusual knowledge of song and ballad stanzas and rhythms; she has as fine an ear for poetic movement as one can easily find in English. Her weakness is domestic sentiment, which sometimes goes all the way to sentimentality. It appears not in her subjects, but in her diction and only fragmentarily; it ruins few poems, probably none, and her book as a whole is far more distinguished than most, but it weakens a good many poems and often her most ambitious.

He then lists those poems "which succeed most fully," remarking in summary, "All of these save the last four and "Love Poems" are very slight; none, I suppose, is a great poem; but most of them are masterly." He then explicates two of her poems, comparing one which he finds "the slightest"—"Girl Help"—with one which he approves:

Lines with a Gift of Herbs

The summer's residue
The aromatic leaf,
Shrunken and dry, yet true
In fragrance, their belief,

These from the hard earth drew
Essence of rosemary,
Lavender, faintly blue,
While unconfused nearby

From the same earth distilled
Grey sage and savory,
Each one distinctly willed,
Stoic morality.

The Emperor said, "Though all
Conspire to break thy will,
Clear stone, thou emerald, shall
Be ever emerald still."

And these, small, unobserved,
Through summer chemistry,
Have all their might conserved
In treasure finally.

His analysis considers the "moral" interrelationships of all of the elements of the poem: theme, content, form, image, diction, and tone; and it ends with a final "unique judgment" which brings it close to his ideal:

> The herbs and the gift of herbs are a charming but small matter; the manner in which each herb preserves its identity, while drawing on the same sources of nourishment, is familiar—but odd when one pauses over it. But it is more than this: it is one of the permanent and reassuring beauties of the world immediately around us. The language is precise, I would say perfect, at every point. The fourth stanza, with its momentary suggestion of rhetorical irrelevance, as it actually moves into the moral, with its sudden citation of the imperial Stoic as an authority for the moral, raises the poem to something very near greatness.[46]

The conclusive criterion for the entire body of Winters' criticism is, in his words, the simple basic principle of "exhibiting the truth." As absolutist philosopher, he thought he knew what that truth was; as traditional poet, he thought he knew how to express it. As human being, he was willing to risk personal dislike to fight for it. In one of his most celebrated critical battles in the columns of the *American Scholar*, he defends this absolutist stand taken in the introduction to *In Defense of Reason*. "I believe in the reality of absolute Truth; that true judgment and true knowledge reside in God, that it is the duty of every man to approximate them as closely as his particular talents permit."[47] This affirmation places the responsibility for any writer's *own* development—and perhaps salvation—squarely on himself, and it indicates that any arbitrary interference with his assuming that responsibility is evil. "I write on *literary* ideas," he says proudly. However, the literary ideas in his criticism always reflect the basic philosophic and religious ideals of this man.

These literary ideas resulting from such absolutism color the entire body of his criticism, whether he is writing specifically about a single poet or generally about a literary theory. In his earliest important review of E. A. Robinson in *Poetry Magazine*, he commented in an aside, relevant to *Merlin and Lancelot*, "Perfection in its nature is unchanging; it is desirable, and presumably we labor to come close to it; and in that labor is the narrative of the spiritual life and its drama, and in the disastrous failure or frustration of that labor is tragedy. But perfection is an unchanging abstract ideal."[48] His subsequent criticism actually *was* the narrative of his spiritual development.

In another essay from his middle years, he states his disgust with another famous poet, Robert Frost, for what he considered "philosophical and religious relativism," though he is quick to admire artistic prowess. He entitled this essay: "To the Laodiceans: Robert Frost, Spiritual Drifter"; and he berated Frost for his inconclusive, ruminative style:

> Poetry is the most difficult, the most revised of utterances . . . . Frost, the relativist, still trusts impulses too much . . . is skeptical, uncertain without having reformed; and the skepticism and uncertainty do not appear so much the result of thought as the result of the impact upon the sensibility of the conflicting motives of his own era, taking the easy way out, drifting with the currents of his time. . . . He is whimsical, accidental, and incomplete- . . . has thus cut himself off from understanding most of human experience.[49]

The necessary proof of being *Homo sapiens*, Winters thought, was in coming to rational conclusions about absolute truth, not in escaping to any oblique, sly relativism. He spent his lifetime taking a definite stand; thus, he even eventually disavowed his own most successful student, J. V. Cunningham, whom he had originally called, "The most consistently distinguished poet writing in English today." But Mr. Cunningham made one fatal error in Winters' eyes; when he used his own poetry as example in his "The Doctrine of Haecceity," he suggested that choice was evil . . . "since it implies 'this' only and rejects all the other 'thats'. . . . Any realized particularity is in fact evil since perfection is only an ideal possibility."[50] The word "only " convinced Winters that his pupil had swerved so far from the truth that he wrote a special monograph to state his reservations. This essay became an integral part of his last volume of criticism. From it he takes off again on his firm principle of absolutism that has held stable whenever he has been tempted to look over "the brink of darkness," whether poetic, philosophical, or personal.

As might be expected, his absolutist criticism gained him many enemies; only his friends could believe that it was something deeper than intolerance or bigotry. In a century when absolutes were definitely out of fashion, many of his critics considered him dated, prejudiced, etc. Only a few farsighted new friends, sensing a shift in the future direction of twentieth century poetry, looked to him as leader. Two examples of the negative criticism are representative of its limited vision. William Barrett, in his early essay entitled "The Temptations of St. Yvor," wrote,

"Winters, like St. Jerome, is tempted into literature, yet he disguises his temptation and makes it look more innocuous than it really is; he seeks to extract so much morality from it that he gives it much more autonomy and significance than it really deserves. . . . He cannot see the historical necessity and value of experiment at certain periods."[51] (One can only wonder if Mr. Barrett ever read Mr. Winters' early writings where he *did* change his own pattern as a result of just such experimentation "at a certain period" in his life and poetry.) Twenty years later Stephen Stepanchev criticized *Forms of Discovery* on the same score: "His commitment to a wooden rationalistic dogma prevents him from recognizing excellence outside his limited sphere of interest. He seems incapable of that sudden surrender to a beautiful new poem that is like falling in love. . . . He can be fouled by his own rationality."[52] Yet Winters had spent a lifetime developing control of those "sudden surrenders" that he knew so well.

For so controversial a man to have more positive than negative support is indeed surprising. Yet by actual count there seem to be more professional critics who admire some part of Winters' absolutist doctrine than those who completely reject it. All of his critics, negative and positive, are in awe of the erudition that forms its basis. Louise Bogan wrote admiringly of an early volume: "Winters has that rare sense: the cool power to appraise evil. He does not reject it, or try to laugh it off, or try to streamline it into acceptable form. He looks it in the eye and brings a sober sense of compassionate justice to bear on it."[53] Howard Kaye assessed the last Winters volume thus: "He is one of the few critics with the temerity to trust his own judgment, for he knew that the significant history of poetry must deal with the great poems, not with the mere typical or familiar ones."[54] Allen Tate, himself a distinguished critic, wrote in *Sequoia*'s tribute-to-Winters issue: "His essays showed me things that my own less developed critical apparatus could never have revealed. I put these discoveries into a different context, but I had to get them from Winters before I could put them anywhere at all."[55]

Finally, his own publisher, Alan Swallow, in that same *Sequoia* issue, rehearses the interesting historical development of Winters' critical reputation as reviews came back to him: "One attitude early became traditional in Wintersian criticism. This custom was to offer admiration for his work but to think him 'touched' in his appreciation of the work of friends or others hardly known to the intellectual coteries of the day. If these critics will take a look at the poems, they will find he is right! A closer look will prove that he has discovered something very good indeed. I have watched with despairing amusement this bit of folklore repeated over and over. . . . His is a great honesty that has been badly reviled."[56]

Winters' own assessment of the state of contemporary criticism, his own as well as that of others, is in a typical series of letters addressed to one of his more benighted critics in *Poetry Magazine*:

> Mr. X displays, for one so uncertain of his facts, his readings and his thoughts, a self-assurance that is mildly perturbing; the more so as his case is not unique but typical of contemporary book reviewing and criticism. His method of careless examination, amateur thinking, pretentious pedantry and aimless innuendo is the method which is rapidly bringing the whole profession of literary criticism into contempt. Sincerely, Yvor Winters.[57]

When Winters could rise above this frustrated critical bickering in the press, he achieved heights of literary insight rarely attained in our century. Passages from his three major critical volumes represent this "defense of reason" and illustrate the high ideals of this fastidiously "moral" connoisseur of literature. Their chronology illustrates their evolution. The first is from *Primitivism and Decadence* in 1937. It expresses his ideal:

> It will be seen that what I desire in a poem is a clear understanding of motive and a just evaluation of feeling; the justice of the evaluation persisting even into the sound of the least important syllable. Such a poem is a perfect and complete act of the spirit; it is difficult of attainment, but I am aware of no good reason to be contented with less.[58]

The second is from "Poetry, Morality and Criticism" in *The Function of Criticism* in 1957; it suggests his own pragmatic approach.

> Poetry as a moral discipline, in the sense in which I am trying to show it to be a moral discipline, should not be regarded as one more doctrine of essays. It should offer a means of enriching one's awareness of human experience and so rendering greater the possibility of intelligence in the face of future situations involving action. It should, in other words, increase the intelligence and increase the moral temper.[59]

Finally, in the last volume published during his life, *Forms of Discovery*, he looked calmly over the final brink and announced with his usual candor the summary of his life's work:

> I am aware that this book will gain me few converts; but my faithful reader may as well face facts: I know a great deal about poetry![60]

One can never hope to analyze the "morality" of criticism and poetry that he defended through any single essay or explication. Such synthesis is only achieved in the totality of his work.

PART THREE

"I was now essential wood"

Winters' Poetic Practice

"Yvor Winters: poet, professor, critic . . ." This original sequence still holds when one turns from critical theory to actual practice in the development of Winters' double career. One need always remember that he developed his particular theories of criticism as a result of certain necessary practices in the creation of his poetry. His first published works were all poems, and his later critical canon is the direct result of his practical poetic experiments. His introduction to *The Function of Criticism* contains his *apologia* for this interrelationship and his insistence upon it:

> The poet as poet tries to write as well as possible. Every moment of his poetic life is concerned with exact and minute literary judgment, with evaluation, and he reads other poets as he reads himself, to discover what is really sound, to discover what may be improved, and in this way to improve his own intelligence and his own composition.[1]

It is ironic that he has been more widely acclaimed as critic than as poet since his controversial critical career was actually always secondary for him. He hoped people would read his poetry first and thereby better understand his criticism, since that was the order of its genesis; but few ever did. (One reviewer of *Forms of Discovery* remarks with naïve amazement that "a fine Winters poem appears on its dust-jacket," and he goes on to hope that this poem will lead people to look further into Winters' poetic work.) It is a fact that his poetry was consistently read through the years only by other poets who understood how much might be learned here: Marianne Moore, Allen Tate, Robert Lowell, Louise Bogan, John Crowe Ransom, John Ciardi, Donald Justice, Thomas Gunn, J. V. Cunningham.

Allen Tate, in "Homage to Yvor Winters," wrote,

> There are no great American poets today, but there are in Winters' sense of the term, major poets; and of the poets of my generation—

> say fifty-five to seventy—he is one of the major poets. An ignorant and stupid generation has chosen to be unaware of Yvor Winters' powerful verse. He is never quite dismissed; he is kept at a distance with the kind of magic word one uses to ward off the evil eye. That word is 'formalism'.[2]

His "formal" poetry succeeded, not only in the critical eyes of other professional poets but of fine contemporary critics as well. When his *Collected Poems* first came out in 1953, they were hailed by David Daiches as "the equal of anything in the United States since Emily Dickinson." He praised them as poems that "work by limitation . . . precise, restricted, remarkable technical accomplishment and control . . . rank with the finest of their kind to be written by modern American poets."[3] Richard Elman called them "strong, masculine, poetic statement that is not anachronistic . . . as engaged with human experience as the most robust of his contemporaries . . . potent with meanings, impeccable of diction; something strongly and deeply believed and understood."[4] And finally Rolphe Humphries summarized his reputation in the modern world: "The thanks of his contemporaries are due Mr. Winters for his energetic, theoretical, and practical defense of neglected values in his criticism and his poetry."[5]

Winters' reputation as poet is just now beginning to be felt in contemporary anthologies. Robert Lowell lamented this lack of attention to him in a "Tribute" in *Poetry Magazine* at the beginning of this decade:

> Dim-wits have called him a conservative. He is the kind of conservative who was so original and radical that his poems were never printed in anthologies for about twenty years. Neither the avant-garde nor the vulgar had an eye for him. He was a poet so solitary that he was praised adequately only by his own pupils.[6]

His own proud reticence was partly to blame for some of his lack of poetic acclaim. His publisher Alan Swallow remarked about Winters' reluctance to print anything except his carefully selective *Collected Poems*, and how he had insisted that this volume not be printed until every single copy of the earlier restricted *Giant Weapon* had been sold. Winters' distrust of most anthologists' taste led him to scorn their invitations, and only now after his death has his own anthology, *The Quest for Reality* (a companion piece to *Forms of Discovery*), been published. So any student of his poetry must acknowledge the fact that—for better or worse—he deals with the highly selected canon which Winters' careful eye has reduced to a minimum. The 1961 *Sequoia* tribute issue carries Swallow's high confidence in his poet from whom two small volumes were to be the total production: "I believe that Winters is an even better poet than he is a critic. It seems to me that with the death of Wallace Stevens, Winters must be acknowledged as the greatest living poet in America today."

But Swallow's faith came only after Winters' long years of trying to get a single publisher who would be willing to risk even a first volume. His first experimental Imagist free verse was finally published in 1921 by Monroe Wheeler of Evanston and entitled *The Immobile Wind.* His second volume, *The Magpie's Shadow*, was brought out by Musterbookhouse, Chicago, in 1922; and his third, *The Bare Hills*, was printed in Boston in 1927 by The Four Seas Company. Finally a series called "Fire Sequence" was published in *The American Caravan* in 1927; but none of these received any wide attention.

Then came the literary climate of the thirties which reflected T. S. Eliot and which was hardly aware of Winters' growing work as it began to appear in a number of periodicals. Nonetheless, this proved the truly formative decade in Winters' development as he shifted from experimental free verse in the Imagist tradition to his necessarily formal classic patterns; quite naturally his writing became less acceptable to publishers as he wrote more and more out of the current fashion. He tried three other small publishers in this difficult decade, with three resulting small volumes: *The Proof* in 1930 by Howard McCann did not yet reflect his change of mode; but by the time *The Journey* came out from the Dragon Press, (Ithaca, New York, 1931), it was obvious that he was developing a new method. The change was evidenced in more detail in *Before Disaster* from Tryon Pamphlet Series in 1934. Only one anthology—his own *Twelve Poets of the Pacific*—in this entire decade carried a small sampling of his work. Despairing in the late thirties, Winters himself printed his poems for private circulation. ("I have printed these poems by hand on my own Gyroscope Press at Los Altos, in the years 1939 and '40.") These volumes were reviewed in only a very few places; indeed review copies in the usual sense were not sent out. They had small chance of attracting critical awareness, led to no anthologies, and made small reputation.

In the early forties Winters' *Giant Weapon* was published as a pamphlet in a cumulative volume entitled *Poets of the Year* (Norfolk, Connecticut, New Directions, 1943). Here Winters was at last in distinguished company. New Directions billed the volume as part of "a series of booklets, each number being printed at a different fine press: $5.00 per year; fifty-cents per copy." (Earlier titles included John Donne, Rainer Maria Rilke, W. C. Williams, John Berryman, R. P. Warren, Mark Van Doren, Dylan Thomas, Arthur Rimbaud, and Berthold Brecht.) Winters wrote with his usual critical candor in its introduction: "This book represents a selection from what seems to be my best work of the past twelve or fourteen years, although a few poems that seem to me better than some here included have been omitted for reasons that it would take too long to explain."

Alan Swallow, who was later to expand the Winters canon into a full collection, has written that this New Directions pamphlet did an unintentional disservice to the eventual career of Winters, poet. It whittled down the great work to too small a compass, giving it the appearance of a minor collection, so that, again, the reputation-making anthologists and reviewers could, with a kind of impunity, neglect the work or pay only token service to it. By that time, the large body of Winters' poetic production had been completed, and what should have appeared—had the publishing mood been at all receptive—was a collected volume. In despair, Winters, at the end of the decade of 1949, published his second anthology, *Poets of the Pacific*, and included none of his own poetry.

By this time, however, a young independent publisher had noted Winters' early writing and was determined to get in touch with him. Alan Swallow of Denver had written an article called "The Sage of Palo Alto" for the *Rocky Mountain Review* and sent it to Winters, who received it kindly but offered some professional advice on criticism. Swallow next proposed a full book of Winters' poems. He describes the poet's reaction in his *Sequoia* tribute essay thus:

> But with that great honesty for which he has been so badly reviled, Winters refused to entertain the notion until *The Giant Weapon* had sold out. For almost a decade the matter stood: the work inadequately presented and therefore having little chance to secure a reputation which would sell it quickly. It was a glad day for Winters' admirers when his own *Collected Poems* could appear in 1952. Its career almost gives one hope that critical intelligence *does* have an effect, that time can right some wrongs. For the volume not only persists; it looms even larger in the consciousness of all those concerned with important poetry. . . . We shall gradually learn to acclaim the great poet who has been so long with us and whom we have neglected.[7]

Small revisions and additions were made to the carefully selected *Collected Poems* in the 1963 edition, and it was brought out in paperback in 1960 and 1968. Winters himself in his late years sorted and collected his *Early Poems: 1920–28* in an effort to control which ones should be saved and which destroyed. The volume spans his writing from age nineteen to twenty-seven and provides autobiographical notes. The Winters career in poetry and criticism came full circle with his final work, *The Quest for Reality*, an anthology collected and edited with his student Kenneth Fields; it served as supplement to the critical *Forms of Discovery* published in 1967. After his death, the Swallow Press persuaded Mrs. Winters to select certain poetry for a new *Collected Poems*. This was published in early 1980 and shows a certain revision of his "all-I-wish-to-keep" attitude. Some of the hitherto uncollected pieces occur here and make this posthumous volume the richest treasure of all.

The publication survey of Winters' poetic career clarifies its historic shift of method in the thirties. Having compressed experimental free-verse forms and impressionistic, symbolic effects to their limit, Winters began to turn very gradually through three more volumes to a more patterned formal style. He was still writing free verse as late as 1930, though using a more controlled technique, and by the end of the volume entitled *The Proof*, 1930, he was actually ready to entitle one poem "Sonnet." Thereafter, practice and theory were consistent and simultaneously developed. The emphasis before the thirties had all been on imagistic intensity: the specific, the particular, the concrete. His new style of verse, remarkable for its precise rhythms and for an imagery of electric vividness, seemed to impel him to state a new theory. He said in his introduction to *Early Poems* that the shift was not due to academic influences at Stanford or to any sudden religious conversion, but that it had become increasingly obvious to him that the great poets had practiced formal control as a discipline, and that he could never hope to approach their quality unless he accepted the same limitation.

By 1930, he had become increasingly interested in certain traditional forms of English poetry: the sonnet, the heroic couplet, and the iambic line of three or four feet. *The Journey* (1931) was written entirely in heroic couplets, and after this volume all of his poetry appeared in traditional forms. A key passage explaining this change occurred in Winters' retrospective lecture at the Johns Hopkins Poetry Festival given in 1958. "It ought to be possible to embody our sensory experience in our poetry in an efficient way, not as ornament and with no sacrifice of rational intelligence." His development through the *Collected Poems* shows this effort to control emotion by reason and form. As his expression of sensory experience moved toward a more logical order, so did his themes become less personal and more seriously universal. Richard Ellman observed this development in a review of *The Early Poems*. "These beautiful, queer little gems of eye and ear composed in the early free verse, imagist style, that he was later to rail against, actually had in them certain tones which eventually harmonized to form some of the great, fully orchestrated later compositions."[8]

It should be noted in summary that the development of his verse and criticism has followed a curve of great historical interest—from the early short poems in the Oriental and American Indian patterns, then the experiments in free verse; next, the explosive one-line projections of single perception, and finally the reversal and gradual shaping toward ordered, traditional forms. It was a deliberate progress as Winters' own study and practice developed with a dedicated care for composition. In "The Morality of Poetry" he spoke of the experience as the "ever-fluid complex" that is a poem. Until the end of his career he was determined to harness this force by grasping his subject in the coherent terms of his neat equation: "The relationship in a poem between rational statement and feeling is thus seen to be that of motive to emotion." Against this standard he constantly measured his own work of a lifetime and preserved or destroyed it on that basis. (For instance, he entirely omitted on the basis of their "softness" *Four Poems* originally published as a suite in *Poetry Magazine* when he compiled his *Collected Poems*.) In 1937 he gave himself "twenty years to be a winner by default" if his arguments were merely brushed aside, or declared a loser if proved wrong. Thus far, no critic has been able to prove his loss in poetry *or* to ignore his *dicta* in criticism.

Before the poetry of Winters can be properly examined, it is necessary to review his own conception of the nature and function of poetry. "I believe that a poem is a statement in words about a human experience. In each work there is a content which is rationally apprehensible and each work endeavours to communicate the emotion which is appropriate to the rational apprehension of the subject. The work is thus a judgment, rational and emotional, of the experience—that is, a complete moral judgment in so far as the work is successful. . . . We regard as greatest those works which deal with experiences which affect human life most profoundly and whose execution is most successful."[9] In every poem Winters ever wrote he literally stood trial for such a judgment, and he expected all serious poets to submit themselves in their work as he did. He could take the slightest subject ("Elegy on a Young Airedale Bitch Lost in the Salt Marsh" or "On the Dedication of a Book of Criticism") and develop it into a full-scale, universalized theme with carefully-wrought images and emotionally-controlled tones.

He sought for his own poetry that style which he was eventually to call "Post-Symbolist"—intellectual, plain, pure, precise, yet highly charged with emotional tension; he acknowledges that few readers will be able to comprehend it fully. After abandoning his early Symbolist-Imagist poetry of the thirties, he analyzed his later style as having been influenced by a disparate group including Wallace Stevens, Emily Dickinson, Robert Bridges, T. Sturge Moore, Lecomte de Lisle, Baudelaire, and Valery. He saw himself in a "counter-romantic" mode of writing and sought a final style that could use "abstract words in descriptive context."

For these demands he chose the medium of the short lyric poem—"the most essentially poetic, the most powerful, the most sensitive." This form left no room for the dangerous habit of reverie or associationalism. It could never allow the poetic mind to be casual or contingent, thereby denying its purposive nature in which he believed so completely. Rather, it cultivated the mind's better qualities: its stringent, economical, self-contained, restrictive, ascetic, orderly processes. Poetry from such a mind and spirit would reach its greatest heights, he thought, when its sensory perceptions and its philosophical themes were combined—not as ornamental background or metaphysical abstraction, but in simultaneous visual and intellectual synthesis. His ideal Post-Symbolism combined carefully controlled association with this new image ". . . in which sense perception and concept were simultaneous, in which phrases contain certain image and idea together."[10] These were the requirements for the ideal poems that he sought in his own creative practice. The final marks of the true artist were, for him, constant care and correction for reasoned control.

So Winters in his mature years set himself to the immense task of changing his style and developing it as inspired by the masters of the sixteenth century lyric. Of these men he had written: "Only a master of style can deal in a plain manner with obvious matter. . . that kind of poetry that is hardest to compare and last to be recognized."[11] He did not demand for it a striking or original subject; rather something merely true or universal. Its rhetorical procedure need not be striking or necessarily original, but always economical and efficient. Its originality would at best be stated only in a most restrained, subtle diction and cadence. But its universals would show their full value of experience by virtue of these subtleties. He knew that he would risk for the insensitive reader a tone which might appear too plain or even brusque; but in the minds of the more sophisticated, he hoped to be acclaimed "laurel, archaic, rude. . . " in the finest sense. One such sophisticated poet-reader, Robert Lowell, wrote of his poems: "They have compassion and are made of iron. . . . He is a writer of great passion who has been praised adequately only by his own pupils."[12] When Winters admonished those pupils, "Write little; do it well," he spoke from long years of experience, "blotting ten thousand lines" as his sixteenth century master had recommended long ago.

When he sifted through his work for "everything I wish to keep," he left only those poems whose style was characterized by their deliberate leanness, studied sharpness, neatness of expression, and epigrammatic tone. They were the poems that avoided soft or blurred images; the only images allowed were those that directly reflected the thematic concept. The most important quality of his style was his ability to cease when he had said enough; and his collections reflected this same control in their compactness. Harriet Monroe's original assessment in 1921 of this "Youth in the Desert" still held forty years later for the old man in the garden. She had called him: "a seeker of austere Beauty in her cool remote haunts with his Pegasus reined by a taut technique."[13]

He achieved that technique by working outward from hard absolutes of meaning and intuition toward sense and sensibility. In process, it was an almost mystical accomplishment for him. Though he tried all of his life to set it down, step by step, in prose, he knew that in the last analysis it belonged only to other poets to truly experience it. His images of stone, for instance, were interrelated with his themes of timelessness in poem after poem and held in the tight control of short form and onomatopoeic diction; if the magic combination happened to come to perfect balance, good poetry evolved. He has written of the startling effect of this cumulative moment: "Good poetry seems, when one reads it, to have been born from line to line, from word to word at the end of a pen. . . ; though inspiration is normally achieved one line or word at a time through hard work over protracted periods."[14] The ideal poet, then, caught up in the ideal moment of his art's consummation would seem to be completely artless, but Winters—priest and mystic though he was—respected and acknowledged the long years of training for the discipline that made the eventual truth possible. His final requirements for success were summarized in *Primitivism and Decadence*:

> The very exigencies of the medium as the poet employs it in the act of perception should force him to the discovery of values which he never would have faced without the convening of all the conditions of that particular act. . . . The poet who suffers from such difficulties instead of profiting by them is only in a rather rough sense a poet at all.[15]

Themes

When one examines Winters' poetry to identify its various themes, there is one striking impression. Most of them are involved in one way or another with "moral" attitudes. His themes always reflect his seriousness of purpose, his assurance that he does know right from wrong, and his absolutist *dicta*. The "moral" quality of his art dictates his choice of poetic themes. He believed that the poet's chief end morally was to exercise judgment so that he could maintain a balance between his understanding of his experiences and his emotional responses to them—avoiding both the primitive and the decadent pitfalls. His system of absolutes centered around a half-dozen themes that recur from his earliest poetry to his latest. In a progressive sequence, half of these concern his own personal experiences and develop in the early poetry first; the other half evolve from them into universals and are more evident in the later poetry. They are all sufficiently interrelated to show the steady growth in this poetic and philosophical mind from groping adolescence to resigned maturity. One of his favorite definitions of poetry—"a spiritual exercise leading toward intelligence"—would make an excellent title for the sequential development of his six main themes. They exemplify the spiritual autobiography which his poetry collections comprise:

1) Perception of *the artist's identity* in the Universe
2) His *appraisal of forces* of truth, wisdom, and justice against evil, ignorance, and injustice
3) His humanistic *relationship of man to nature*: his artifacts versus Nature's laws
4) His *development of stoic strength*
5) His *spiritual search for the ultimate mystery*
6) His *desire for timelessness*

Although all six are interrelated and recurrent in all stages of his development, the first three are predominant in the early poetry, and the last three in the later. His first imagistic exercises—sometimes only a single-line statement of these themes—led eventually to fully developed and integrated poems in his mature style: statement, analysis, and conclusion. Halfway through the canon, he began to write sonnets as developmental exercises, and from these one may watch the themes grow in maturity as this form develops. (One particular sonnet, "The Fable," is a perfect example of transition in form *and* theme from the first half of his neatly balanced canon to the second.) As the style became more formal, the themes became more universal, the feeling deeper, the content less personal and more general.

An examination of his themes shows the first two lending themselves to Imagist treatment; the second two to a kind of academic treatment, and the last pair to a metaphysical treatment. It is significant to note that Winters was well enough aware of this sequential development to entitle the volume that stands at exact midpoint of his shift of theme and method "The Proof." Yet one of his best students, J. V. Cunningham, warns against too analytic a division: "Winters can never be sifted into piles. He is all at once."[16]

Although there is this organic recurrence of all six themes throughout the poetry, it seems wise for practical purposes to consider each one separately before experiencing their varied riches in a complete reading of the *Early* and *Collected Poems*. Winters finally determined to preserve an additional 129 poems of his *Early Poems* after he had collected his first volume of 117. Only about twenty of the best of these early poems had been originally included in the *Collected Poems*, but with his passion for scholarship's perfection, he wanted to make the picture of his *own* development complete. In the posthumous recent publication of the "collected poems," Mrs. Winters saw fit to include some of the poems that had been omitted from earlier volumes. Donald Davie, in his introduction to the book, remarks:

> Winters' poems were not written for classroom use or for polemical purposes; they were composed and made public not as models or *exempla* or illustrations of 'how to write'; but as considered statements of 'how to live,' or of how the business of living has been experienced by one thoughtful and feelingful man. . . . What is the poet inside the poet-critic doing, if not outwitting the critic in him?[17]

Throughout the entire Winters canon, a survey of his six themes shows the first to be his apprehension of the artist's self-identity, his perceptions as a "feeling" person. There is good reason to claim much of this early poetry as autobiographical; *The Brink of Darkness* showed to what lengths this self-awareness might be disastrously carried as the young artist's personality seemed to be gradually invaded by the powers of darkness. His earliest Imagist poetry is full of a young poet's absorption of sense impressions and perceptions for their own sakes; later he begins to worry about their effects, emotional and psychological. He is titillated by the sheer physical ecstasy of "hawk's eyes," "the immobile wind," "the pale mountains," "goats' hooves," "desert sands,"; and the early poetry builds on this "awareness" theme as it is related to its Imagist forms. One of the most beautiful of these simple poems is "Song" in which the form and images reflect the utter simplicity of the theme of artistic sensitivity. But even as early as the second poem in the first book there is the menacing "One Ran Before," where the theme involves more than mere physical image; the final stanza warns:

And this were more
A thing unseen
Than falling screen
Could make of air.

The foreboding silence of this early poem and the "darkness" of the early short story are similar, audibly and visually, in the development of this theme; as the senses rise to higher and higher pitch, the mind is driven to contemplate a possible hysteria which might surrender to the invasion of unreason unless checked. Instantaneous perceptions of the artist's sudden or arrested movement against the universe's implacable background provide tense images for this theme. Kenneth Fields, Winters' friend and collaborator, points out in "The Free Verse of Yvor Winters" how this poet often associates two perceptions in a single-line poem. In his later work, Winters was more complex in images and forms, but this same theme remains: the artist's highly attuned sensibilities confront the universe in time and space with a certain hysteria lest it either be lost to him or absorb him completely. The tightly reined later poetry shows the artist finally in control of both theme and form (see "The Vigil" and "The Proof") but with the same old haunting fear of the Imagists' juxtaposition of irrational, disparate associations. The theme suggests the artist caught up in the constant Heraclitean flux of his physical world: glorying in his super powers of perception; reeling in the terror of his romantic seriousness, but clutching firmly for balance to a classical control of his art form. His second book, *The Magpie's*

Shadow, is the one in which he experiments most extremely with this theme, eliminating everything except statement of the essential perception, describing only the quality of hallucination against the landscape in pure Imagist fashion. This theme of the artist's awareness extends from his earliest Imagist efforts to his last poem in the *Collected Poems* where he draws the mature conclusion of abstraction at the end of "Dream Vision":

> I was now essential wood
> . . .
> Orchard tree beside the road
> Bare to core but living still
> Moving little was my skill.

One of his best mature poems, "Sir Gawain and the Green Knight," tells of the artist-hero's successful war within himself against such sensuality and epitomizes his spiritual salvation after having confronted nature and experience without evasion or submission. If Winters seems to some critics to have dwelt overlong on the control of such temptation, it is only because he recognized its great attraction for aesthetes like himself. The reader of his *Collected Poems* always gets the feeling that he was never able to omit completely this constant theme of the awareness of the artist's own private hallucinatory perceptions. It runs like a dark "remembrance of things past" from first to last as the most personal undercurrent in all of his writing. His sharp apprehension of the physical always seems to end in profound disenchantment. Two of his best, "The Longe Nightes When Every Creature . . . " and "Sonnet" at the end of *The Proof*, show him in complete control of this theme. His dedicatory poems to Melville and Emily Dickinson evidence his intense kinship with earlier writers using this same theme.

Winters' second theme concerns the artist's awareness of his position in the mundane world around him. This involves his appraisal of the forces of truth, justice, and wisdom as they battle in the here-and-now against evil, injustice, and ignorance. And since this is Winters at his most realistic level, it sometimes results in what critics have scoffed at as merely "occasional" poetry. But when one analyzes the total performance, it is obvious that any "occasion" merely serves the poet as touchstone for a full-scale treatment of man's inhumanity. David Daiches has pointed out: "His poetry is more than occasional. It takes off from something observed and remembered, or from a contemporary occasion, and by a combination of perception and meditation wrings some human meaning out of it." There is no impersonal occasionalism about such poems as "Postcard to a Social Muse." Its ponderous title bespeaks the high irony of the situation in which a naïve critic had engaged in an inexact search for wisdom and thus enraged this erudite poet by her shallow claims. Similarly, "On the Death of Senator James Walsh" expresses in formal sonnet cadence the tribute owed by *all* men to those . . . "whose purpose and remorseless sight pursued corruption for its evil ways." Another long-titled poem, "To a Woman on Her Defense of Her Brother . . . ," rails against the "villainy of pride in scholarship" and in "cold impartial hate" debates a case in which Winters himself historically engaged. He uses his cool power here to appraise evil and to seek compassionate justice. "To a Military Rifle" condenses the futile problem of war into a fine, lean poem; "The Prince" laments the irony of a political establishment that breeds corruption from power. The most personal of many poems on this theme is his "Hymn to Dispel Hatred at Midnight" in which he seeks to exorcise his own heart's evil thoughts. One may indeed justify the title of "humanist" for Winters in this poetry—"Nor is the mind in vain"—since his subject is always the dignity of man's commitment in spite of his limitations. There is a tragic force about this poetry as he refuses to abandon the world, but attempts always to subject it to "a lasting proof." He resents each break or defilement of the moral order by general chaos or specific evil, and his poetry predicts doom for our civilization if these continue to pile inexorably on one another. So "occasional" verse becomes universal poetry; and "A Prince" of wisdom and good heart must be found to save us from our fatal drift toward self-destruction. Winters calls us all to such royal ambitions:

> Betray the witless unto wisdom, trick
> Disaster to good luck, escape the gaze
> Of all the pure of heart, each lunatic
> Of innocence, who draws you to his daze;
> And this frail balance to immortalize,
> Stare publicly from death through marble eyes.

The poetry of Winters' second theme is of the mind, as the first was of the senses; yet they both involve the reader and writer in specific personal preoccupations evoked by this poet's great passion for integrity in human relations.

The third theme—man's humanistic relationships in nature—begins to move away from personal references but does not completely deny them. Rather it contrasts the human condition with the vast imponderables of the natural world. It shows the frail human highlighted against the backdrop of nature's vast panorama, contrasts his puny artifacts with nature's laws, and is sometimes reminiscent of the nineteenth century's pathetic fallacy in its longing for nature's kinship. But this poetry often abandons that romantic longing for a thematic irony that is akin to Hardy or Dickinson. This man sees himself in perspective against the flat immensity of cosmic forces and examines his own small niche maintained by scientific technology. "Nor is the mind in vain," he writes. His theme reflects the dignity of man's reason, his commitment to his preservation in spite of his limitations. A poem may take off from any single person, place, or thing; but it will always return to the one great ironic cosmic fact of man's boundaries. Such a Winters poem will usually be a combination of perception first and meditation second, with a highly sharpened focus as the one is juxtaposed against the other. In "Quod Tegit Omnia" one finds the cosmic background given first—"Earth darkens. . . ;" then ". . . the mind, stored with magnificence, proceeds into the mystery of Time." An early poem in *Fire Sequence* entitled "The Bitter Moon" opens with traditional Imagist background and ends with the narrator swearing wistfully, yet recognizing his own futility:

> You are the way, the oath
> I take, I hold to this—
> I, bent and thwarted by a will
> to live among the living dead
> instead of the dead living;
>
> . . . .
>
> Can you feel through Space,
> imagine beyond Time?
> Can you find this end?

In the poetry of his later mode he sets the same theme—"Before Disaster," "By the Road to the Air Base," "At the San Francisco Airport"—where the small artifacts of man take on limited significance as great relativistic ironies are developed. His sharp apprehension of man-made, physical things against the mysterious screen of eternity etches the mind of the reader in such poems as "The Streets" ("I met God in the streetcar but I could not pray to him. . .") and "Rows of Cold Trees":

I have walked upon
the streets between the trees that
grow unleaved from asphalt in a night of
sweating winter in distracted silence.
I have
walked among the tombs. . .

The tragic limitation of the mind of man is here contrasted to its earlier defiance. Both themes are conveyed in strong statement, evading nothing, and accepting failure courageously. They are carried by many subjects: from the historical "John Day, Frontiersman" or "John Sutter"; the mythological "Orpheus," or "Sir Gawain"; the didactic "On Teaching the Young," or "Prayer for My Son." Yet they all remain relevant to Winters' particular age and milieu. This last poem to his son could serve as his summation of the plight of humans striving against an unmanageable universe. It grew from an epigram in one of his wife's poems ("Tangled with earth all ways we move. . ."), and it is one of his most personal statements:

Earth and mind are not one,
But they are so entwined,
That this, my little son,
May yet one day go blind.
Eternal spirit, you
Who guided Socrates,
Pity this small and new
Bright soul on hands and knees.

Such flashes of insight into the relationship between man and nature evoke a tension that is stern and dry and without romantic sentimentality. The poetry of this theme takes a straight look at the horror of "Chaos and old Night" and girds itself with human reason for the inevitable moment "before disaster." It accepts the sparseness of human certainty; yet it has respect for human history. As such, it is a truly general rather than an "occasional" poetry.

The first three themes mentioned all included a personal element: man's artistic perception of his identity, his local human condition, and his cosmic position. The last three themes of Winters' poetry move away from this personal interest in man and seek basic universal truths, more often found in denial of the flesh than in its acceptance or exaltation.

They include a desire for stoic resignation, a search for the ultimate mystery, and a hope for a mystic timelessness. These philosophical themes of the later Winters poetry are in direct contrast to the more personal themes of the early works.

One particular poem, "Sonnet," at the end of *The Proof*, indicates this historical shift from physical to spiritual emphasis in both theme and form. The old madness from high sense impression is controlled, and the poet concludes: "We lose reality in symbolism. / Stripped of our own meaning, / simplified for men . . . . / . . . . The mind escapes." Its escape is from violence and bitterness into calm contemplation that controls his poetry from this point on. The poetry on this theme of resignation marks the beginning of Winters' mature writing; the best of his criticism grows at this same time and carries much the same tone. The style of these poems becomes more sure as the themes grow more complex and universal. They stem from a profound disenchantment with the world in general and himself in particular: "I, crumbling, in the crumbling brain of man. . ." And yet he views the death of pleasure and decay in nature as a fulfilling experience for man. In "Summer Commentary," for instance, he shows a man striding purposefully through a field of fermenting fruit with the constant knowledge of his own simultaneous destruction; this is more than sheer hedonism. This theme is again evident in two poems written from his American literary heritage. In "To Emily Dickinson," he speaks directly to her in a sonnet depicting their common Stoicism:

> Yours was an empty upland solitude
> Bleached to the powder of a dying name;
> The mind, lost in a word's lost certitude
> That faded as the fading footsteps came
> To trace an epilogue to words grown old
> In that hard argument which led to God.

Again, in a pair of poems to Herman Melville, he seeks for his own restless spirit the quiet contemplation that he imagined the older poet had finally achieved. He addresses "A Portrait of Melville in My Library":

> . . . Rest here in quiet now. Our strength is shorn.
> Honor my books! Preserve this room from wrack!
>
> . . . .
>
> Wisdom and wilderness are here at poise,
> But still I feel the presence of thy will:

> The midnight trembles when I hear thy voice,
> The noon's immobile when I meet thine eyes.

The next theme develops naturally in the sequence toward some search for salvation and reconciliation with maturity. In several poems Winters examines the possibilities of a religious experience—even a Christian experience. He wrote as an absolutist in his late criticism that he felt such an experience was impossible for any thinking man in the modern world; yet a good deal of the poetry hints at an active religious hope. In one of his wilder (and worst) poems, he shrieks "Belief is blind!" His sense of the mystery of the universe runs throughout all of the poems: from the early perceptual ones (such as the hedonistic "Song of Advent") to the sophisticated metaphysical ones of the *Collected Poems* ("To the Holy Spirit," "A Fragment," and "A Song in Passing"). These last three indicate his stern compulsion for a religious experience; it is significant that he released these poems as a separate pamphlet through the Cummington Press in 1950. They seem to represent some sort of milestone in his spiritual development. And yet its source seems to elude him. "Thou whom I try to reach . . . to know thee as I ought . . ." He finally asks, "Was there another birth?" and then concludes wistfully, "I cannot find my way to Nazareth. Thy will be done, and let discussion cease." It is obvious that he was attracted by the ultimate mystery of the Christian experience, but as an avowed rationalist he could go no farther than the profound knowledge that the mystery exists; and he is never sure that it exists for *him*. In "To the Holy Spirit," he achieves a kind of reconciliation with the mystery and accepts his own ignorance of it; he finally dismisses the pain and anxiety of his search:

> Only one certainty
> Beside thine unfleshed eye
>
> . . . .
>
> Into irrelevance.

With such a rejection, he was forced to turn to another source for mysticism. His "Sir Gawain and the Green Knight" showed a rational soul in desperate conflict with the forces of subhuman nature. Yet it also showed the spiritual discipline necessary to achieve mastery over it, "though the eye sear with the effort." Winters—a tough, solitary man at the end of his life and career—adopted his own particular variety of mysticism. His earliest reviewer and friend, Agnes Freer, had predicted this development when she wrote of him in 1922: "He expresses himself only to a higher grade of intelligence and to the especially initiated. . . some of a special mystic with the feeling below the feeling that persists in many of his poems."[18] Death was no hopeful religious experience for him; it was full of horror and decay. Yet he recognized his potential immortality in another direction through his poetry.

In the absence of traditional religion, he sought timelessness and perpetuity for his artistic productions—whether in his garden or his poems. His perceptive earliest poems had concerned the timeless present as opposed to the fleeting past; his later poetry repeats this theme as it reaches for the future timelessness that he desired. The theme is often revealed through the use of particular images: the association of stone with the nonliving and wood with the living runs throughout many of his poems. As the one is compressed into the other by time, so is timelessness achieved as this poetry is compressed. In "Hill Burial," for instance, such finality is given to the imagery of the last lines. In some of the early poems of *Fire Sequence* the sheer quality of incantation compresses this theme into a reiterated order. "Quod Tegit Omnia" shows the only true timelessness or renewal to be found in the individual artist's transforming new experiences. If his identity is to be preserved at all, it must be in his art. Hence the poet becomes more alive and "timeless" as his perceptions are more uniquely his own. If Winters were any sort of theist at all, his god would probably be a poet, and a rational one. He was terribly aware of the cold certitude of being "essential wood . . . bare to core, but living still" as he neared the end of his life. Such poems as "The Slow Pacific Swell" indicate his meditations on the mystery of death, and much of his last poetry carries this grave, brooding theme. The recognition of its imminence, its terrible cost, his lack of orthodox belief are all finally surmounted in the poetry that celebrates the dignity of man's commitments to his own limitations. "A Song in Passing" concludes "Death is but death, and not, the most obtuse of ends." "To the Moon" addresses his final deity as he waits for a complete reconciliation with timelessness; this poem appeared as the final one in his *Collected Poems.*

His view of time is ". . . the progression of existence toward meaning that its changing cannot find." He would oppose this and find the secret with his mind's reason if he could; but much of his poetry carries the theme of acceptance and the desire for timelessness. He sought this through cultivation of his particular "gardens": the literal one where he tended the exotic desert plants and tropical fruits around his small study; and his poetic "garden" where he hoped to cultivate the timeless qualities of those masters whom he cherished. The struggle for timelessness in his life is finally epitomized in "Time and the Garden."

I would expand to greatness. No one hears,
And I am still retarded in duress!
And this is like that other restlessness
To seize the greatness not yet fairly earned

. . . .

Unbroken wisdom in a single look,
Though we know well that when this fix the head
The mind's immortal, but the man is dead.

With these last lines, he wrote his own thematic epitaph.

Content

Choice of poetic subject matter for Winters might be any interesting thing that was significant enough to evoke the moral concepts that his critical theory demanded. According to this theory, the poet makes a judgment—final and unique—that the subject of his poem will be a strong enough vehicle to carry the more important theme—"the concept"; and it will be a "moral" poem if all the chosen elements are technically able to produce the proper emotion. This leaves the poet a wide latitude for choice of subject matter, but restricts his use of it stringently. Winters, in reviewing *The Poems of Theodore Roethke*, remarked favorably on Roethke's choice of subject matter which resembled his own: "It requires courage to deal with Platonic abstractions in a season of nominalists triumphant and untrammeled. There is in all of these a comparable seriousness both in the selection of the subject and the desire to render the subject honestly and for what it is worth . . . Roethke is ashamed neither of having subject matter nor of the kinds of subject matter he has; and he writes in a style that is good in this period and would be good in any other."[19]

For Winters, the subject—however simple or esoteric—should carry a new perception, not only of the exterior universe, but of human experience as well. It should, in his words, "add to what we have already seen." And the fact that he so often took commonplace subjects "already seen" is evidence that he asked the sensitive reader to take a *second* look with him at all the important metaphysical perceptions of the artist. He was often accused by superficial critics of using banal, everyday subjects that were beneath the level of his highly abstract themes. This very juxtaposition was often a careful part of Winters' deliberate technique to force the philosophical reader to see the macrocosm around the microcosm. He discussed this technique in his essay entitled "Poetry, Morality, and Criticism":

> The poet in the practice of his art should sharpen and train his sensibilities to render his subjects more acute . . . so that the act of perception should force him to the discovery of values which he never would have found without the convening of all of the conditions of that particular act, conditions one or more of which will be the necessity of solving some particular difficulty of his style. The poet who suffers from such difficulties instead of profiting by them is only in a rather rough sense a poet at all.[20]

For him these "insignificant" subjects are as much a part of the total "morality" of a poem as any of the other blended elements if the critic will take the trouble to consider them seriously.

His subjects are surprisingly wide in range, and their problems are complex; they may be as abstract as his insistence on the worth of reason and discipline or as concrete as his defense of a friend on trial for murder. His treatment of his material, usually restricted to the form of the short poem, makes up in height and depth what it abandons in breadth. It catches the significant germ of the subject stated and develops just that much without any of the padding that more dramatic or narrative poetry might use. Background detail is only suggested; the actual subject stands in high relief. Concentration is all.

The subject matter of Winters' early poetry was suffused with an imagistic ecstasy as the young poet examined every single cause for his own perceptual reactions. The subjects of the first three volumes come mainly from the poet's physical environment; their content was actually a description of feelings and reflections attendant upon a scene, an animal, a plant, a seasonal change, a shift of light. By the time *The Journey* was published in 1933, he had abandoned these acute perceptual moments with their attendant nervous tensions and begun to concentrate on more earthly subjects of a broader appeal. While much of this earlier poetry was apt to use geographical, historical, or seasonal materials, his mature poetry concentrated on more mundane subjects (family relationships, friends, hobbies, events in his professional life, colleagues, students). The *Collected Poems* shows him by the end of his career using cosmic, philosophical subjects. This sequence parallels the development of his themes; however it should be noted that these divisions are based only on tendencies, and that a variety of all types actually occurs in all three periods in his career.

Winters' use of geography and history as subject matter varies widely from the early perceptual poems, such as "Aspen's Song" or "Jose's Country," to the later fully orchestrated "Winter Evening" or "Summer Moon." Early in life he developed into an amateur biologist and was widely read in esoteric fields of this subject. No item of the natural world was too small to escape his use in poetry. Some of the most beautiful examples of the early free verse in *The Immobile Wind* (all written before age twenty-one) used desert and mountain animals as subjects for the one-line nature poems. Coyotes, goats, hawks, butterflies, and dragonflies are all defined in the artist's perceptions. They may be potent enough to cause hallucination, as they are observed against the seasonal panorama of nature in *The Magpie's Shadow:* "pale mornings," "snow curls," "the magpie's shadow," "leaves against a doorframe," "flower patterns," "deer tracks," "summer shadows," "the well of autumn." His next volume, *The Bare Hills* (1927), uses topography and landscape from the Southwest for its organization into four parts: "The Upper-River Country," "The Bare Hills," and "The Passing Night." The emotional *Fire Sequence* of 1927 begins with the highly subjective "Coal: Beginning and End," in which the narrator faces the timeless atomic universe alone and observes the natural elements blending eternally. In "Return of Spring" he laments ironically his inability to sense his own renewal in it.

> This only I can never forget; the shrieking
> steel amid the wilderness of Spring.

The "crystal of the coal," the "bitter moon," the "sweaty sun," "November roaring low along the ground" are all the subject matter of an ironic, disillusioned poet lamenting man's pathetic fallacy. The final volume of *Early Poems* is *The Proof* in 1930; and its specific content includes "The Red Month (July)," incandescent earth, "Orange Tree," the silhouette of Los Angeles, "Song of Trees," "Goatherds," "Bison," "Sunflowers," "Remembered Spring," "The Longe Nightes. . . ," and "The Snow Ghost." His later poetry was more complex, but much of its subject matter was still the natural local world around him: "The Empty Hills," "A View from Pasadena from the Hills," "Green," "The Slow Pacific Swell," "Sonnet to the Moon," "California Oaks," and "October Nocturne." Physical sensation and observation from nature comprised a large share of the subject matter of Winters' early poetry.

General history and geography were more limited in the later poetry, which concentrated on specific local fact or legend for content; though metaphysical themes were developed around such subjects in "The Invaders," "A Fable," "John Day, Frontiersman," "John Sutter," "Moonlight Alert," "Night of Battle," and "At the San Francisco Airport." This local subject matter was always depicted in a minute description of the feelings and reflections attendant upon a scene—such as his thoughts recorded on a train trip up the Snake River in *The Journey*. The narrator was always the focal point of the poem though the geography, history, or local scene is actually its subject. Often there is an ironic tone suggesting that the beauty of this subject is wasted by the constant encroachment of materialistic civilization; theme and subject are thus interrelated. Winters' sensitivity to the art and subject matters of former cultures is evident in his many translations of Indian and Spanish materials and in his use of medieval European legend. He knew that these were too often lost to the modern world, and he deliberately chose their subject matter to try to salvage them in his own poetry. His own sense of solitude gave him an intimacy with history and geography which is reflected in the content of his verse. He saw himself proudly against the background of Nature and in spiritual communion with it:

> I, one who never speak
> . . . creeping through an ancient shell
> I paved a sky
> Beyond the lie.

In a few poems Winters used a more worldly temporal subject matter: that which was avowedly personal or occasional. He has several poems that grow from subject matter within his own family: "Marriage," "For My Father's Grave," "Inscription for a Graveyard," "To My Infant Daughter," "A Leave-Taking," "The Cremation," "Prayer for My Son," and "At the San Francisco Airport." These all testify to the seriousness with which he took his family relationships and the depth of his affection. In these poems there is no modern mawkishness, no Freudian frustration; simply honest dedication. Though his friends are honored with several titles, these are never just personalized tributes, but full-scale "universalized" poems. "To William Dinsmore Briggs Conducting His Seminar" and "For the Opening of the William Dinsmore Briggs Room" pay homage to one of his own great teachers, and thus to all great teachers. "A Dedication in Postscript to Agnes Lee" and "To Howard Baker" are beautiful paeans to true friendship. Even his hobby of dog breeding and his civil defense activities during the war inspired poems which transcend their mundane subjects: "Elegy on a Young Airedale Bitch Lost Some Years Since in the Salt Marsh," "Moonlight Alert," and "Defense of Empire." Three poems epitomize a humanistic civil *cause célèbre* that Winters supported in defense of an unjustly accused citizen of his neighborhood: "To Edwin MacKenzie," "To David Lamson," and "To a Woman on Her Defense of Her Brother Unjustly Convicted of Murder."

His academic career was a fertile field for subjects handled in both positive and negative tones: "On Teaching the Young," "To a Young Writer," and "Anacreontic" offer cryptic mature pedagogy of the most positive sort; but "To William Dinsmore Briggs" and "Ode to the Despoilers of Learning" show to what bitterness he could be driven by academic negligence and hypocrisy. "Two Old-Fashioned Songs" assess his scholarly career at the very end of *The Collected Poems.* The most interesting poems from his academic career trace his autobiographical development influenced by his poetic masters. An early poem "To Emily Dickenson" and two later ones "To Herman Melville" pay tribute to those literary personalities for whom Winters felt a great affinity. He often used literary material of myth and legend as the subject for poetry, but always with universal relevance or focus on an immediate concern—never just as narrative verse. Examples of this type are "Apollo and Daphne," "The Castle of Thorns," "Midas," "Orpheus," "Chiron," "Heracles," "Alcmena," "Theseus," "A Trilogy," "Socrates," and "Sir Gawain and the Green Knight."

Perhaps the most important category of his subjects is that which is religious or aesthetic in temper. The stated subject itself may be, as in the early poetry, a well-known place or artifact, but the actual subject is its poignance for the poet that sends him off into a religious perception of higher relevance. Such specific content turns later to abstract subjects: from "Hill Burial" to an individual's death, from "The Invaders" to an individual's solitude, from "The Empty Hills" to his fears. Finally in the most mature poetry, this same sort of transformation becomes the subject of "To the Holy Spirit" and "Time and the Garden." These subjects ultimately symbolize the tension between mortality and immortality, and they represent the peak of his virtuosity. He takes a last honest look at his subjects in these poems and concludes humanistically:

> And I, alas, am bound
> Pure mind to flesh and bone,
> And flesh and bone to ground.

Forms

Come, write good verses then
That still from age to age
The eyes of able men
May settle on our page

With this advice in "Anacreontic," Winters exhorted himself and young writers to "Peace at last," and turned his back forever on formless poetry. His search for form had been an autobiographical and philosophical odyssey as well as a literary one, and for Winters it represented a long and arduous struggle. Near the end of his fourth volume, *The Proof*, is a poem simply entitled "Sonnet" and arranged to stand in the midst of some of his most violent free verse. The subject matter of "Sonnet" is as perceptual, as sensuous, as any in the surrounding poetry, but the concepts have been brought into the order of a modified sonnet form. The rhythms and stanzaic patterns escape as "the mind escapes" from time to time, but the finale is a triumph of control. Shortly thereafter he drew theoretical critical conclusions from practical poetic experiments; he wrote in *The Function of Criticism:* "The difference between poetry and prose is verse . . . verse is metric or measured language. The resulting form is more expressive of emotion than is the relative loose rhythm of prose." And he sought ever after the most formal patterns for this expression.

"Form," then, is what makes "great" poetry for Winters. His main themes and subjects all evolve eventually from one concept: his confrontation with confusion. His horror of instablilty of all sorts—from the purely personal, through the mundane and social, to the cosmic—is the total and constant preoccupation of this man. His biography as "poet-teacher-critic" is dominated by it; his one short story reveals it; and all of his poetry reflects it. He turned gratefully at midpoint in his poetic career to the security and discipline of form in "good verses," and he developed his particular "morality" around it. He chose to clarify confusion by imposing an order on it; that order was form.

The major primary source for the critical development of this theory comes from his fifth essay in *Primitivism and Decadence*, entitled "The Influence of Meter on Poetic Convention." Here he states his basic premise: "The morality of poetry is inextricably involved in its form and is related to the norm of feeling." If the poet makes a wise choice (or is happily intuitive) with a "form" which can best control the theme and evoke the proper emotional feeling toward the subject, then the poem is aesthetically "moral." It is then under the control of the poet's reason. By "form" Winters means primarily verse pattern, meter, and rhythm, though he does include in his theoretical remarks some random comments regarding rhyme and syntax.

His own shift from his early style of free verse to his later formal verse was made because of what he conceived to be the paradoxical fact of *greater* freedom in traditionally patterned verse. In *In Defense of Reason* he concludes, "In traditional verse, each variation, no matter how slight, is exactly perceptible, and as a result can be given exact meaning as an act of moral judgment."[21] This "moral" choice of variation is thus strongest for the poet who purposefully holds his poetry in the tight rein of the short poem and never loses control of the possibility of freedom. When Winters first rebelled against the Pound-Eliot associational school of free verse in *Primitivism and Decadence*, he condemned experimentalism for its incompleteness, its confusion, its ultimate emptiness: a poetry without either proper subject or form, no matter how hallowed its theme. He called for a reiteration of objective substance and the proper forms to preserve it: in other words, he wrote "in defense of reason." John Crowe Ransom assesses Winters' symmetry thus: "Every syllable must be recognizably in or out of place: each one's full sound value must be willed to its particular end. Experimental meters will never exploit the full possibilities of the language."[22]

His general aesthetic theory rests thus on the "moral" evaluation of experience conveyed through all possible details and variations of versification and rhythm; control of form is the secret of success. His practice befitted his preaching—indeed promoted it—from his earliest amateur statement to his "Gyroscope Group" at Stanford where he was "Maestro." J. V. Cunningham recalls his pronouncements there: "What was explicit became an implicit part of the conception. Qualities of sound and meter served as comment and perception. True simplicity was the last resolution of inherent and recognized complexity."[23] Winters' final insistence on control of formal patterns brought that clear simplicity to his poetry. From that time on he strove for technical perfection. Metrical patterns became eventually accentual syllabic; strictly so, with significance of variation in direct proportion to its rarity. Where "freedom" occurred, it meant a distinct shift of thought or accentual emphasis. Words were assembled and sounds juxtaposed so that no value was lost as the form was meticulously contrived. Mechanical slickness or shoddiness was intolerable for this master of form who had learned his lessons from the great sixteenth century lyricists. Certain modern critics have called Winters a "synthetic classicist" because they felt this insistence on form to be out of rapport with his chaotic times. But Winters merely shrugged this off as a dated, "immoral" analysis. He felt that his formality was a necessary corrective in the thirties and a harbinger of the future for contemporary poetry. For him, *all* details of form: stanzaic pattern, meter rhythm, rhyme, and syntactical device have moral significance and must be chosen, managed, and evaluated as they contribute to the "morality" (the aesthetic balance between rational statement and feeling) of the poem.

This balance between motive and emotion—which is evident in the paraphrasable theme and subject of his poems—is achieved through the skillful manipulation of form. Howard Kaye, in his perceptive essay, "Yvor Winters: 1900–1968," assesses over a half-century of Winters' work and concludes that his poem "Sir Gawain and the Green Knight" is actually a summary dramatization of this constant struggle for control in his poetry; in the allegory Gawain represents the rational soul in desperate conflict with forces of subhuman nature. As the hero struggles for control, the poet struggles for form; and, as in all of Winters' poetry, form and reason win in the end, with wisdom the ultimate crown. The poem represents Winters' own autobiographical development as artist. His mature poetry's adoption of form begins about half way through *Collected Poems*; in *The Early Poems*, it is first apparent in the last section of the collection—"The Proof," (1930). In that year he wrote a letter to the editor of the *Saturday Review* which actually paid tribute to what free verse had meant to his development; at the same time this conscious artist was beginning to abandon it in his own writing.

> The matter of free verse has always been in a cloud and seems at present likely to sink back into total darkness. I believe it is a legitimate if superlatively difficult medium that has produced its masters and enormously enriched our rhythmic consciousness.[24]

He understood it, as few poets have, to be a highly technical medium when properly developed, and he had his own theory of scansion for its proper use. When the *Times Literary Supplement* of February 9, 1967, reviewed these *Early Poems,* patronizingly, as "five-finger exercises which are clues to Mr. Winters' development," they did not understand how seriously he took them. His own statement in the preface credits them as "very good of their kind." Two eminent fellow poets understood more about them than the reviewers. Donald Justice, reviewing

Collected Poems in 1954, wrote perceptively of Winters' development of this form:

> He began as an experimental poet working backward through technique then in fashion toward the traditional styles he would eventually formulate. Early Imagist poetry led to experiments in a system of free-verse scansion. . . . As the style becomes surer, the content grows richer, the feeling deeper. . .[25]

And J. V. Cunningham reviewing *The Journey* in 1940 commented:

> The density of his poetic line indicates that the wide range of forms does not come from facility or defect of integrity. Indeed he seems capable of adopting a poetic form, realizing the experience it offers, and deliberately choosing another, different one. He is among the masters of free verse . . . and of the sonnet.[26]

The best work to date on the transitional development of Winters' poetry is contained in "The Free Verse of Yvor Winters," a pamphlet by his student and collaborator, Kenneth Fields. Fields believes that Winters' free verse is more vigorous and varied than that of any other writer of our time. He observes how Winters managed to introduce complexities of feeling into his poems with a variety of rhythmical devices, such as placing two perceptions syntactically in a single line with juxtapositions in an Imagist form (a technique that he kept even after he returned to traditional patterns), or by using runover lines and elisions that caused a sense of hurried, nervous motion. When Winters did return in the thirties to the control of traditional forms he wrote of the transition thus:

> I changed my method, explored the new method, and gradually came to understand the theoretical reasons for the change which I had made as a practical necessity. . . . One final word of warning. My shift . . . was not from formlessness to form; it was a shift from certain kinds of form to others. . . . I have always been preoccupied to achieve it in my own work. Form is something that one perceives or does *not* perceive; theory in itself is insufficient . . . . These early poems are rhythmical not merely from line to line, but in total movement from beginning to end; and the relations between the meanings of the parts is an element of the rhythm, along with the sound. . . . In the long run, however, free verse proved severely restrictive. . . . I had pushed this method past the limits of its efficaciousness. . . . I found myself unable to write what I wished, and I therefore changed my method.[27]

His famous "method"—of which he writes so much in his comparative criticism—involved his control of form in versification, rhythms, meters, rhymes, and syntactical devices. He was skilled in the practice of a great many verse forms, and the *Early Poems* include a range from single-line poems to full-length verse plays and prose-poems. His transitional volume, *The Proof* (1930), also shows a wide virtuosity of form: free verse, blank verse, short lyrics, sonnets . . . all vigorously and carefully handled. Prior to this collection, he had used traditional patterned verse forms in his first book (*The Immobile Wind*, 1921), single-line perceptions in his second (*The Magpie's Shadow*, 1922), moderately free verse in his third (*The Bare Hills*, 1927), and a looser free verse in his fourth (*Fire Sequence*, 1927). After *The Proof*, 1930, he turned to form in the strictest sense of versification—the heroic couplet—which he uses with great facility for writing didactic, satiric, and allegorical poems; they invite comparison with accepted eighteenth century masterpieces of this classical mode. Some of Winters' longest poems occur here. The last three volumes (*Before Disaster*, 1934, *Poems*, 1940, and *The Giant Weapon*, 1943) exhibit Winters for the most part completely converted to the shorter traditional verse forms; "Theseus, A Trilogy" is the one long, blank-verse exception.

His preference for the form of the short poem was announced first in *The Function of Criticism* where he stated:

> Is there a form of literature which is essentially poetic?. . . I believe that there is such a form: the short poem—unfortunately called the lyric poem. It reached its highest structural perfection in English in the late sixteenth and early seventeenth century. Its structural principle—that of logic—was inherited from the Middle Ages. Its decay reached its peak with Pound and Eliot. . . . Its form is not merely imitative or narrative; yet it is exploratory. It may deal with trivial subjects, but it is never confined to them for effect. It is the raw material of generalization. . . . The master of the short poem is the poet who deals primarily with the understanding of action, and since his medium is verse, he can render as fully as possible the total understanding, not merely the rational, but the emotional as well.[28]

This "raw material of generalization" was controlled in this most condensed of verse forms: the short lyric. Winters preferred that it be stringent, self-constrained, restrictive, ascetic in tone and theme; and the stern, dry, sharp, narrow form of these poems on the page made the balance between motive and emotion a truly "moral" one in his estimation. This form for him best reflected the truly purposeful mind behind the poem.

His particular preference for the short poem produces an interesting visual, audible, and philosophical effect upon the reader of Winters' poetry. It is so concentrated that it is best read in small quantity; and he preferred always that it be read aloud, so that all the nuances of form would be evident. Its printed image is short-lined, rhymed, strong, "masculine," and abstract. Its theme, moving always toward the philosophical and the general, is usually succinctly held to an almost epigrammatic finale. His virtuosity with this verse form creates an intensely organic poetry. It allows a wide variety of tone—from the warm depth of its pastoral passages to the rugged austerity of its more heroic measures. It is sometimes filled with homely certainties in a lighter vein; yet it can rise in its stark simplicity to an overpowering mystical height. Some critics have felt that the typical Winters short poem is too "cubistic"—that he restricts too much in the conjunction of lines—"block form, cemented by rhythm and rhyme." But such critics have obviously only read a limited number of his poems. Even his most "blockish" poems are filled with delicate variety by the sensitive use of runover lines, elisions, anaphora, and alliterative devices. Read aloud, as Winters insisted, they are anything *but* cubistic in effect.

He opened his famous essay on meter in *In Defense of Reason* with the statement: "The creation of form is nothing more or less than the art of evaluating and shaping a given experience." This shaping of experience into form meant for him the ordering of a poem's "rhythm"—its broad, prevailing accentual pattern; its "meter"—the measure of its lines and stanzas; its "pace"—the variation of speed through syntactical devices; and its "cadence"—its rise and fall by phrase and line placement. The poet, even in his earliest free verse, was constantly preoccupied with this audible impression of his poetry. In 1949 he gave a lecture and a reading at Kenyon College in which he emphasized this interrelationship:

> I mean to indicate the reading of poetry not merely for the sensual ear, but for the mind's ear as well, yet the mind's ear can be trained only by way of the other. Readers who read rapidly without hearing are barbarous; literature is closed to them; they understand little. . . . To master an art—even to understand it—one must labor with all of one's mind and with at least a part of one's body.[29]

He encouraged listening audiences to distinguish between meter and rhythm as he had done in his own transition from experimental to traditional patterns and to assess the difference: "Meter is the arithmetical norm, the purely thematic structure of the line; rhythm is controlled departure *from* this line." His adoption of traditional meters for his mature poetry gave him the *real* freedom of rhythm that he felt was lacking in his early so-called free verse. When he was making this transition, he wrote somewhat bitterly of the poetic milieu in which he and other young poets struggled for true freedom of form:

> The writer of today finds himself tempted, on one side, by the roads to rhythmic salvation offered by the various sects of tree-climbing mystics, and on another by the faint, moribund murmurs of transatlantic, Middle-Western, middle-aged Whitmanisms. These and related manifestations of our democratic era or of its Pragmatic Providence, our educational system, have to be avoided.[30]

Since for him the real difference between poetry and prose was "verse . . . metric or measured language whose resulting rhythm is more expressive of emotion than is the relatively loose rhythm of prose," his final judgment was made in favor of traditional poetic rhythms to express and modify emotion, to modulate and define it. Only with this form could the poet truly "shape experience," he concluded. The ultimate end of poetry was the most precise rendition of emotion and the most precise relationship of it to rational content that was possible. Since meter controlled rhythm and made it more orderly in both its general outlines *and* its variations, he eventually opted for highly metrical verse forms. It is significant to note that at the transition stage from free to metrical verse Winters' poetry had reached its highest emotional pitch. With free verse—violent and vigorous though his was—there was literally no other place to go. (See the transition between *The Proof's* "Fire Sequence" and *The Journey* to observe this dramatic shift of form.) He found it necessary in his practice and his subsequent theory to turn to traditional metrics if he would develop further. In his early essay on "The Morality of Poetry," he had spoken evocatively of a poem as "an almost fluid complex." In *Forms of Discovery*, he summarizes this concept:

> The proportions of a poem, like the proportions of a musical composition are rhythmical, for both compositions exist in time . . . if the proportions of a poem are "pleasing," they are pleasing because they further the intention of the poem; they

> contribute to the definition of the emotion to be encouraged, and this, in turn, is related to the matter with which the poem began.[31]

To analyze Winters' poetry metrically one must understand his insistence upon the theoretical necessity of rhythm. When he writes of structural analysis of meter, he speaks from actual practice and careful study of the masters. (Two early critical essays in *Primitivism and Decadence* demonstrate this examination: "The Experimental School in American Thought" and "The Influence of Meter upon Poetic Convention.") After long analysis and example, he concluded that a metrical phrase is nothing at all in poetry unless it is capable of variation within the definitive scheme of a regular pattern. He believed that meter was the frame of reference against which we can locate and define such phrases. A successful poem should be, then, a complex of meaning with two distinguishable features: a logical structure and a texture made up of sound through meter and musical phrasing. The relationship between the two from moment to moment makes for this success.

In the introduction to *Early Poems*, Winters analyzed his "free verse" (which he says he learned from Williams, Miss Moore, H.D., and Hopkins) and found it to be mainly two meters actually running concurrently, providing a kind of counterpoint between "free" and "iambic" (as he said, ". . . often balanced on a particular tight-rope thus"). He scanned two poems, "Quod Tegit Omnia" and "The Bitter Moon," to illustrate his system and remarked, "The foot which I used contains one heavily accented syllable and an unlimited number of syllables of secondary accent." He claimed that most of his really good free verse could be scanned this way. (He had little use for verse that was *more* free than this, or for what he called "Websterian" verse, a long-lined combination of free and blank as used sometimes by Pound and Eliot.) He observed that the nature of the English language and the difficulty of abandoning old forms had led him inevitably to this system, and he concluded that the extremely abnormal convention was seldom necessary. Since in free verse, the only *norm* was perpetual variation, the free versifier was actually handicapped by a lack of substitutions and variable degrees of accent. His own experience as a young writer exhausted by emotion and experimentation had led him to conclude: "The nearer a norm a writer hovers, the more able is he to vary his feelings in opposite or even in many directions, and the more significant will be his variations."[32]

As he made the shift to traditional patterns, he sharpened his techniques on translations from French and Spanish in traditional meters and exercised with the strict demands of sonnets (See *Collected Poems*, pp. 33–50). He experimented with the four historical systems of measurement which he described in *Primitivism and Decadence*: the quantitative (classical), with a given number of recognized feet; the accentual (Anglo-Saxon), with a certain number of accents and the remainder unmeasured; the syllabic (French), with a certain number of syllables; and the accentual-syllabic (English). Always he returned to his basic premise that the merely mechanically perfect was lifeless; but that the merely "free" was impotent.

The ultimate importance of meter for Winters was, of course, its "moral" significance. He saw it as an opportunity to bring each work as close to a true judgment of rational choice as possible; in *Primitivism and Decadence* he gave an elaborate set of techniques for detecting any lack of balance in the analysis of meter. His own mature poetry demanded of him a respect for and a return to such a balance.

So much for his theory; what of his practice? In 1930—close to the end of his free versification—he wrote in despair to the editor of the *Saturday Review*.

> The matter of free verse has always been in a cloud and seems at present likely to sink back into total darkness. I believe it is a legitimate if superlatively difficult medium that has produced its masters and enormously enriched our rhythmic consciousness. Mr. Pound once claimed that one should master the standard meters before attempting free verse; but free verse has given us so much that the poet of the future may have to go near to reversing the process.[33]

As though he were somehow a prophet ahead of his time, he was actually describing his own future development. He left what he considered to be the best examples of his early free verse when he collected his poems in 1952—a bare 23 poems in a volume of 120—which he culled for his definitive volume. When he later published *The Early Poems* in 1966, he included the full canon of free verse for purposes of developmental study. However, he cautioned that the ones he considered inferior in quality certainly obscured the principal issue: "That of how the best poetry can be written."

His first volume, *The Immobile Wind* (1921), is generally traditional in its rhythms: trimeters and tetrameters, some rhymed, some not, but most coming back to the basic beat with only a few experimental metrical excursions such as those in the title poem, "Two Dramatic Interludes for Puppets" and "I Paved a Sky." It was as though he were testing the press with a few free verse experiments to see how they would be received. By the second volume in 1922, he devoted the entire collection to twenty-eight single-line perception poems in as free a verse as any poetry could be. The young poet by this time had abandoned any early attempts at traditional verse and determined to be as revolutionary as possible. In the third book, *The Bare Hills* (1927), the amateur begins to show a maturing skill in the variation of his accent and the flow of his free cadences. The virtuosity of range here shows from single-word lines (as in "Flesh of Flowers") to long cadences of twelve-syllable lines (as in "Rows of Cold Trees" or "The Streets"). This book also includes two prose-poems which are highly poetic though set in the typography of prose—"The Passing Night" and "The Fire Sequence"—which juxtapose spot images of perception strung together in single long lines. The final poems in this collection and the first ones in *The Proof* push free verse to its ultimate of irregular run-on lines of various accentual and syllabic lengths. (See "The Longe Nights When Every Creature . . .") Finally, just before the end of the last volume in this collection, Winters includes the milestone poem formally entitled "Sonnet." But here he makes no sudden reversal; instead he subtly and experimentally combines the verse pattern of the Elizabethan sonnet with some of the remaining irregular cadences of free verse, as though trying to create a nostalgic composite of the best of both worlds: his old free and his new traditional meters. As a result, this sonnet has the unique quality of hurry and excitement first, then a calm quiet climax as it finally settles into traditional patterns.

When Winters chose the poetry for his *Collected Poems*, he followed the few early free verse examples with a section of translations ranging from thirteenth century Spanish poets to nineteenth century French ones. He practiced traditional forms and meters here from such masters as Baudelaire, Verlaine, and Mallarmé, from whom he learned stern lessons in the use of accent, elision, and caesura ("The Skeleton Laborer," "Green," and "A Sigh"). Yet he included also in this section one beautiful example of cadenced free verse translated from Rimbaud ("Marine") as a nostalgic literary farewell to his former style. The early Spanish translations in this section include ballad refrains ("The Lady's Farewell," and "Cossante"), prayer chants ("Poem," and "Cantabria") and sonnet patterns ("Death's Warnings," and "Rome"). All of these provided metrical discipline and thus gave him the freedom for the all-important variation that he felt made poetry infinitely interesting and "moral." The translation of Mallarmé's "A Sigh" is a particularly fine example of these variations of audible sound patterns with run-on lines, cadenced phrases, and elisions of accent. The next practice exercises to be included were seven Petrarchan sonnets carefully wrought in form, yet containing the all-important few variations that make them uniquely Winters'.

One-third of the way through the *Collected Poems*, the best of Winters' mature poetry begins in a variety of traditional meters. From this point on he seems capable of adopting any poetic form, realizing the experience it offers, then deliberately choosing a different one and exhibiting progressive prowess with it. It is as though he had proudly organized the book by genre and subgenre in a very rational exemplification of his own virtuosity. For instance, he includes one group all written in the strictest of iambs, but he varies them from poem to poem, from dimeter through pentameter ("Marine" through "The Fable"). In other sequences of a single stanza, he varies rhythms from quick trimeter to slow dimeter and thereby creates an emotional and rational synthesis of this theme—or, in his words, makes the proper "moral" choice of meter ("Hymn to Dispel Hatred at Midnight" and "Moonrise"). The completely rational mind of the critic shows in the logical precision of this volume's order as the poet displays his verse.

He next includes a half-dozen long poems in heroic couplet—a measure that exhibits an accumulation of prosaic detail and low-toned effect. Here there is none of the old nervous tension which characterized his earlier work. These are descriptive poems, calmly setting down his physical and psychic reactions to "The Slow Pacific Swell," "A View of Pasadena from the Hills," "A Journey in the Snake River Country." And as if to show that he *could* even maintain the dignity of this meter in less prosaic, more passionate "recollections in tranquility," he even molds into this form such subjects as "The Marriage," "A Vision," and "The Grave." These are followed by short, cryptic, epigrammatic verses ("Anacreontic" and "To a Young Writer") in trochaic trimeter twelve lines long. The short lines are made *more* cryptic by internal stops and caesuras: "Come, write good verses, then," or "Write little; do it well."

The remainder of this carefully organized volume—whose poems are grouped often by subject matter, theme, and even tone, as well as by form—is a *tour de force* of metrical virtuosity. Their range shows Winters' skill with the tremendous power of rhythm and meter over subject and tone. For instance, "Before Disaster" uses its jerky trochaic tetrameter with monosyllabic words to evoke the nervous speed of modern crowded highways, while "The Prince" has the lengthy spacious iambic pentameter lines to fit the rhetorical tone of the pompous, self-conscious ruler. "To Herman Melville in 1951" uses the epigrammatic couplet to spin its high irony; while "At the San Francisco Airport" exhibits an unusual five-line stanza of iambic tetrameters, often interrupted by midline stops, to demonstrate the precarious father-daughter relationship whose generation gap can scarcely be bridged, even at parting. The book ends with two strongly ironic pieces entitled "Two Old Fashioned Songs: Danse Macabre and A Dream Vision"—again in his five-line stanza and in trocaic tetrameter. Their tone of nostalgia, as the poet assesses his career, is heightened by the run-on unpunctuated lines in "Danse Macabre" and by the tremendously final quality of the fifth-line coda in "A Dream Vision."

Certain metrical devices of variation should be mentioned as examples of that important controlled freedom that Winters sought in both his experimental and traditional poetry. One is the short line that frequently runs over for the effect of rapidity and intensity of feeling—as in "The Morning" in *Early Poems*, or "Night of Battle" in *Collected Poems*. Conversely, he could write very slow free verse by lengthening the syllables in long vowel tones ("Hill Burial"); and this phonetic variation shows up later in such a traditional poem as "To the Moon." Kenneth Fields, in his fine study of Winters' *Early Poems*, cites the one-line six-syllable poems of *The Magpie's Shadow* for their sense of arrested movement and their speed. These effects come from two perceptions being dramatically juxtaposed in a single line. "The Walker," "Still Morning," and "Sunrise" all exemplify this variation. Winters later used this same technique held within the traditional meters of "Moonlight Alert," "Much in Little," and "Midas." The nervous energy of despair is epitomized in the abrupt short rhythms of the early poem "The Longe Nightes When Every Creature . . . ," and this effect is used later with distinction in the more measured verse of "To the Holy Spirit" and "At the San Francisco Airport."

Certain other metrical devices occur mainly to reinforce meaning or mood by heavy emphasis. In "Phasellus Ille," he shifts rhythms so dramatically for a slowing effect that he feels it necessary to mark the desired monosyllabic accents for the reader. In "Post-card to a Social Muse", he flays the social *poseur* with the cryptic rhythm of a startling dimeter close to each regularly trimeter stanza. In "On Teaching the Young," he actually syncopates accents in midline for effect on a particular word that marks his point ("It is what one *should* say"). He achieves the desired conversational prosaic quality within short meters by his use of run-on lines in "Socrates," and he captures the rhetoric of legal language with the long lines and the use of series in "To Edwin MacKenzie in His Defense of David Lamson." His keen sense of placement of unaccented syllables (that he learned so well in his free versifying) shows to advantage in "Summer Commentary," where they help achieve the "full," ripe effect he wants in his long lines. This single example is also representative of his sensitivity for the weights and measures of unaccented syllables. However, there are some few cases where Winters struggles for metrical precision without quite making it. Certain forced rhymes ("Hymn to Dispel Hatred at Midnight"), awkward inversions ("Nocturne for October 31st"), and archaic abbreviations ("Chiron") occasionally appear. "A Testament" seems actually to have suffered padding in several lines; but these are in such small minority that one still marvels at the vast majority of metrical successes that the full Winters canon displays.

One such complete success is "Before Disaster," which serves as a good example of Winters' virtuosity with rhythm, meter, pace, and cadence. In this poem fresh perceptions of theme and subject shift familiar traditional verse patterns into new, personal movements. The violence of contemporary life by which all balance is threatened is caught up in the very rhythm of this poem. Composed in 1933 as a result of an experience with heavy traffic on the California freeways, it couples the narrator's immediate local terror with a frightening historical forecast of things to come. Here indeed Winters proves that choice of meter has "moral" significance; it is not merely arranged, but "true"; and there is an interpenetration of meter *and* meaning. In this poem he uses the octosyllabic couplet for the basic meter; but he cuts off the line abruptly at the end of seven syllables to evoke the nervous tension of the precariously poised line of traffic; this rhythm is carried from the first stanza's local specific threat to the second stanza's universal general foreboding, where "ranks of nations" move as delicately as lines of traffic. The meter here is the agent for the organic fusion in the poem; as such it is one of the many good examples of Winters' metrical "morality."

In summary, it can be said that the emphasis before 1929 was on Imagist intensity, and for this he chose a free verse of electric vividness with a precise rhythm appropriate to each poem's cadence ("Requiem for Bees"). His earliest reviewer, Pearl Andelson, had noted the organic quality of his early poems, each of which had a unique form determined by its own subject, even in its most free experiments. By 1930, his free verse had become irrational (and therefore, according to him, "immoral") to the point of hysteria ("The Fire Sequence"). So the shift to *The Journey*'s heroic couplets in 1931 marks the real metrical turning point in the Winters career from free verse to traditional patterns. Many of the techniques that he had mastered in free verse served him well in these more traditional patterns and actually showed off to better advantage as they were highlighted against a more regular pattern. Although for Winters the element of "form" is primarily a matter of stanzaic pattern and meter, he is also interested in certain other devices that create formal order through sound patterns such as rhyme, enjambment, anaphora. As might be expected, his critical studies on these matters all stem from his basic philosophical premise which he liked to state paradoxically: "flexibility through inflexibility." The poems in his first volume, *The Immobile Wind*, combine rhymed and unrhymed lines; then he abandoned rhyme entirely in his free verse period until after *The Proof*. When he decided to return to traditional forms in *The Journey*, he typically adopted the most rigorous of all rhyme schemes—that of the sonnet and the heroic couplet—to be sure that he had learned his lesson well.

His critical remarks on the value of rhyme are summarized in a passage from *In Defense of Reason* in which he analyzes the strength of the heroic couplet in literary history. He concludes that its versatility in didactic, satiric, descriptive, and lyric poetry is greater because of its rhymed formality: "What makes the couplet so flexible? Its inflexibility . . . "

> The identity of the line is stronger in rhymed verse than in unrhymed because a bell is rung at the end of every second line; the identity of the line will be stronger in the couplet than in any *other* stanza because the couplet is the simplest and most obvious form of stanza possible. This mathematical and almost mechanical reverence for line and stanza provide an obvious substitution and core of connotation over which other poetic variations may move, from which they derive an exact identity. . . . The full sound value of every syllable must be willed for a particular end, and must be precise in the attainment of that end. As language has other values than those of sound, this ideal will be always forced into some measure of compromise with the other values; nevertheless,

> the essence of art, I take it, is that no compromise should be very marked, and the perfection of art, though rare and difficult, is not unattainable.[34]

Thus rhyme—as well as all other factors of form—became a "moral" agency in Winters' poetry, a way of willing choice; and he adopted it as one more means of achieving aesthetic perfection in his mature work. A few examples of this moral choice in rhyme can demonstrate his theory. The first seven sonnets in *Collected Poems* are set in the traditional Petrarchan mold; and yet Winters is unwilling to follow the carefully wrought pattern too far without variation. He follows it exactly through the octaves, then changes the rhyme scheme of the sestets (through an act of choice) to show his control over its *in*flexibility. He comes up with three different rhyme schemes for seven sestets, all skillfully followed as an act of willed sound. About two-thirds of the way through *The Collected Poems*, he placed his blank verse trilogy, "Theseus," as if to add variety and show his mastery of another controlled unrhymed form. Here the sound patterns are arranged through skillful repetition of vowel and consonant repetitions.

Other exhibitions of his virtuosity with rhyme include stanzaic patterns set up with certain alternating and consecutive rhymes within a single stanza, all carefully repeated in exact sequence in all subsequent stanzas ("Hymn to Dispel Hatred at Midnight"). Again he may use three regular rhymes in irregular order repeated in exact sequence ("The Cremation"). His fondness for the five-line stanza is understandable because of the strength of finality given by that last exact rhyme of the coda which always matches the first-line rhyme, thereby willing the stanza to a climactic end in sound as well as sense ("At the San Francisco Airport"). It is characteristic that he almost completely avoids slant rhyme or feminine rhyme in his poems; he doubtless thought them a sign of weak morality.

His careful use of the heroic couplet shows unending variation through the technique of enjambment ("Time and the Garden") or the closed pattern in a formal grouping such as three stanzaic units of five couplets each ("The Grave"). In "The Marriage" he wills a powerful climax, after a sequence of ten closed couplets, with a series of three lines exactly rhymed, and then a return to the original pattern for denouement. Working closely in the tradition of the form, he avoids repetition of effect and obviously delights in using it for a variety of subject matter. It serves him for love poetry in "The Marriage"; for description in "The Journey," "The Slow Pacific Swell," and "On a View of Pasadena from the Hills"; for didactic verse in "To Edward McKenzie"; for satire in "To a Woman on Her Defense of Her Brother Unjustly Accused of Murder"; and finally for dream narrative in the enigmatic lines of "A Vision."

Two poems in particular should be mentioned for their magnificent control of enjambment: "Socrates," which manages the pure flexibility of dialogue within immaculately rhymed quatrains; and "The Slow Pacific Swell," where the very cadence of the sea comes through the carefully wrought phrases of varied length all fitted together with a tidal regularity of rhyme and rhythm. The couplets remain intact, yet the will of the author manipulates them to accept his direction to freedom. (Note the line "That was the ocean . . . " with its heavy pause and its substituted trochee for effective dramatic use of change in rhythm for summary.)

Robert Lowell, in praising *Collected Poems* as a "marvelous book" in a *Poetry Magazine* review, calls Winters "the greatest master of anaphora in contemporary poetry."[35] A good example of this repetition of words or phrases at the beginning of lines or clauses occurs in the last three stanzas of "John Sutter," a tragic lyric poem about a local "patriarch" destroyed in the mania of the California gold rush. The repeated words "knives," "gold," "reviled," and "ruined" in successive phrases at the end of the poem build it to a dramatic climax of theme and tone. Another example occurs in "To My Infant Daughter," in which Winters advises: "True love is slow to find," in stanza two, then repeats the line effectively in stanza three's conclusive variation: "True art is slow to grow." A more complex use of it is in the last stanza of "Elegy on a Young Airedale Bitch Lost Some Years Since in the Salt Marsh." Here the anaphora of two interrogatives is repeated in an answering declarative statement for alliterative climax:

> Led by what heron cry,
> Lies by what tidal stream?—
> Drenched with ancestral dream,
> And cast ashore to die.

A final example comes from "Dedication to a Book of Criticism: To W. D. Briggs" where the ritual form is set by anaphora at the beginning of the poem:

> He who learns may feed on lies:
> He who understands is wise.
> He who . . . .

The poem ends with a syntactical variation on this device:

What is good from you I took:
Then, in justice, take my book.

Winters' scrupulous dedication to all aspects of "form" seems to stem from his philosophical desire to set his poetic world in rational order, however fragmented may be the rest of it. He felt himself living in an age "in which the insistence of the contemporary has obscured the vision of the permanent." He saw other poets of his age writing formlessly with over-emotional, irregular, rhymeless regularity. He diagnosed their problems as symptomatic of the great artistic malaise that came from social and moral decay. In his essay on "Poetry, Morality, and Criticism" he wrote:

> I cannot grasp the contemporary notion that the traditional virtues of style are incompatible with the poetry of modern subject matter.[36]

If modern consciousness is more complex (and he doubts that) or merely less educated (and he knows that), then poetry can proffer moral support to a sick society only when its form is *not* loosened, but more scrupulously willed than ever.

Other critics have sensed his extreme awareness of his own moment in time. Robert Lowell's praise of his new classicism mentions Winters as "a stylist who exemplifies two hundred years of American culture." (Lowell adds a personal tribute: "His voice and measures still ring in my ears. They pass Housman's test for two poetry—if I remembered them while shaving, I would cut myself.")[37] Keith McKean acclaims "the moral equilibrium of his form in a formless time."[38] F. O. Matthiessen admires his poems "which come closest to success when fresh perceptions stir the familiar verse patterns into new personal movement."[39]

Winters himself summarizes best of all his dedication to form and tradition in a succinct statement in *In Defense of Reason*: "Form is expressive invariably of the state of mind of the author. . . . Form, insofar as it endeavors to imitate the formless, destroys itself."[40] In his lifelong search to will and maintain rational form, he suffered many personal setbacks and much professional criticism. It is significant and poignant that the last poem in his *Collected Poems* should be a survey of this particular pilgrim's progress. Entitled "A Dream Vision," it expresses with clarity and stamina (and in traditional "form") his magnificently defiant, yet nostalgic apologia for his life and practice. The second stanza contains the most poignant statement from it:

> I had grown away from youth,
> Shedding error where I could
> I was now essential wood,
> Concentrating into truth;
> What I did was small but good.

Imagery and Symbol

The imagery of Winters' poetry includes a complete range: from the simple word pictures of his early poems, through the precise metaphors of his mature works, to the highly complex metaphysical symbols of his later "Post-Symbolist" verse. At all levels they are chosen with great care and a sense of clear perception: so clear that at times they almost seem to frighten the poet himself as they reflect his own personality. The young poet had realized early in his artistic development that his delight in external image for its own sake might take away some sense of his own identity. While he indulged in the pure aestheticism of the image in his early poetry, he predicted in the very first volume the direction this imagery would take toward a metaphysical symbolism. He seemed determined to "keep it in its place" and to understand how it might eventually be turned to "moral" purpose.

One early poem (written before he was twenty-one years old) from *The Immobile Wind* plainly states his problem and becomes a kind of credo. Poet speaks directly to reader on the subject of "the image"; comparing the images' various reactions, listing some of his favorites that excite and haunt him, and warning against their seductive allurement. (It is interesting to note that these same images recur throughout his poetry and are still being used in a metaphysical way in the last poems of *Collected Poems*.)

> Where My Sight Goes
>
> Who knows
> Where my sight goes,
> What your sight shows —
> Where the peachtree blows?
>
> The frogs sing
> Of everything,

And children run
As leaves swing.

And many women pass
Dressed in white,
As thoughts of noon pass
From sea to sea.

And all these things would take
My life from me

Though the young poet has trouble with form and rhyme, even at this early stage the perception of pure image delights him; yet he is aware of his vulnerability to it and determined to direct it lest it conquer him.

An analysis of Winters' use of image shows an historical development in his management of its varying levels: image, metaphor, symbol. The imagery in his first book is defined mainly in terms of the landscape of the Southwest, to which he had gone for physical cure. The young poet's images here are recorded with a sense of hallucination; he seems unable to get beyond his own private perceptions, and he fears them as he savors them in a kind of youthful romanticism. In the first poem, "Two Songs of Advent," he records two precise images, one visual and one audible, then warns his readers: "Listen! Listen! for I enter now your thought." All through this volume he seems to wonder whether or not his perceptions are more than his own; and in "The Morning," his exquisite, painful, solitary identity is contained in the image of the directionless insect, with no meaning beyond its beauty:

The dragonfly
Is deaf and blind
That burns across
The morning.

And silence dinned
Is but a scream
Of fear until
One turns in dream.

I see my kind
That try to turn:
I see one thin
Man running.

With this same frightening awareness "Two Interludes for Puppets" contrasts the blue, black, and white "wisdom" that he would hope eventually to gain; but toward the end of this volume—after all of its beautifully recorded images of "wizards from golden hills" and "women walking scarlet-flowered in a thin valley"—he cries desolately in "Death Goes Before Me":

> Weeping I go, and no man gives me ease—
> I am that strange thing that each strange eye sees.

These earliest poems, for all their youthfull awkwardness, point the direction that this sensitive young man takes for his own poetic development.

The second volume, *The Magpie's Shadow*, is the one of purest Imagism with no metaphoric intent at all. It is an experiment in pure compression, eliminating everything except the essential perception. (Winters has written that the primary influences here were certain translations from Oriental and American Indian poetry.) These poems give instantaneous perceptions of imagery caught in arrested movement or juxtaposed in a single line—very much in keeping with Pound's *dicta* for "an intellectual and emotional complex in an instant of time." "Still Morning" is one such line-poem:

> "Snow air—my fingers curl."

"God of Roads" is another:

> "I, peregrine of noon."

The third volume, *The Bare Hills*, displays many of Winters' pure images developed to their highest point; yet some of these poems often suggest through metaphor the metaphysical trend that the mature poetry will take. In this collection, he often sets visual against auditory images for a haunting effect, as in "The Moonlight": "A train droning out of thought / The mind on moonlight." Frequently images from the atomic universe magnify the hallucinatory effect: "Atoms seethe into / The sun. . . ", or ". . . the / chlorophyll booms . . . " in "Primavera." His exercises in metaphor and simile become more specific in this volume. In "Genesis," he writes: "The door became a species of mystery / It opened inward and stood closed." / It was a two-faced god that was able to learn nothing, save its own reversible path." In "Digue Dondaine, Digue Dondon," he uses this same technique in a more cryptic form: "Sun on the sidewalk / for the corpse to / pass through like the / darkside of a leaf." In "The Muezzin," he compares the traditional prayer ceremony to the modern newsboy crying his wares to the red sun. And "The Bare Hills" become a psychological threat: "some grating horror." In the last section of *The Early Poems*, ("The Proof"), the explicit image becomes an implicit part of the entire poem's conception and mingles skillfully with other elements of sound and rhythm to achieve tone and emphasize theme. Though these poems seem more "simple," they are actually more organically fused than the elaborate Imagist poems of the early books. "Orange Tree" is a good example of this type:

> Hard, oily,
> sinuous,
> your trunk,
>
> black serpent,
> struggling
> with your weight of gold—
>
> great strength
> massed
> against Time,
>
> in angry pride
> you hold out
> lacquered life
>
> the classic leaf.

In "Snow Ghost"—near the end of this book—the poet assesses his position as Imagist and even tries to escape his image, though he cannot disavow it:

> I look both ways and wait
>
> Behind the window, waterclear
> volcanic trees of winter
> against crumbling sky

In "Sonnet," enamored of his candle image, which he draws to perfection, the poet then warns:

> We lose reality in symbolism
>
> . . . .
>
> stripped of our own meaning
> simplified for men.

And in "Vigil," he takes the final step to move completely away from pure to metaphoric image:

The thought, the leap, is measured: madness
will return to sanity. The pendulum. Here.
Trapped in time.

In this volume's final poem, "Simplex Munditiis," the poet first uses one of his favorite animal images—a young, impulsive goat; then he contrasts its freedom to his own mature, controlled directive:

The goat nips yellow blossoms
shaken loose from rain—
with neck extended
lifts a twitching flower
high into wet air.

One must think of this
in quiet. One must
bow his head and take
with roughened hands
sweet milk at dusk,
the classic gift of earth.

It is at this point in the development of his poetry that Winters gave up "simple adornments"—and turned to more complex ideas—and to more traditional forms.

From this point on Winters uses imagery, not for its own sake, but always to enhance the philosophical theme of the poem. It becomes *his* willed agent to serve *his* purpose rather than some tantalizingly beautiful external object for its own sake. The images in the remainder of *Collected Poems* precisely serve the organic concept behind every poem, and as such they contribute to its all-important "morality." In this mature poetry, Winters is still a lover of nature and its precise observer, but here he sees the image as a partial symbol for the whole, as emotion is gradually held in tighter check by intelligence.

In his most successful poetry, Winters' concern is always to isolate perception with no softness or blurring, and then to relate it to mood or thought so that both intellectual speculation and emotion are distilled from his deftly handled imagery. Often he will add some propositional statement of studied simplicity after a sharp, clear collection of images. This aphoristic addition may turn them into symbols by reflecting back on them to give new meaning of great poignancy, such as that at the end of "The Fable." In this poem the sound and sight of "the steady sea" are described as "a slow obscure metonymy of motion . . . Lending a sheen to Nothing, whispering." Later he writes, "I found a fable here, but it is gone. / The mind alone is mind, and it must wait."

Babette Deutsch commented on Winters' ability to use metaphysical imagery in a perceptive review of his poetry for *Bookman:*

> The integrity of his poetry derives from his metaphysical passion, colored by his sharp apprehension of physical things. . . . Having its issue in a profound disenchantment with the world, he conveys it by means of a few spare, precise images. In thirty words he will give you the essence of the moment. But these moments are an ineffectual screen for Eternity. Time, Space, and the Mind are his ultimate concern. . .[41]

The metaphorical images of such poems as "The Streets," "The Rows of Cold Trees," and "Prayer Beside a Lamp" invite the reader to share his tragic awareness. ("I, crumbling in the crumbling brain of man.") Another critic-poet, Allen Tate, praises Winters' finesse in symbolic imagery and cites "Sir Gawain and the Green Knight" as one of his most successful metaphoric poems:

> It takes an enviable gift that can only be called genius to use the least figurative distortion for the greatest imaginative effect.[42]

He compares Winters' use of image with that of Marvell and Donne, and he concludes that such mastery leads to "massive, complex effects."

Winters' critical comments on the importance of imagery for other poets elucidates his own practice. He says that his masters of imagery are William Carlos Williams and Marianne Moore. Yet he writes in relation to Williams:

> Stenographic reports are not enough. One must look for relations and conceits . . . intellectual relationships between two objects physically unrelated, one of which fuses with the second and takes on an imagic existence . . . and find the sharpest way to set them down.[43]

Poems in which Winters manages this especially well are "The Castle of Thorns"—where the old, mythic water image from medieval romances is juxtaposed against the sound of the local goat-herder watering his flock, and "Before Disaster"—where imagistic sights and sounds of superhighway travel reflect the spiritual panic of the individual and national mind.

In a review which Winters wrote of Marianne Moore's *Observations* for *Poetry* in 1925, he paid high tribute to her use of imagery, and he advanced his theory one step further:

> The emotional unit of a poem may be divided into two general types: the image, in which all sound and meaning elements fuse into a single physical whole; and the anti-image, in which the relationship of at least one element to the rest is non-physical. That symbol is most intense which, provided it be fresh, sets into harmonious action and reaction the widest possible range of life—connotations in the smallest possible space—purely a matter of specific density.[44]

Such anti-images as Winters' poetry occur in "The California Oaks" and "On Re-reading a Passage from John Muir," in which the natural descriptive images take on added spiritual dimension as they are contrasted to the non-physical. Years later, Winters praised his own pupil Edgar Bowers for this particular technique:

> The result is sensory perception not for its own sake and not in the form of the traditional metaphor or simile, but sensory perception offered as sensory perception yet charged with perfectly explicit meaning by the total context. This is imagery as it should be . . . the mind and the matter . . . the two are inseparable, complex and profound.[45]

He criticized Hart Crane, whom he admired with reservations, because he felt that Crane never got to this complex stage of the metaphysical symbol. Though he admired Crane's boundless catalogues of simple images, he wrote:

> One feels no fluid experience bathing these images or perceptions and giving them a significant relation; rather only one after another. . . . In the best Imagists a wholly concrete statement *may* have poetic value *if* the feeling is implicated in the pure perception. The danger inherent is Mr. Crane's almost blind faith in his moment-to-moment inspiration.[46]

Winters had experienced years of writing such poetry, and he knew its dangerous quality. He felt that he had saved himself from its particular hypnosis, but he could never completely give up the old excitement of pure image for its own sake—even in his last book.

Winters' philosophical theory and artistic practice of imagery are best defined by an actual classification of his favorite images. These fall into three categories and seem naturally related to the classifications of his themes and subjects. Together they all reveal the personality behind the poetry. His images come first from the world of nature, of which he was a close observer with highly attuned senses. An ever-abiding interest in science—from botany, through protozoology, to physics—shows in his careful descriptions. The second category includes images that come from the human, mundane world around him: everyday things such as doors, lamps, newspapers, automobiles, houses. Finally, the third category has to do with the visionary imagery of the spirit: those recurring hallucinations that were always returning to him in a certain form. These seem to hold more than merely sensual quality for him, and they are the main source of the metaphysical and philosophical poetry of his later years, though predictable from certain early poems.

Winters was always intrigued with the change of season; he devoted one entire book to this natural phenomenon. The images here are sense impressions of the simplest sort: "At night bare feet on flowers," or "The tented autumn, gone!" He set them up as single-line exclamations to call intense attention to them. In the later poetry these images of the natural world are interwoven into theme and content for "moral" purposes, and the poet wills more than just the particular sense impression involved. For instance, in "Time and the Garden," the exotic fruit trees which he lists come to represent in a symbolic way his life's own esoteric efforts. In other words, they serve a metaphysical purpose and, as such, are his "anti-images." He is obsessed with particulars in his nature imagery: "*scarlet* flowers," "*decaying* leaves," "*whispering* wind," "*foaming* water," "*creaking* winter," "*writhing* sunlight," etc. He recalls in one of his poems, "Rows of Cold Trees," this impulse for the specific:

> It was the dumb decision of the
> madness of my youth that left me with
> this *cold eye for the fact*; that keeps
> me *quiet*, walking toward a
> *stinging* end. [Emphasis mine.]

The change of seasons ("The Fragile Season" and "Snow Ghost") and the turn of day to night ("Nocturne") elicit images of dazzling light on the desert ("Incandescent Earth") or of snow on the mountains ("The Precincts of February"). He makes delicate use of sensations of temperature and light change to intensify his poetry. One excellent example is from "The Cold":

> Frigidity the hesitant
> uncurls its tentacles
> into a furry sun.
> the ice expands
> into an insecurity

that should appall,
yet I remain.

And in "The Barnyard" there is the frightening image of a child ". . . that staggers / straight into / the clotting cold / with short fierce cries." Sun and moon images are used over and over again as the source of all energy; one particular poem entitled "O Sun!" extols its massive, blinding potential in a sensuous hymn:

O Sun who makes
the earth sweat
shadowy and acid
. . . . .
red carrots tumble
in a rigid shoal
. . . . .
great cabbages
roll from the dark
. . . . . .

In another entitled "Bitter Moon," the same reverence is elicited:

Dry snow runs burning
on the ground like fire—
the quick of Hell spin on
the wind . . . Earth burns with a
shadow that has held my
flesh. . . .

Similar examples of this complex precision of nature imagery can be cited in which Winters uses animal freedom in contrast to human limitation. He was especially fond of certain winged creatures for this purpose: butterflies, dragonflies, hawks, grosbeaks, goldfinches, bees, and of shy, small animals such as fieldmice, hares, snakes, toads. He admired strong, graceful animals for their tension in action: dogs, horses, goats, mules. His imagery cites more than their mere physical prowess in descriptions which use the added dimension of their potential liberation and explosive energy ("Song for a Small Boy Who Herds Goats," "Jose's Country," "April," "The Mule Corral," "Bison," etc.). One of the most beautiful poems of this type is "Song" in which animal imagery is deftly juxtaposed against human emotion:

When I walk out
to meet you on the
cloth of burning
fields

the goldfinches
leap up about my
feet like angry
dandelions

quiver like a
heartbeat in the
air and are
no more.

One final example of this transition of Winters' developed nature imagery will indicate how the later poems still maintain the Imagist precision, but turn it to philosophical ends. Here, as in all the later poems, the images are chosen for metaphysical idea, not for sense alone:

Moonlight Alert

The sirens rising, woke me; and the night
Lay cold and windless; and the moon was bright,
Moonlight from sky to earth, untaught, unclaimed,
An ice nightmare of the brute unnamed.
This was hallucination. Scarlet flower
And yellow fruit hung colorless. That hour
No scent lay on the air. The siren scream
Took on the fixity of shallow dream.
In the dread sweetness I could see the fall,
Like petals sifting from a quiet wall,
Of yellow soldiers through indifferent air,
Falling to die in solitude. With care
I held this vision, thinking of young men
Whom I had known and should not see again,
Fixed in reality, as I in thought.
And I stood waiting, and encountered naught.

His use of imagery from the everyday world—in both early and late poetry—includes such specific things as books, puppets, lamps, pictures on walls, miners' shacks, farm houses; but these are used for more than mere local color. Always there is the added human dimension involved in juxtaposition to the image. The poem that uses newspapers also involves the newsboy—as "muezzin"; the puppets become their puppeteers; the narrator who observes the portrait on the wall finds himself reflected back in its image; and the compassionate observer finds his own loneliness increased by the drab, austere exterior of the miners' shacks or the farmers' houses. (Winters' years in the mining camps and the ranches of New Mexico provide the recurring images of the "pale blue shacks" of the miners and of the "gray clapboards" of the desolate ranches.) In one poem he identifies his title character—"Bill"—with accurate profanity and coarseness; in another he describes "A Miner" with "granite strength"; and he obviously patterns "The Schoolmaster in Spring" on himself: ". . . my books / Like colored stones / Are hard to move." He uses the characters "John Day, Frontiersman" and "John Sutter," goldminer, both as physical and spiritual images of their time and function in Southwestern history. In another local color poem "See Los Angeles First," the images are used to heighten the synthetic artificiality which the poet derides: "red-rock plaster hollyhocks," "spit crackling mamas," "dark, wettish plushy leaves," "The Temple glitter-gates," "Jagged geometric current," "concrete Egyptian nakedness," "watertower of cleanliness," etc.

This category of "everyday" images evidences Winters' preoccupation with spatial relationships. He has a great passion for doors—their mystery, their double function, etc.: ". . . the two-faced god that was able to learn nothing, save its own irreversible path," "Spring is the world's door," etc. He is also interested in the areas of rooms and houses in which he has lived ("The Schoolmaster in Spring" and "Return of Spring"); the close density and dimension of his small study in his California garden ("Of Time and the Garden," "The Cold Room," and "To a Portrait of Herman Melville in My Library.") Upon occasion he may broaden these images from private to public rooms where people converge around him. Often there is a heightened threat of intimacy, yet at the same time a fear of losing his own identity in some foreign space relationship: ("At the San Francisco Airport," and "For the Opening of the William Dinsmore Briggs Room").

In many poems the physical images of the mundane world are elevated to symbols. In "To a Military Rifle," the gun, which is minutely described in all of its physical characteristics, becomes by the end of the poem the symbol of all modern warfare. In "Before Disaster," the contemporary auto becomes the lethal symbol of contemporary civilization. In "On a Portrait of a Scholar," the physical aspects of the single painting eventually become the symbol of all mankind's ephemeral transition from flesh to spirit.

One particular group of poems from both *Early* and *Collected Poems* uses images of passion. In the first volume these are recorded as precise images of the senses; in the second, they are elevated to a spiritual dimension. One of the earliest is "Flesh of Flowers":

> Your body
> bare
> alive
> on slow-veined
> feet
> that trod
> the swollen floor

Another from *The Early Poems* is "Under Rain":

> Your deep thighs
> heavy with white
> wade toward me—
> and the mind thins in a
> wave that floods
> the edge of Time

When he selected *The Complete Poems*, he left none of these purely physical poems and included only *The Marriage* where the fleshly images are transposed into metaphysical symbols:

> Incarnate for our marriage you appeared,
> Flesh living in the spirit and endeared
> By minor graces and slow sensual change.
> Through every nerve we made our spirits range.
>
> . . . . .
>
> Wild Spring in dream escaping, the debate
> Of flesh and spirit on those vernal nights. . .
> And when I found your flesh did not resist
> It was the living spirit that I kissed,
> It was the spirit's change in which I lay:
> Thus mind in mind we waited for the day.

The poem concludes with a philosophical comment on the metaphysical transition that has taken place through the years of marital experience.

The final category includes Winters' favorite images from his inner world of mind and spirit. These occur in both *The Early Poems* and later in *The Collected Poems*. They are unrelated images which seem to grow to symbol as they recur again and again from the early poems of dream and hallucination to the spiritual and artistic meditations of his later years. They are highly specialized and personal, individual to his poetry alone. They include a vision of pale women walking toward him, the play of shadow and light, the sound of bees swarming, the impalpable void of the desert, the sense of atoms disintegrating , and finally the permanence and lifelessness of metal and stone as it is contrasted to the "crumbling" mind and body of the human creature. These unrelated images are woven in one way or another into a large body of Winters' poetry and seem to represent in their recurrence some personal kaleidescope or collage that might be used for psychological analysis. Without any attempt to draw psychic conclusions, a few examples will illustrate.

The first example of the dream women occurs in an awkward early poem, "My Memory," in his first volume:

My memory is falling
Like the snow—

. . . . .

I found sheer women talking
Like surf on a shore
. . . . . they
Bore me as upon a pall
Out of life and into death.

The women—like King Arthur's dark women of Avalon—seem always to be appearing to bear him off to some unknown—perhaps to death, Nirvana, or another sort of release. In another early poem—"I Paved a Sky"—it is a single woman who comes:

. . . . .
Down thin
Valleys, scarlet flowered;
Nor in
Nor out my name.

I never know
Where to stand
I turn and go
Increasing numb. . .

He seems in all these poems both entranced and fearful as though they somehow threaten his sanity. In the supersensitive poems of *The Bare Hills*—preoccupied with his own sense impressions—he writes in "The Crystal Sun":

> I screamed in sunrise
> . . . . The Chinamen
> Amid the lemon grove
> Lived with pale women
> And ate dogs and sang
> All night.
> What wonder, then,
> That I went mad
> Amid the cloudy stone
> And look at
> Print
> more beautiful
> Than women, till
> The earth took form
> In my place
> at my feet

In "March Dusk" the alluring yet threatening woman is "only one thought—of a naked girl / beneath black eaves / that thunder / in the rain / like risen wings." In "Dark Spring" she is ". . . my love, / Her hand upon the sill / White, as if out of earth; / And Spring, the sleep of the dead." Finally, back to the original image, in "Where My Sight Goes":

> And many women pass
> Dressed in white
> As thoughts of noon pass
> From sea to sea.
> . . . . .
> And all these things
> Would take my life from me.

This image of pale women recurs in the later poetry as one mythic Lady in "Sir Gawain and the Green Knight"; here she is symbolized to haunt him with all the pleasure of the flesh. Finally, in his "Goddess of Poetry" whom he calls "maiden of icy stone / with no anatomy . . . " he epitomizes the alluring female spirit whom he could never refuse and concludes plaintively: "What is your pleasure now?"

A second image from Winters' private world of mind and spirit is that of his own recurring shadow—either hovering behind him or running before him or directly submerged in him. Three examples in this sequence are found in "God of Roads," "One Ran Before," and "The Crystal Sun." In the last, he gives an added dimension for this all-pervasive "shadow":

> . . . . . and my God
> Lay at my feet
> And spoke from out
> My shadow.

Later poems incorporate the shadow image into the symbol of the dual-self, the alter ego, as suggested in "To the Holy Spirit," "To a Portrait of Herman Melville in My Library," and "Sonnet to the Moon."

Most of the animal images earlier discussed were used in a purely physical, descriptive way. One, however, seems to be a part of Winters' inner world of the psyche, much as the fly that buzzed whenever Emily Dickinson imagined dying or Dostoevsky's Raskolnikov sensed his guilt. Winters' symbol here is also an insect; he uses bees swarming and buzzing throughout his consciousness for such critical moments' evocation in his poetry. In the early hallucinatory poem "Alone" he writes:

> I, one who never speaks, . . .
> My own eyes did not exist,. . .
> My brain is a thousand bees.

In "Sunrise" from *The Magpie's Shadow*, there is a one-line perception in which he asks the recurring image for psychic guidance. "Pale bees! O whither now?" In "The Crystal Sun," "God eyed me from the bees." In "The Upper Meadows," the narrator admires "the clustered fur of bees." One of his earliest published poems in *Poetry Magazine* of 1922 is entitled "A Requiem for the Memory of Bees (Lake Michigan)," and it incorporates many of his recurring images:

> A brown flowering tree
> On twilight
> Was but a farther spinning of
> the sprinkled blackbirds.
> A woman walking,
> The evening dying.

Her dress among low blossoms.
Among low blossoms
Lake water humming

Later he uses this insect image as a symbol for a warning as the beautiful yet violent world of sensation threatens his rational identity.

The image of the desert, to which he went for physical cure in his youth, occurs frequently in his poetry as a symbol for his soul's loneliness and solitude: "Two Songs of Advent," "The End," and "Man in the Desert." It is in this locale that he seems most poignantly aware of the atomic writhing of the precarious universe in which he exists. The interchange of matter and energy is epitomized in such images from "Primavera"—"Atoms seethe into / The sun." In "To the Crucified," he examines his own dearth of spiritual fervor as opposed to Christ's in a passage of frenzied imagery:

I read my paper
. . . . .
Three nights in Hell
your flame of solid gold
rolled over all the surface
lifted atom
after atom
and burst through space

The arid literal desert becomes the sterile soul's desert, and the thirsting spirit laments—like Hopkins or Newman or Eliot—its lack of refreshment. In "Genesis," he regrets his inability to join this spiritualized atomic fusion with the universe of which he spoke in the earlier poems. He rejects it, yet he wishes he could accede to it:

. . . . this
Crystallized electric hatred
bitter with no sense
it is a dream

The sources of this universal energy and force—the sun and moon—are used symbolically in the later poetry; however, here they are not merely descriptive of states of mind, but actual symbols, as in "The Rows of Cold Trees," "Sonnet to the Moon," and "Time and the Garden." Two poems—"The Longe Nightes . . . " and "Snow Ghost"—present the plight of the poet's identity as he confronts the "feigned rigidity" of the atomic, material world. Constantly he seeks a symbolic way to avoid the frightening prospect of being absorbed into it; and the old quarrel of reason versus madness persists to the last volume.

Winters' most constant, useful images and symbols are those of metal and stone. His years in mining camps provided the details for the early imagery in "The Fire Sequence" in which "Coal; Beginning and End" shows his great respect for the permanence of matter and energy thus compressed: "The pressure of the years," ". . . writhing heart," ". . . driving downward / atom after atom," etc. Another favorite metallic metaphor is brass; its "sheen" and "hard, cold glow" is celebrated in "Moonrise" and "The Lamplight." The permanence of metal and stone and their inanimate qualities are always used by the poet to symbolize peace, immobility, death, and eternity as opposed to the terrifying confusion of flux, change, and inconstancy, which he epitomizes in metaphors and symbols such as light, water, flame, etc. Stones are described in the early "Hill Burial" as "inevitable" and "rare," and the hero sinks to his grave in "Wet air / The air of stone." "February's" winter scene is full of "steely shadows" or "stone-pierced shadows"; and the "Tewa Spring" lies quiet in deep valleys with "shadows deep as stone." In "The Crystal Sun," the stones are made the source for strength:

> . . . the stones
> that hold the hills,
> The sun that holds the
> Sky with all its
> spreading rays, were of one
> Substance.

In "The Solitude of Glass," the poet finds permanence in the ". . . " 'fringed rock,' the 'stiff rock' / . . . "iron filings / Gathered to / The adamant." In "To the Painter Polelonema," he uses the rock image in an onomatopoetic stanza as the symbol of the artist's struggle with his medium:

> You wring life
> from the rock
> . . . . .
> crush, smell it,
> temper it
> in a single grip
> that lasts for years
> . . . . .

with love—
of rock!

And finally in one of his own dedications to his own mistress—poetry—he speaks to his muse, "Maiden of icy stone," thus evoking the permanence and immortality that he seeks for his art form. In the last poem of his *Collected Poems*, he closes with a characteristic symbol. "The early flowering orchard trees" of his early poetry have finally become the permanent, inevitable stone of truth.

I was now essential wood
Concentrating into truth
. . . .
Orchard tree beside the road
Bare to core, but living still!

In one poem that he rejected for *The Collected Poems* (probably because of its too didactic and nonimagistic quality), he sums up his life's ambition with this same symbol. He wishes to be one of a select company of those who, in defense of reason, maintain the permanence of stone. The last stanza of "These Walls Are Brown and Faded" concludes:

While those whose minds are living
Grow hard and cold and gray,
Elude the unforgiving,
And somehow have their say
In words no fool can touch
Because they mean too much.

The sequence of Winters' poetic development from early Imagist to later "Post-Symbolist" is recorded as he remembers it in a poem called "Summer Commentary." It is one of his last poems, and as he looks nostalgically back on his long poetic journey—he meditates:

Where is the meaning that I found?
Or was it but a state of mind,
Some old penumbra of the ground,
In which to be but not to find?

Winters acknowledged his progressive development and named his final style "Post-Symbolist." This term seemed to identify a more calculated, controlled use of his original sense impressions, now elevated from simple image to complex symbol. Some critics and poets have failed to recognize his emphasis on imagery; John Ciardi observed, "He is a poet who seems to refuse to engage the senses."[47] It can only be assumed that they have never completely read either *The Early* or *The Collected Poems* of this highly sensitized poet.

Diction and Syntax

In the Foreword to his most important book of criticism—*In Defense of Reason*—Winters defined his "absolutist" theory of literature in terms of diction, which he considered one of the most important elements of poetry:

> I believe that a work of literature insofar as it is valuable, approximates a real apprehension and communication of a particular kind of objective truth. The poem exhausts the inherent *possibilities of language* more fully than any other form: hence my thesis can be extended to them. . . . The poem is a statement in words about a human experience which employs both concept and connotation, has formality, etc. (Italics mine)[48]

The "possibilities of language," through precise word choice, make the diction of poetry one more integral part of the poet's "moral" will to choose words precisely for exact connotation and denotation. (It is significant of Winters' *will* that he used the words "exhaust" and "possibilities" in his definition, since *their* very connotations as a diction suggest the totality of his effort.)

He wrote this prescription as a teacher years after he had already successfully practiced the Imagist art in his early experimental poetry. He had learned from his wide reading of Pound, Williams, and Marianne Moore the value of *le mot juste*. He had practiced this art with translations from Mallarmé, Baudelaire, and Rimbaud. He had reached a selective precision and a verbal finesse in the diction of his still-life paintings in poetry. Yet somehow this had not seemed enough. Having reached the ultimate of language possibilities through the spare, precise images of his early poetry, he then sought an extension of language for a type of poetry that would go beyond simple clarity and precision of image. He sought a diction that would add the metaphysical dimension of abstraction through denotation and connotation in his later poetry. An examination of his poetic practice reveals his theory of language through denotation and connotation; his use of words in terms of style, syntax, and onomatopoetic effects; and certain passages from his poetry that exemplify his art.

He had written in *Forms of Discovery* of his admiration of the "plain style" of the sixteenth century lyricists; yet that *plain* style was achieved by a very selective choice of diction which includes consideration of both denotation and connotation. The "moral" rational poet will use both and will not abandon either of these important faculties at his command; for words cannot have associations without meanings, and it is the nature of associations that they are associated *with* something. Words must be chosen, then, so as to achieve due proportion between denotation and connotation. Winters felt that the basis for this proportion was "the rational assessment of the feeling engaged." If the feeling is *not* rationally assessed, the result will be a sentimental, over-emotional choice of diction, without the fine adjustment of denotation to connotation necessary for the contemporary "plain style." This theory, first elucidated in *Primitivism and Decadence*, is elaborated in *The Function of Criticism* and finally summarized in *Forms of Discovery*:

> Words require connotations of feeling, since human experience is not purely conceptual. The good poet makes a statement in such a way as to employ both concept *and* connotation as efficiently as possible, but concept is the master. . . .[49]

In other words, "It is what one *should* say."

Winters' practice of diction shows his choice of language for "what one should say" to be in keeping with the doctrines of his sixteenth century masters and yet highly contemporary. It is an "open" diction in the modern mode, using the everyday patterns of speech of our time ("muscles," "sediment," "traffic," "mineral," etc.). It is unmannered and unidiosyncratic except for a few archaic abbreviations and contractions in his early writings before he was sure of his rhythms. When appropriate, he varies the diction to the subject and its time. His directives in "To a Young Writer," for instance, are couched in the plain language he would have his pupil use in today's businesslike, no-nonsense world ("arrears," "discreet," "knowledge," "discern," "dispel" etc.). On the other hand, the poem "Anacreontic" is full of old words that give a sense of the ancient tradition of dignified classicism from which the substance and the form of the poem comes. ("Tuscan," "Grecian," "swathed," "august," etc.) In both cases the diction has been chosen "morally" to fit content and form with appropriate language.

Choice of diction is also directly related to tone and may well be its determining factor. Although Winters' poems generally use contemporary language, they do not partake of any particularly contemporary idiom or jargon. Their diction is neither innovationist nor tricky; neither is it dated. Generally it has a rather formal tone as befits its high seriousness, but it is never anachronistic. Often it is a direct blunt "masculine" diction uniquely suited to the movement of its plain speech style. In Winters' mature poetry, he works as hard at achieving just the right rational word in this terse, nonfigurative language as he had worked for the exact, colorful imagist word in his earlier verse. This quality of direct forthrightness is often achieved by a heavy emphasis on monosyllables to compose a phrase or even a clause in his aphoristic poetry ("On Teaching the Young" and "A Leave-taking"). Generally it gives the semblance of spoken language because it never gropes for ingenuities. Even in "Elegy to a Young Airedale Bitch" he manages to contain the relatively slight subject matter within the context of the theme of high seriousness because of his choice of diction. As the subject and theme of a Winters poem grow more complex, so the syntax becomes correspondingly more involved; "The Lie" compared with "Quod Tegit Omnia," or "April" compared with "Midas," exemplify this progression. Generally his language becomes more elevated as his ideas become more "mystic"—as in "To the Holy Spirit" or "The California Oaks"; yet it is significant to note that his last two poems added to the latest edition of *Collected Poems* ("Dance Macabre" and "A Dream Vision") use a purposefully cryptic diction whose clipped syllables emphasize the stark clarity with which he sees his final position. ("Who and who and where were they?" and "What was all the talk about?") When necessary and proper, he addresses himself directly in plain language to his subject, however delicate the content. There is no mawkishness or dissimulating jargon in his poems of sex and passion. ("Sir Gawain" and "The Marriage").

One of his most interesting techniques of diction is the use of abstract words in a descriptive context. In *Forms of Discovery*, he named this as one of the most important hallmarks of his "Post-Symbolist School." Thus he combines sensory vividness and abstract meaning so that the imagery achieved from this connotative sensory diction is not just description or illustration, but is in itself the embodiment of the idea. For instance, the diction choice for "The Slow Pacific Swell" becomes by the extension of its very sound (its alliteration, onomatopoeia, etc.) the threatening forces of the unconscious, which always haunted him. The poem begins with simple descriptive monosyllables—"Far out of sight forever stands the sea." The choice of diction here controls the stately rhythm and the mystery of the content. But it is merely observed here. As it continues to explore the subjective sensations of the narrator, it reflects *his* growing complexity of mood, as observation becomes contemplative and as diction become more sophisticated:

> That is *illusion.* The *artificer*
> Of quiet, distance holds me in a *vise*
> And holds the ocean *steady* to my eyes (Italics mine)

The poem continues to build into a cadence of diction, similar to that of Melville, and eventually the forces of evil and darkness threaten all landsmen who see its peril and promise. Concept and context are intermingled:

> I have lived inland long, The land is *numb*
> It *stands* beneath the feet, and one may come
> Walking *securely*, till the sea *extends*
> Its *limber margins* and *precision* ends
> By night a *chaos* of commingling power,
> The whole Pacific *hovers* hour by hour. (Italics mine)

The precise choice of diction here with the onomatopoetic syntax makes this a *tour de force* of sound and sense and shows Winters is a truly "moral" dictionist. Other poems noteworthy for selectivity of diction and syntax are "To the Holy Spirit" and "My Father's House," where the "stitching" of vowels and consonants adds to the organic essence of the poem's sound and sense.

The contemporary poet-critic Howard Nemerov recognizes Winters as one of the few modern poets able to use abstract words in a descriptive context, and he praises his skill in diction choice ". . . that has a dry, literate, mature, adult intensity."[50] It could be called "academic" in that the discourse is absorbed in the illustration and vice versa. The syntax is supple enough to balance both emotional and rational diction in a final act of aesthetic morality.

Winters' early poems show as much care in their choice of diction as the later ones; but, as might be expected, the language of his Imagist period is more youthful, passionate, and exuberant than that of his more formal mature period. The early poems use the open diction of the contemporary world ("antennae," "monsters," "compression," "reversible," etc.), with only a few archaisms and abbreviations when rhythm demands them ("thou'rt," "ere," etc.) Some particular word choices show his selective discretion for the use of sudden abstraction even in these Imagist poems; these suggest the experimental early attempts at a technique that became so important to his later poetry. In "Hill Burial" he writes "The only *mean* / was borne by men. . ." In "The Crystal Sun": "The stars . . . the sun . . . / were of one *substance* / spun." In "Song" he writes of the "precise," "remote," and "striking" "coolness" of fine wood in a progressive sequence of search for just the right abstract adjective. In the same poem he writes of birds in a "stiff, wild hall of light." These words are chosen not to mix the metaphor but to add an abstract and sometimes even paradoxical dimension that will clarify the philosophical concept of the poem, "Imagist" though it be. In the same poem he speaks autobiographically of this poetic effort to which he has dedicated himself:

And I preach to them of
the mystery of this my
sacred craft but no one
listens
I a poet
stand about the streets
alive for any audience
and shivering at quiet
as at pure thin morning.

Verbs and adjectives are chosen in this early poetry for their colorful precision. In "The Precincts of February" he writes of a man "Heavy and ironblack . . . *threading* the grass"; in "The Rows of Cold Trees," ". . . the pipe is *haired* with *unseen* veins; cold *lies* on his eyelids." In "The Resurrection," "Spring *penetrated*"; in "The Crystal Sun," "the mare *spun* knee-high in yellow flowers," etc. In "The Muezzin" the poet paints his word pictures with a mixture of abstract and specific diction: ". . . *swarming* clouds . . . *cobwebbed* with pale *beatitudes* / a *certainty* of evening." In "Wild Sunflower" he describes the bloom as "*gross* of leaf and *porous* / *gummy, raw*, with *unclean* edges . . . / It leers beside our doors. . . / *gulps* the sun and earth, will not be *beaten* down."

Onomatopoetic effects are achieved by careful word choice of alliterative and syntactical arrangements. "The Fragile Season" is a good example of the *s* sound of autumn throughout:

The scent of summer thins
The air grows cold.

One walks alone
And chafes his hands.

The fainter aspens
Thin to air—
The dawn
Is frost on roads.

This ending of the year
Is like the lacy ending
of a last year's leaf
Turned up in silence.

Air gives way to cold.

Another poem in which sound is made to fit sense through choice of diction is "Quod Tegit Omnia." Here the tentative, precariously balanced nature of the subject and theme—time versus timelessness—is emphasized by the *t, k,* and *p* repetitions throughout, as the plosive consonants literally tick the time away; in the same lines the *l, m,* and *n* sounds draw it out into a timelessness:

. . . . When
Plato temporizes on the nature
of the plumage of the soul the
wind hums in the feathers as
across a cord impeccable in
tautness but of no mind:
Time,
the sine-pondere, most
imperturbable of elements,
assumes its own proportions.

Some of Winters' poems achieve their Imagistic precision through the combination of onomatopoetic connotations that are evoked by the words themselves. "The Immobile Wind" is full of such diction choices. Here the images are not only of physical sound but of emotional sense, and the diction is chosen accordingly:

Blue waves within the stone
Turn like *deft wrists interweaving.*
Emotion, undulant, alone
Curled wings flow beyond perceiving
Swift points of sight,

mystic and *amorous* little hands,
The wind has drunk
as water *swallows sifting sands.*
[Emphasis mine.]

Such a combined effect of diction chosen for sound and sense is also evident in the starkly monosyllabic, short-lined "Cold Room":

The dream
stands
in the night
above unpainted
floor and chair.

The dog is
dead asleep
and
will not move
for god or fire.

And from the
ceiling
darkness bends
a heavy flame.

A final device of diction often used in these early poems is that of mixing images to stand one against the other, thereby suggesting the first in terms of the second. Hence the choice of diction for the second image adds a new dimension to the first. In "Orange Tree," the poet addresses it as ". . . *black* serpent / *struggling* / with your *weight* of *gold*—you hold out / *lacquered life*." The tree becomes infused with serpentine evil as the diction develops it beyond the merely botanical descriptions. In "Bison" the poet exclaims, "O bed of burning / horns / O swarming / blood that stored black / honey in your flesh / thighed with a storm!" The magnificence of the physical animal is transcended only by its mystic quality of elemental godliness given by the poet's diction choice.

These same techniques extend into the later poetry of *The Collected Poems*, but the selection of diction there is more formally integrated to suit the sedate, reserved tone of this traditional verse. In the final "Sonnet to the Moon" the techniques of onomatopoetic precision, abstraction with sensory connotations, and syntactical arrangements all exemplify the finesse Winters had reached within the strict confines of traditional forms. Certain particular passages show his ability to handle these techniques so that the choice of diction is a willed, "moral" element, organic in the entire mature poem. Even in an occasional poem such as "On the Death of Senator Thomas J. Walsh," he adopts the appropriate timbre and sedate order necessary to his content. "One *old* man *more* is *gathered* to the *great*." The long vowels and the slow gutterals add dignity through word choice. He even adopts and adjusts a quotation when it serves his tone and subject: "How sleep the great, the gentle and the wise! / *Aged* and *calm*, they *couch* the *wrinkled* head . . . . Dwellers amid a peace that few *surmise*, / Masters of *quiet* among all the dead." (Italics mine) Another good example of Winters' ability to make diction fit his content and tone occurs in "Postcard to a Social Muse. . ." whom he scorns with biting monosyllables:

> Madam, since you choose
> To call yourself a Muse,
> I will not be too nice
> To give advice

In "Midas" the effect of wonderment and awe is emphasized by diction that contains the intense assonance of long vowels and dipthongs:

> Where he *wand*ered, dr*eam* en*wound*,
> Br*igh*tness took the pl*ac*e of s*oun*d.
> Sh*i*ning pl*a*ne and mass bef*o*re
> Everywhere the s*ea*led d*oo*r. (Italics mine)

And again later in this poem sound is made to fit sense with the slowing *m, n*, and *l* consonants in such lines as "Mineral his limbs were grown / Weight of being not his own . . ." / Immortalized the quickened shade / Of meaning by a moment made." In the poem "The Prince" the theme is balance; the content is advice to rulers. The diction choice and its syntactical arrangements suit precisely the *double entendre* with pairs of balanced nouns and adjectives: "love with hate," "craft and hardihood," "witless unto wisdom," "disaster to luck," etc.

Winters is a master in choice of diction for exact emotional connotation of feeling. For instance, in "Sir Gawain and The Green Knight" he describes the knight's throat as the head is struck from his body as "reptilian," "wrinkled," etc.; while the lady's body "clung" and "swarmed" around the knight as he loved her. In another poem inspired by "The Portrait of a Scholar," the poet chooses to describe the very painting in the visual language of its medium: "fluent oil," "flesh luminous as pearls," "eyes ingenuous but intense." He summarizes in a bridge to his philosophical finale by using this same "occupational" diction appropriate to the medium:

> This is a *vision* in a frame,
> *Defined* and *matted* down with *gold* (Italics mine)

At the end of the poem he frames the traditional "Ubi-sunt" theme in a combination of well-chosen image and diction:

> Our names with his are but the *lees*
> *Residual* from this *clear* intent;
> Our *finely grained* identities
> Are but this *golden sediment.* (Italics mine)

In an occasional poem written in praise of wisdom and scholarship, but ostensibly "For the Opening of the William Dinsmore Briggs Room," he chooses words for the climax of the poem which contrast the sequential consonant *s* and *ch* sounds with *l*'s for a distinctly "moral" dignified, slow finale:

> That in this room, men yet may read
> By labor and wit'*s* *s*u*ll*en *sh*ock
> The fina*l* *c*ertitude of *s*pee*ch*
> Whi*ch* He*ll* itse*l*f cannot un*l*ock. (Italics mine)

Here the words with *s* and *t* sounds seem to suggest the slow effort—as the connotation suggests—of learning and scholarship; the climax comes with the rolling *l* sounds of the last line of permanence.

One final example of his virtuosity is found in the last stanza of "On Teaching the Young." After the two formal, cryptic, first stanzas have stated the qualifications for this art, the poet concludes with three exact adjectives that sum up completely his theme and tone. They connote his complete dedication to his muse and his reverence for teaching the classical tradition to his young scholars and writers:

> Few minds will come to this.
> The poet's only bliss
> Is in cold certitude—
> *Laurel, archaic, rude.* (Italics mine)

Here are connotation and concept deftly combined: a truly "moral" artistic choice of diction.

In 1932 Winters wrote an essay in praise of Robert Bridges, which he entitled "Traditional Mastery." In it he complimented Bridges for his "purity of diction. . .":

> . . . a diction so free from any trace of personal idiosyncracy that a successful imitator of it could never be detected as an imitator but would appear only as that most unlikely of phenomena, a rival; that he should, I say, in all likelihood be recognized as the most valuable model of poetic style to appear in the language since Dryden.[51]

It is this same pure "open" diction, dictated by the very "morality" of his art's organic quality, that makes the poetry of Winters a likely rival for either Dryden *or* Bridges!

Tone

Tone is the most personal element in poetry, the one by which the poet establishes his own identity behind the poem. By means of it he draws a "sympathetic contract" with his reader and either gains or loses rapport. Delicately balanced, it reveals how the poet takes himself. In this sense it is not really a single element at all, but rather the synthesis of all the others. It is by this evanescent "tone" that a connoisseur recognizes his favorite poet's work even though single moods shift from one poem to another.

To try to identify any single tone for a poet's complete canon is, of course, impossible. But if one were to try to generalize about most of Winters' mature poetry, one might conclude that the one tone most often struck is that of the voice of authority. Variations of this occur, but as in all the distinguishing elements of his work, one finds in its tone the necessary assurance of the authoritative "moral" judgment. Even in this nebulous area of tone, he comes through as rationalist, mistrusting the completely emotional. He once used his early poem "Nocturne" as an example of a bad poem with too much tone and not enough idea. He divided the emotional unit of any poem into two general types: "the image, in which all sound and meaning elements fuse into a single physical whole; and the anti-image in which the relationship of at least one element to the rest is non-physical."[52] Hence "tone" in a mature Winters poem should grow from a combination of the emotional *and* the rational if it is to succeed.

After his emotional experimental early verse (whose tone was mainly terror and uncertainty), his poetry began to take on the tone of authority as it adopted formal patterns. He achieved this mood in a variety of ways: declarative statements, short, cryptic lines, tight stanza patterns, periodic sentences, formal diction, rhetorical questions and climactic exclamations, close rhymes (such as those of the heroic couplet), etc. All of these devices added to the image of the "single physical whole"; and all were set off by the "tone" of pure reason in concept or "motive," so that the total effect was one of dignified verse, *ex cathedra*. His defense of reason in these later poems was not always successful, though he strove for rationality constantly; sometimes the prevailing temper seems to be a strong stoniness, a bitter stoicism, a resigned endurance that is not actually reasonable at all; but it *is* authoritative. Critics whom he has antagonized have called it "priggish, and pedagogical"; others, who admire it, go so far as to call it "mystic." Whatever the term, Winters *knew* he knew. But when he was occasionally frustrated in communicating his absolutism, he wrote some of his most successful poetry out of the stoicism to which he turned in his despair. Having passed beyond foreboding, he turned to authority for endurance.

This tone of authority often put off his critics and readers, and Winters was well aware of their resentment. He seems to have intended this tone to emphasize the validity of his judgments, but it frequently impeded or irritated his audience instead. Taken in large doses, it may well grow wearing; but in the individual poem, it most often succeeds in evoking respectful attention from the reader who is attracted by the highly intellectual theme. It is the quality of his tone that establishes his esoteric coterie of readers who would not be interested in lesser matters taken less seriously.

His faculty for controlled discernment was slowly developed through the self-conscious, frenetic free-verse of his early poems. His mature work took confusion for its main subject and disciplined it by this tone of authority achieved through the order of form. The later work of the older poet reflects a resigned stoic endurance as time ran out and current style shifted in literary matters.

The earliest poetry is full of self-conscious nervous tension. Its tone is precarious, excited, tentative—full of hurry, excitement, and hysteria, charged with either beauty, horror, or both. This tone often condensed the subject into separate perceptions or expanded it into kaleidoscopic meanderings. But however involved, these psychological odysseys were never relaxed. After the orgiastic effects in the first three volumes, the tone in *The Proof* settles to a lower key and a more sophisticated repose. The old laments are still here—a consuming resentment of waste of time and talent, a feeling of rejection by his peers, and a loss of the great tradition by his literary generation. But as a whole these poems show a calmer sense of self-assurance. They no longer ask about life; they tell about it. While they may scorn it, they do not rage against it. The darkness at the brink has receded, and the mind and spirit have recovered themselves. Authority begins to speak out in its own voice after *The Journey*. Sometimes it is sarcastic and irritated in many of the small occasional poems; it can also be affectionate and poignant, depending on its subject. But whatever the subtone, there is always the major voice of authority that was based for him on sweet reason. His formal poems often use the devices of rhetorical question or exclamation to assist the elevation. The final ones, whose themes and subjects are of a highly spiritual nature, take on the lofty tone of a seer who has seen truth, is condemned to tell it, and suffers through the telling. The tone here reflects his double vision of time ("as a progression of existence toward meaning / that its changing cannot find") and of the opposing timelessness in the rational mind of man. In seeking this latter nirvana, the tone of the poetry becomes that of some mystic voice of finality. In the very last of *The Collected Poems* the reader senses a peaceful resignation, a "stoniness" that will endure. It is finally a compassionate authority, still convinced of its own reason, but willing to let the unreasonable go their benighted ways. The self-conscious, subjective, youthful quest has come full circle to this mature objective voice of authority at the close of the Winters canon.

It is a fact that this one element of tone, more than any other, has earned for Winters his most negative criticism. To some he has seemed dogmatic, bigoted, and sullen in his pronouncements. And yet what he actually says is that we know we *cannot* know. Though a shy man personally, he felt impelled to a public stance of bravado. He is a sort of contemporary Socrates without the grace of the Greek. Yet he speaks with such knowledgeability and authority that the message is often confused by those who mistake tone for them. If no solution is offered to our mortal problems save endurance, at least this is proposed vigorously and with conviction. It is natural that professional critical reactions to Winters' tone all emphasize the uncomfortable candor of this twentieth century gadfly in their midst.

Dennis Donoghue attributes Winters' authoritative tone to his search for order in a dark confused world:

> If much of Mr. Winters' is dour and sullen, the reason is that this is the only kind of order he is prepared to invoke, darkness being what

> it is. . . : The stupidity of powerful men and the conspiracy against the intelligence.[53]

Howard Kaye suggests that even in the later Winters poetry there is still the old threat of madness. "It surges constantly against the constraint of poetic form and spiritual discipline."[54] As a result, it is a grave, brooding poetry—full of high seriousness because it recognizes the terrible cost of spiritual discipline. Howard Baker attributes Winters' stoicism to the Protestant American tradition, plus contact with the more humanistic traditions of English and French letters. "His is an austere and not too congenial voice . . . with an awareness of the dark experiences of life by a poet who charges his lines with passion as he controls them with tempered, classic sweetness."[55] Hayden Carruth observes Winters' tones of "rationalism reconciled with mystery."[56] Babette Deutsch describes them as "gaunt, grey, and harsh, having issue in a profound disenchantment with the world, inviting us to share his tragic awareness."[57] Richard Ellman finds them "gruff, blunt, irascible, stony, and masculine . . . sometimes humorless, portentous, sommolent. . . .but only sometimes."[58] Edward Honig suggests that Winters' tone "risks banality, flatness, and oversimplification to obtain the illusion of 'cold certitude' ";[59] and Rolphe Humphries finds the tone "cold—or anyway cool."[60] Morton Zabel concludes: "Too much abstraction and grandiloquence, tiresome pontificality, over-ambitious gravity."[61] (These critics omit attention to the many humorous and tender poems such as "See Los Angeles First," "Postcard to a Social Muse," "To My Infant Daughter, "For My Father's Grave," etc. when they make such generalizations.) The most discerning and knowledgeable critic of Winters' tone seems to be Donald Justice, a poet himself, who commends Winters for being able "to adjust his tone perfectly to whatever his matter of the moment."[62]

Indeed it is this ability to adjust that shows Winters' virtuosity within the overtone of authority. "The voice of experience" does encompass a great range: the affectionate in "For Emily Dickinson" or "On a View of Pasadena from The Hills"; the ruminative in "The Journey" or "The Slow Pacific Swell"; the didactic in "To Edward MacKenzie" or "For the Opening of the Wm. Dinsmore Briggs Room"; the sarcastic in "Ode to the Despoilers of Learning at an American University" or "Danse Macabre"; the reverential in "To the Holy Spirit" or "To the Moon'; the mysterious and terrifying in "The Vision" or "The Longe Nightes When Every Creature . . . "; the regretful in "John Day" or "John Sutter";

the whimsical in "Prayer for My Son" or "In Praise of California Wines"; the mystical in "Time and the Garden" or "Sonnet"; the passionate in "Sir Gawain and the Green Knight" or "The Marriage"; and finally the fatalistic in "A Dream Vision" or "A Song in Passing."

Winters' late poetry in particular carried this tone of the fatalistic. It was a final tone after long and bitter endurance in a life that had tried to balance "wisdom and wilderness" through reason and form. In *The Early Poems*, "Prayer Beside a Lamp" concludes with his most irrational line of the sheer wilderness that he had so often sensed and feared: "I, crumbling, in the crumbling brain of man!" But in the last poem of *The Collected Poems*—"A Dream Vision"—he could state authoritatively:

> I was now essential wood,
> Concentrating into truth;
> What I did was small and good.

The timelessness of this last poem closes the work on a cautiously optimistic note . . . optimistic, at least, for Winters. The rest he will leave to the judgment of time, and such critic-poets as Robert Lowell, who describes Winters' tone as ". . . compassionate, made of iron."[63] In the last analysis, like all the other elements of his poetry, his tone is strongly autobiographical. Like his hero in "Heracles," he could say passionately and proudly: "This was my grief, that out of grief I grew." Yet his rage for order held in the end contained even that grief.

What can be said in final assessment of Winters' poetic practice? It is natural—even tautological—that it follows the tenets of his criticism because his criticism was literally developed as a result of his practice. His final "style" was ultimately determined after years of experimentation with free verse, Imagism, supercharged perception, emotional and psychological orgy. When he finally selected "everything I wish to keep," he printed mainly the poems that were characterized by a deliberate leanness of line, a careful neatness with studied sharpness of expression, and a formal epigrammatic tone of authority. It is a poetry that has been guided by a rigorous and isolated critical intelligence, in almost direct opposition to the patterns of his contemporaries. From his earliest one-line poems to his most complex formal sonnets, he has sought to arrest both intuition and sensory perception in one stroke; then to make the idea and its physical realization coincide with a "moral" accuracy of judgment which makes for truly metaphysical poetry.

Allen Tate first wrote that Winters had as few mistakes to live down as any living poet, but it is true that there are some. It would seem that most of them stem from his effort to be too purely reasonable and too firmly controlled. It is true that this taut technique gave him a firm sense of order and direction, but it has also limited his freedom of movement, for all his sense of variation. Sometimes the poems are *too* full of abstraction, tiring in their pontifical tone and diction; but these are all faults of the lesser poems, and since even they are full of high gravity, his faults, as such, merely point up the serious, courageous intelligence behind them. As a matter of fact, many of the poems wrestle with this absolutist tendency, and sometimes the didactic treatment robs the meaning of the symbol (as in "To a Military Rifle") or taints the imagery (as in "Portrait of a Scholar from the Italian Renaissance") to unfortunate distortion.

When one looks on the positive side of the Winters achievement, one finds that rare species—a poet who works by limitation rather than by expansion. He does not reach out through deliberate symbolic echoes or ironic parallels of associational techniques. His references are crystal-clear and refined for one particular citation only; hence the meaning of each poem is precise, restricted, and technically controlled. He is in no sense a sterile formalist yearning for the past though he adopts classical forms. His is a completely contemporary conservative poetry whose conservatism is so original and radical that his poems are still not reprinted in any great quantity in anthologies. Some of his best poetry is that which comes out of the world of formal occasions, in touch with the tragic circumstances of our public times as they reveal the personal terrors of our private psyches. This poetry reveals a fine fusion between the personal and the universal. Allen Tate summarized his accomplishments in three words: "Clarity, elegance, and power. Clarity, because he respects the limits of language more than inner light; elegance because he does not invite the reader into the irrelevance of his private sensibility; and controlled power, because his insights are not asserted but earned."[64]

This is, after all, a poetry of self-preservation: the preservation of the poet's identity by the very act of writing. His student colleague Kenneth Fields said of him: "This poet becomes more alive as his perceptions are unique, more specifically his own."[65] His main theme is always the predominant mystery of existence, particularly his own. It is his "style" to be preoccupied with his own unique relation to the universe and to seek his rational position in it. As such he is completely contemporary. In *Maule's Curse*, Winters wrote: "Poetry is truth and something more.

It is the completeness of the poetic experience which makes it valuable."[66] Praised by such brothers in the priesthood of poetry as Allen Tate, Robert Lowell, J. V. Cunningham, and Donald Justice Winters—who always prized poets over critics or scholars—could be justly proud of his poetic accomplishment.

PART FOUR

"Laurel, archaic, rude."

Explications of Selected Winters' Poems

Twenty of Winters' poems have been chosen for analysis to show the development and range of his creative ability. This process of "unfolding" a poem was a serious critical business for him. For such explication one must make a "moral" judgment of "the simultaneous relationship between rational context and feeling." It is this delicate balance that he sought in all of his poetry and criticism and that he demanded of his Post-Symbolists for the future. The criticism of good poems was for him a civilizing influence because "they train our powers of judgment and affect the quality of daily judgment and actions."[1]

These poems are not grouped by genre but in sequential order as he printed them. (They may be followed in the pagination listed from the tables of contents for eight of *The Early Poems* and twelve of *The Collected Poems.*) They sample Winters' wide range of interest, mood, attitude, style, and craft. Actually, he wrote in a very wide variety of genres: Imagist perception poems of a single line, or long descriptive pastorals; occasional heroic poetry on public events, or highly personal emotional lyrics; tragic poetry of religious and philosophic depth, or satiric epigrammatic verses on the mundane state of the world.

In all of them, he felt "called" to speak out as a contemporary seer. It should be remembered that they are all highly autobiographical and personal. The narrator barely conceals the poet, if at all; and they are all highly serious. This series begins with an early dedicatory poem from his first book, written before he was twenty-one years old. It requires no explication other than the poet's own statement of the *raison d'etre* of his entire life. Written in his simple, youthful traditional style, it embodies the meaning of his existence as a creative artist.

The Priesthood

We stand apart
That men may see
The lines about our eyes.

We perish, we
Who die in art,
With that surprise

Of one who speaks
To us and knows
Wherein he lies.

The Crystal Sun

Lean spring came in,
A living tide of green,
Where I, a child,
Barefooted on the clear sand,
Saw the sun fall
Straight and sharp in air—
I screamed in sunrise
As the mare spun
Knee-high
In yellow flowers.

The stones
That held the hills,
The sun that held the
Sky with all its
Spreading rays, were of one
Substance
                    and my God
Lay at my feet
And spoke from out
My shadow, eyed me
From the bees:
And he was not, or
Else I—none could
say.

The Chinaman

Amid the lemongrove
Lived with pale women

And ate dogs and sang
All night.

What wonder then,
That I went mad
Amid the cloudy stone
And looked at
Print

more beautiful
Than women, till
The earth took form
In my place

at my feet.

This poem is typical of some of Winters' early Imagist verse techniques, yet it mixes personal lyric qualities in its combination. It comes from his third volume *The Bare Hills* and shows the return to more than the sheer Imagist one-line perceptions of feeling-states that made up the second book, *The Magpie's Shadow*. It presents one of his most common themes: the search for self-knowledge. It is sought not only through constant high-pitched sense perception, but also through a kind of transcendence to mysticism as a result of this recalled perception. The poem opens in reverie—"rememberance of things past." The diction recalls the physical sense impressions "*Lean* Spring . . . a living *tide of green*," in pure Imagist fashion. The childhood memory includes not only the physical sensations, but the hallucinations and the emotional trauma as well. The scream in sunrise is evoked again along with the concurrent, precise image of the mare—its "knee-high" spinning motion among the "yellow" flowers. Many of Winters' poems of this period contain such an association of two perceptions juxtaposed against each other in an instant of time, in good Poundian tradition. The words become highly charged by their juxtaposition and their interaction: "screamed" and "spun," "in sunrise" and "in yellow flowers." The second stanza moves with a slower pace of the sort of free verse that Winters preferred—where single accented patterns of rhythm are set against an indefinite number of unaccented feet. Monosyllables predominate to hold back the inexorable feeling of the weight of the universe. The repetition of the verb "held" adds to this impression; and the sun, stones, and hills are all interdependent—"of one substance"—as the sensitive narrator is aware of his awe and hallucinatory state. The rhythm moves the lines to their inevitable climax of "one substance"; "My God / Lay at my feet / And spoke from out / My shadow, eyed me / From the bees." Favorite images of Winters are used here to signal his near madness. "Shadow" and "bees" accompany this condition both visually and audibly, and his God seems a part of his own being, yet *not* of it. "And he was not, or / Else I—none could / Say." After this stanza the poem makes a rapid shift of pace and mood, as though the narrator would shake himself out of his hallucination by another memory of something he had read or dreamed from another reality. He forces himself to think on this other narrative, the story of the Chinamen. But it does not last long, and it only sends the narrator back to his own preoccupation. "What wonder, then, / That I went mad. . ." If Chinaman ate dogs, lived with pale women, and sang all night, this hedonism seems to be some sort of justification for the narrator to seek control, to look at "Print / more beautiful / Than women . . ." Here he is saved from madness by his association with the one reality of his life, "Print"—something to be understood by the use of reason rather than passion. Lemon groves, pale women, dogs to eat, songs all night—all represent a wild mélange exotic enough to drive one to stark madness of emotion "amid the cloudy stone." But he will not be left there in it. With the short, single word "Print" alone on the line, the narrator is brought back to reality and the world of reason. It is the symbol for things learned and reasoned and recorded. It is "more beautiful than women," and it causes the earth to take form again in its proper place at his feet. Wholeness is restored; sanity is preserved once more; the threat of being engulfed in the imagistic wildness of "lean spring" and "tide of green" is over.

This is a good example of the free-verse Imagistic patterns that are representative of this early period of Winters' writing. It also introduces certain images that recur throughout all of his poetry and eventually take on the character of symbol. It concerns his early fearful delight in the sensuous world and projects his hope of finding self-awareness, not in emotional orgy but in cool reason and knowledge. It was not included by Winters in *Collected Poems*, but it is used here to show the genesis of this technique. The next poem was included, and it shows the Imagist style perfected, refined, and condensed.

Jose's Country

A pale horse,
Mane of flowery dust
Runs too far

For a sound
To cross the river.

Afternoon,
Swept by far hooves
That gleam
Like slow fruit
Falling
In the haze
Of pondered vision.

It is nothing.
Afternoon
Beyond a child's thought,
Where a falling stone
Would raise pale earth,
A fern ascending.

Here the Imagist technique is more closely adhered to: less authorial comment, more precision of image, tighter syntax. The initial image of the pale horse is observed visually against the unusual silence. Winters' interest in perceptions and their juxtapositions is emphasized here as the observer expects the usual sound to accompany the sight and does not receive it. The river has also absorbed the normal expectation; and the quality of the occult, the ghostly, the weird is interjected into the tone immediately. "A *pale* horse," "mane of *flowery* dust" adds to the effect; and the image fades from the sight of the beholder in this silent country where images are set against the widest of landscapes. The tone of meditation is added in the second stanza as the observer ponders the vision he has had. The verbs "swept" and "gleam" and "falling" add the "proper" emotion to the motive: the rational theme of the poem is self-identity through wonderment; its subject—the recalled image of the horse running silently away to some never-never land. The afternoon seems in trance, suspended without sound. It is "swept" by far hooves, yet the observer does not hear them. His sight becomes a "haze of pondered vision." The juxtaposition of "pondered" with "vision" projects Winters' theory of Post-Symbolist techniques. The adjective is abstract, mental; the noun is literal, physical; together they evoke a metaphysical combination. The total metaphor—"Hooves / That gleam Like slow fruit / Falling / In the haze / Of pondered vision"—completes the transition from physical "image" to spiritual "vision." Then the narrator comes back. Willing suspension has ended; "It is nothing." In characteristic Winters fashion, the rational mind takes over. But the narrator is denying at the same time that he is savoring the vision. Indeed it is only "afternoon," but it is "beyond a child's thought." There is more to it than that. The last lines can be read with a double meaning for the "beyond." It may mean "*only* a child's thought;" or it may be "afternoon beyond a child's thought"—with a deeper metaphysical meaning than the simple images "Where a falling stone / Would raise pale earth / A fern ascending." "Pale horse," "*pale* earth;" "*falling* fruit," "*falling* stone," and one "*ascending* fern." The image evokes audible disbelief and visual belief. It leads the narrator to question his senses, to mistrust his impulses, to savor their intrigue, but finally to disavow them in a single stroke of reality. Perhaps, in the distance, it *is* only a fern ascending in the dust from a falling stone. But who can determine the reality of such a vision?

The rhythm of the free verse is slow and ponderous. It has mainly a double-accentual beat, but there are many unaccented syllables between them to heighten the nervous effect against the silence of the scene. There are also many end-line pauses, as though the observer were stopping to take longer looks, to try to hear the ghostly hooves that he is denied in the reality of vision. The brevity of the entire poem and the short lines—often of single words—add to the tone of meditative, silent wonderment. It is an aberration from the norm, to be believed or disbelieved, but remembered from this silent upper-river country of the Rio Grande, where Winters spent some of his most desolate years.

"Quod Tegit Omnia"

Earth darkens and is beaded
with a sweat of bushes and
the bear comes forth;
the mind, stored with
magnificence, proceeds into
the mystery of Time, now
certain of its choice of
passion but uncertain of the
passion's end.

When
Plato temporizes on the nature
of the plumage of the soul the
wind hums in the feathers as
across a cord impeccable in

tautness but of no mind:

Time,

sine-pondere, most
imperturbable of elements,
assumes its own proportions
silently, of its own properties—
an excellence at which one
sighs.

Adventurer in
living fact, the poet
mounts into the spring,
upon his tongue the taste of
air becoming body: is
embedded in this crystalline
precipitate of Time

Time and timelessness are favorite themes of Winters; "the mystery of time" is investigated here: "that which touches all" and is yet a mystery. And as the subject of time is meditated upon, the subject of man's own mind and passion *in* time is considered. The poem opens with the image of Earth in its darker moment, where passion is recalled in the mind, "stored with magnificence." Reason is its glory, and yet in this moment, when earth is "beaded with a sweat of bushes," it is the bear's image that brings the clumsy, physical, awkward, brutish aspect of that human mind into the poem. "Certain of its choice of passion, but uncertain of the passion's end," the mind proceeds to investigate time.

The philosophical mind of the poet recalls Plato's temporizing on the subject in *The Phaedrus*; the "plumage of the soul" represents for the philosopher-poet those "multi-colored passions which are mindless" and therefore dangerous. They are attractive, and they are intuitively satisfying; but they are not to be trusted. "The wind hums in their feathers as / across a cord impeccable in / tautness but of no mind." The crisp plosive consonants here literally sing the delight of the passionate experience, but the climactic judgment at the end deflates it. Onomatopoetically, the poet creates a *tour de force* here where the very sound of the line adds to the sense of attraction. Plato's theories are investigated, assessed, and dropped.

The "free verse" is held to a limited regularity of line with two main accents, around which many unaccented feet cluster. The stanza patterns are interconnected with the last word—the beat of the last line becoming the first word-beat of the next first line. The word "time" rings a kind of knell throughout to restore the mind to the proper focus; it serves as link with "when," another "time" word, and operates as an organic element of the poem's structure. "Time, the sine-pondere" is no atomic structure here? And yet the poet knows it is an element of the universe to be considered for its own proportions and properties. Yet how can one investigate it scientifically as he might another element (by atomic weight) when there is no atomic structure here? And yet the poet knows it is an element of his very being. Imperturbable, it will not be disturbed; it *assumes* its own proportions *silently*, it does not give off rays or gas or whatever might be measured by modern scientific skills. Its independence is "an excellence at which one sighs" in admiration. Its very abstraction is indeed perfection.

Alas, it is not for the poet to be so abstract or so perfect. He is "adventurer in living fact"; he deals with images, metaphors, rhythms; has weight; is perturbable; knows the limits of his own proportions; thus time to him is mystery. He mounts into the spring—Empyrean or otherwise—and professionally seeks those definite images which *will* give weight and substance to his verse: "Upon his tongue the taste of air becoming body." But eventually he too is "embedded" / in this crystalline / precipitate of Time." The last two lines show Winters at his best with diction choice. It is aesthetically a "moral" choice that leads him to the consonant repetitions of *d* and *k* and *p* and *t*—sounds that literally thrust the idea in the reader's ears and mind as they eventually evoke the "motive": the merely human mind of the poet in the inanimate mystery of time. His passions, his images, indeed his very mind are all finally absorbed in "That Which Touches All," and for Winters—as for all poets— this was a constant threat during his entire lifetime. The observer is alone in time; it is the only stability; all else is flux, even the poet's best efforts. The only constant feature is his own identity. How best to preserve it as he feels the crystalline timeless precipitate surround him?

Another poem from *The Bare Hills* carries this identity theme even further:

The Rows of Cold Trees

To be my own Messiah to the
burning end. Can one endure the
acrid, steeping darkness of
the brain, which glitters and is

dissipated? Night, the night is
winter and a dull man bending,
muttering above a freezing pipe;
and I, bent heavily on books; the
mountain, iron in my sleep and
ringing; but the pipe has frozen, haired with
unseen veins, and cold is on the eyelids: who can
remedy this vision?

I have walked upon
the streets between the trees that
grew unleaved from asphalt in a night of
sweating winter in distracted silence.

I have
walked among the tombs—the rushing of the air
in the rich pines above my head is that which
ceaseth not nor stirreth whence it is:
in this the sound of wind is like a flame.

It was the dumb decision of the
madness of my youth that left me with
this cold eye for the fact; that keeps me
quiet, walking toward a
stinging end: I am alone,
and like the alligator cleaving timeless mud,
among the blessed who have latin names.

The title has little to do with the poem except to set it in the locale which evoked the mental torture. The rows of cold trees dropped their leaves on the asphalt "in a night of sweating winter," and the tortured poet-narrator walked under them "in distracted silence." The theme of the poem is again the search for self-identity, the fear that it may not be found, or that once found, it may not maintained. The tired, mature narrator looks back on himself as the brash youthful narrator who had decided long ago to be his own Messiah. Echoes of Eliot's *Gerontion* in the "dull man bending / muttering above a freezing pipe" and of *Prufrock* in "I have walked upon the streets . . . " weave through the poem's meditative lines. The narrator recounts the "dumb decision" of the madness of his youth; he ponders the worth of it. Should he preserve it to the "stinging end"? The Messiah that he would create for himself demanded sacrifice: a "burning," "stinging end," "with a cold eye for fact." His was the unusual, unpopular way. This narrator's acrid, steeping darkness of the brain seems now incapable of retaining the youthful vow of reason and fact. Sense impressions creep in: the emotional overrides the rational, glitters, and is dissipated. He bends heavily over the books that should save him, but the mountain "iron in my sleep" is ringing; the frozen hairs of the pipe intrigue him, and "cold is on the eyelids." Who can resist the temptation of the senses so alerted? (It was about the time of this in the autobiographical accounts of Winters' introduction that he *did* begin to doubt the wisdom of a life of image only, of pure fact; yet his dedication to a life of reason kept him "quiet, walking toward a stinging end.") The narrator leaves the present vision still seeking a remedy at the end of the first stanza.

The two internal stanzas shift time and place and take the narrator back to meditations from his past locales. Neither the asphalt streets of the living nor the rustling tombs of the dead have provided any answer for his quandary. The rows of cold trees in both places—unleaved along the streets, or rich pine in the graveyard—have brought him neither surcease nor answer beyond their sight and sound. Senses alone operate here. Diction such as "unleaved from asphalt," "sweating winter," "distracted silence" and "rich pines," "rushing air," "sound of wind like flame" all appeal to emotional, sensory reactions and serve as organic links with the theme itself. Here again the motive and feeling are properly balanced—"morally" balanced, to use Winters' term. These two stanzas provide a developmental exposition of the theme stated in the first stanza, an apologia for the present from the past. The sudden shift from ordinary diction to formal, archaic language serves to heighten the dignity and seriousness of tone—"That which ceaseth not nor stirreth whence it is"—being almost direct Biblical quotation. The rhythm of these interval stanzas is highly metrical within the limits of Winters' free verse technique: a certain number of accented feet with an unlimited number of unaccented ones. The beat is again Biblical and sonorous. "I have walked . . . etc." is repeated with chantlike effect, and the main rhythmic progression is in a context of a three-accent line. However, it is purposely hurried when necessary with an extra beat and with such elisions as "the rushing of the air / in the rich pines above my head."

At the end the exposition is completed; the narrator returns to the rhythmic and philosophical status of the beginning. He asked in the first stanza; explained in the second and third; and answers in the last—much as a sonata structure develops in music. He concluded that having set his life in the particular direction of his youthful vow, he has permanently altered it. He savors his solitude; though as he examines it now, it seems a "dumb," "mad" decision without voice or reason. But it left him with "this cold eye for the fact." It also left him with this cold eye for his art and its development. The poem becomes something of an apologia not only for Winters' life-style and personality but for his *ars poetica* as well, in which he admits ruefully but proudly, "I am alone." The final metaphor is startling; purposely awkward and grotesque. Classical formalists who have Latin names *are* timeless—though like Winters, they are constantly cleaving muddy elements of disbelief and scorn in his century. But he is among "the blessed," and his cold eye for fact never forgets it, in spite of the morass of sense impressions into which it is so easy to slip. The poem begins with the narrator's brave vow to be "my own Messiah"; it ends with the narrator as an awkward reptile. It is paranoic to the extreme, and it is brutally honest and brave.

This poem and the next two show Winters at his most nerve-wracked state—his most hallucinatory, and his most beautifully Imagistic. By the end of the sequence in *Early Poems* he had shifted to sanity for art and reason's sake, to a totally different type of poetry.

The Bitter Moon

Dry snow runs burning
on the ground like fire—
the quick of Hell spin on
the wind. Should I believe
in this your body, take it
at its word? I have believed
in nothing. Earth burns with a
shadow that has held my
flesh; the eye is a shadow
that consumes the mind.

Scream into air. The voices
of the dead still vibrate—
they will find them, threading
all the past with twinging
wires alive like hair in cold.
These are the nerves
of death. I am its brain.

You are the way, the oath
I take. I hold to this—

I, bent and thwarted by a will
to live among the living dead
instead of the dead living; I,
become a voice to sound for.
Can you feel through Space,
imagine beyond Time?

The
snow alive with moonlight
licks about my ankles.
Can you find this end?

This poem is another of the Imagist, free-verse style of Winters, but this basic pattern is modified more and more by the meditative and metrical interpolations that occur. It is too contemplative for an Imagist poem and too regular in its metrical pattern to be truly free verse. It shows the beginning of the end of this early style in theme, content, and pattern. The poet is more and more concerned with a didactic self-analysis directly stated and more and more regular in his metrical beat. The old impulses and nervous reactions to image and sense impression are still there and are indeed the impetus for the poem: "Dry snow runs burning / on the ground like fire, etc. . . " but the poem soon shifts to the narrator's psychological reactions rather than allowing him to remain as a purely physical reactor. Indeed the narrator denies the old way and concludes that he has "believed in nothing." This disavowal is the reality that all is "shadow." Substance is somewhere else. And yet he is still somehow associated in an organic way with his old life though it is dead. "These are the nerves / of death. I am its brain." "You"—the bitter moon—are the way. And the image of the moon goddess as his muse is first indicated here and concluded in one of the final cryptic poems of the *Collected Poems*. Through poetry, through art, through "The *Bitter* Moon" as his constant goddess, he has "become a voice to sound for." His oath by the moon has been taken at great cost—"bent and thwarted by a will / to live among the living dead / instead of the dead living." Its cost will be greater before he has reached that final poem, and he knows it. But the moon will be the same: bitter yet constant. He prefers the living dead of the past—the classical heroes of art and literature—rather than the dead living of the insensitive world around him. Here he affiliates himself with the "fit though few," and he takes the oath willingly, but with full awareness of its pain.

By some hallucinatory, near hysterical affiliation he hopes to "feel through Space, / imagine beyond Time" and so guarantee some sort of eternity for himself. Identity may be lost, but eternity will be gained through his poetry. The poem returns at its end to the "snow-alive-with-moonlight" image and rises to a climax with the magnificently onomatopoetic phase, *licks* about my *ankles*." He asks the fatal question in the first stanza: "Should I believe / in this your body, take it / at its word?" He associates the private poetic vision with the insubstantial light of the moon and contrasts it to the turn of the unrelieved and immediate universe. And the agnostic who has "believed in nothing" vows at the end of the poem his dedication to a formal art as his means of self-preservation. Diction adds much to the tone here: "*Dry* snow runs *burning* / on the ground like *fire*—the *quick* of Hell *spin* on the *wind*," etc. The "shadow," the "scream," the "twinging, vibrating, threading," the "wires," the "nerves," the "hair," are all a part of the old hysteria. And the poem returns at the end to the last image inscribed in this onomatopoetic diction of "moral" choice: "The snow *alive* with moonlight / *licks* about my ankles." The metrics are basically trimeter but "free" in the particular Winters way: variation within the pattern of "freedom" which allows a certain number of accented feet with an unlimited number of unaccented ones. It is full of the agony and the ecstasy—the imperatives and the interrogatives—of the youthful narrator's search. It turns eventually to the calm, collected voice of reason, and the way has been found.

The last of Winters' "Early Poems" were published in *The Proof* in 1930, and they show the end of the totally free hallucinatory verse and the beginning of the more reasoned, formal patterns. The transition takes place within this single volume. One final example of the exclamatory, perceptive hysteria from this volume is allowed in *The Complete Poems*: Winters doubtless kept it as a kind of museum piece, however embarrassing; for it represented the violent rhythmic patterns, the urge to record the ultimate sense impressions, and the drive to associate with the elemental and the timeless. Here were the lessons learned from Pound and Fenellosa—his early masters—carried to their conclusion: swift perception of relations, words highly charged, and juxtaposed for interaction. After this, there was no place else to go; it is self-explanatory, or rather self-impressionistic, and needs little explication other than its own experience:

Song of the Trees

Belief is blind! Bees scream!

Gongs! Thronged with light!
And I take
into light, hold light,
in light I live, I
pooled and broken here,
to watch, to wake above you.
Sun
no seeming, but savage
simplicity, breaks running
for an aeon, stops, shuddering, here.

The "Song of the Trees" becomes somehow the song of the agonized poet—also living in light, but pooled and broken—to watch, and finally to wake. Kenneth Fields refers to Winters' poems of this variety in the language of contemporary physics. He finds the reactions of physicists who split the atom very much like those of the poet who seeks some sort of atomic oneness with the universe. He quotes James Franck: "The only way I can tell that a new idea is really important is the feeling of terror that seizes me."[2] Poets from Plato to James Lowell have reiterated this seizure, and Winters here describes his final attractive yet fatal dementia. The world of sensation impinges upon the identity. Plato warned against it; Winters took the warning. Instead of throwing himself into his own private Empedoclean Mt. Aetna, he threw himself into a "Defense of Reason" and changed his poetry's style along with his life style. Both shifts are evident by the end of this last volume of *The Early Poems*. The last two poems printed here from this book—"Sonnet" and "Simplex Munditiis"—are a kind of autobiographical and artistic hiatus: an "Ave atque Vale" as this poet of the older mode meets the personal of the new.

Sonnet

The table softly flames with flowers and candles
flame in wax and wax in flame and flame in flesh
and flaming flesh in silver
and your hand draws fruit from air

grown substance. And beyond the pane
moonlight is eating into earth—where the night
glimmers. My eyes will not rest.
We lose reality in symbolism,

stripped of our own meaning,
simplified for men. Beyond elision,
tragic if displaced! God stalks

in my living hand the mind,
the prey equivocal. The mind escapes.
You, set before me on a shaft of night!

The title of the poem states Winters' determination to adopt a formal pattern, a traditional mode; yet the actual implementation shows his independence within the form. He is not ready to give up the old or completely adopt the new; and the poem is a kind of synthesis. It was written when he was beginning to return to traditional verse and regular sonnets; yet at the same time he was writing some of his most violent final free verse. Many of the same themes in the *Early Poems* are hinted here; the poet's predicament is articulated as he seeks his identity as poet between the sense impressions of Imagism and the control of formal verse. There is the underlying norm of the iambic pentameter, the fourteen lines with heavy slow stresses of formal sonnet form predominating; yet these are not constant in every line. (See line two for metrical variation.) There are runovers, elisions and caesuras to vary the norm and to free the poet. The first stanza is an unpunctuated stream of consciousness into the second. The rhyme scheme can hardly be called "scheme" at all, and is certainly not in any Petrarchan or Elizabethan sonnet pattern; yet the octave and sestet are there in philosophical spirit if not in poetic order. Stanzaic patterns are varied, however the unusual spacing does not entirely deny the stated sonnet form.

The poem opens with the beautiful description of the candelabrum. The first five lines are visual shimmer of flame, flowers, wax, flesh, silver, fruit, and "your hand." Substance is finally achieved and outline is defined by the opening of the second quatrain. The external world offers a similar mélange of sense impressions; ". . . And beyond the pane moonlight is eating into earth—where the night / glimmers." The eyes of the poet are insatiable, and he fills himself with the glory of the exotic scene. Then the flat statement: "We lose reality in symbolism, / stripped of our own meaning, simplified for men." It is as though he has meditated and concluded that once and for all he must make the painful confession. Reality and "our own meaning " must avoid such temptations of simplification by sheer enjoyment of the senses without reason. The fate of such an imbalance would be "beyond elision, tragic if displaced." The rational voice speaks here; then immediately after it, the ironic alter-voice of emotion and sensation answers back: "God stalks / in my living hand the mind, the prey equivocal." The lines are full of careful high irony as the living hand of senses almost conquers the prey—the equivocal mind that is not yet as rapid or certain as the involuntary senses. (God is still anti-mind!) The mind escapes for the time being, and the enigmatic "you" is idealized on a spiritual "shaft of night." The violence of the older Imagist poems is gone; the bitterness is softened to meditation; and the poet is finally resigned and entranced by the pure contemplation of beauty which he cannot rationally understand, but can still admire. The poem ends on a classical note with the regular iambic pentameter varied only with the opening emphatic "you." It is a synthesis of all Winters has been and proposes now to be.

The final poem in this volume is a survey of the poet's new resolve; in effect a prayer for support in his new classical mode. He defines his position as man-poet and his new stance set against the old free Imagist pattern. Humbly he takes on the task before him with its yoke of form, knowing that it will bring him a larger freedom.

Simplex Munditiis

The goat nips yellow blossoms
shaken loose from rain—
with neck extended
lifts a twitching flower
high into wet air. Hard
humility the lot of man
to crouch beside
this creature in the dusk
and hold the mind clear;
to turn the sod
to face the sod beside his door,
to wound it as his own flesh.

In the spring the blossoms
drown the air with joy,
the heart with sorrow.
One must think of this
in quiet. One must
bow his head and take
with roughened hands
sweet milk at dusk,
the classic gift of earth.

So the simplest things of the world become the most complex: the gift of life and art are epitomized as the milk to be drawn for sustenance from nature. And the human milker must humble himself before the simple animal giver. The sensual poet observes the goat in her natural habitat and describes the scene with the same old delights in the simple sensory images of nature and the same lust for the right word or phrase: "nips," "yellow blossoms," "shaken loose from rain," "neck extended," "twitching flower," "high into wet air." But as soon as the image has been fully absorbed, there comes now to this artist the new corollary of responsibility to form, and it is a hard lot "to hold the mind clear." This farmer of verse must face the sod beside his door, wound it, plant the right seed for the right blossoms which will "drown the air with joy," and alas, "the heart with sorrow." The simplest things are the hardest; the poet, tilling his poetry and his mind for fruit, contemplates his task. He speaks of it in a short, simple line, in a humble third-person impersonality. No more of the raving first-person madness. "One must think of this / in quiet." Hands and head are again the sources of the right combination—senses and mind—but always in the proper synthesis and never one exclusive of the other. "One must / *bow* his head and take / with *roughened* hands . . ."; and the poet accepts the necessary sacrifices if he would gather the "sweet milk at dusk" and thus collect with his reasonable endeavour "the classic gift of earth." The poem hushes to silent imperative, and the tortured volume ends on this resigned note.

It is significant that Winters published this larger selection of his early poems long after he had included only a few of them in his *Collected Poems*. He said in the introduction that he viewed this early collection as a developmental study, and that he was protecting himself from someone else's making the improper selection. But the poems for which he had the most respect were those which followed the short early section in *The Collected Poems*. They are the poems of his maturity, and they contain the wisdom of the older man who has found his freedom within the variation of classical form. He allowed 23 of his early poems in the collected volume of 125. This sequence is followed by a section of translations, and then the mature Winters poems begin. The first section of these are the sonnets with which he disciplined himself as he took his new way into formal verse. The poems discussed next from this volume will follow the order in which Winters printed them. They are often grouped by genres, by themes, by subjects, but most often they represent the current shifts of the poet's mind as he sees his philosophy developing along with his art. They seem to demand explication in that same order rather than in some artificially imposed scheme; however, there is an effort to represent as wide a variety as is possible.

The first is from the sonnet section of seven exercises in growth as he sharpens his techniques in form after the years of free verse. He published these just after his translations from the French and Spanish. Their subjects are various, and in this one he recasts myth and legend in a brilliant discipline.

Apollo and Daphne

Deep in the leafy fierceness of the wood,
Sunlight, the cellular and creeping pyre,
Increased more slowly than aetherial fire:
But it increased and touched her where she stood.
The god had seized her, but the powers of good
Struck deep into her veins; with rending flesh
She fled all ways into the grasses' mesh
And burned more quickly than the sunlight could.

And all her heart broke stiff in leafy flame
That neither rose nor fell, but stood aghast;
And she, rooted in Time's slow agony,
Stirred dully, hard-edged laurel, in the past;
And, like a "cloud" of silence or a name,
The god withdrew into Eternity.

Winters frequently used myth as the basis for his poetry, but he usually added some touches of his own to the traditional legend. So here he bases the sonnet on the tragic tale of Daphne, pursued by the dazzling sun-god Apollo. She tried to flee, stood struck by the sun's flame, and was turned into a laurel tree. The theme—timelessness versus time—represents the constant struggle of the human to preserve his own identity in the face of universal or godlike pressures. Daphne seeks that preservation, is denied it, but is transcended in her mental state before she is completely transfixed or conquered.

The poem opens with the lovely description of the wood in which the chase occurs. Winters uses one of his favorite Post-Symbolist techniques here; the combination of physical with nonphysical, specific with abstract words: "Deep in the *leafy fierceness* of the wood." The combination of the two makes for the metaphysical reaction. The same sort of combination is evolved with "*cellular* and *creeping* pyre," where the invisible atomic energy is juxtaposed against the visible, moving flame. "Sunlight" and "cellular" give off the steaming, hissing onomatopoetic effect of initial consonant sounds as the description for the chase is made more frightening. The repetition of "but it increased" repeats the inevitable and adds to the suspense which is finally climaxed with six short monosyllabic words: "and touched her where she stood." After this, all is lost though the human struggles hard and long for release. The caesural effects of midline stops bring the effect of struggle into lines five and six as their rigorously regular rhythms are interrupted. The powers of good struggle in Daphne's effort to maintain her identity. The final effort is explosive as "with rending flesh / She fled all ways into the grasses' mesh / And burned more quickly than the sunlight could." The words "rending flesh," "fled," and "grasses" contain onomatopoetic consonants that make the physical flight and effort more real in the very mouth and ear of the reader. These are followed, as the descriptive octave ends, with a swiftly paced last line that literally brings the poem to a temporary halt as Daphne is transformed.

The sestet, in good sonnet style, adds a philosophic dimension to the physical problem posed in the octave. Now it is no longer just the physical battle between the two—the human and the superhuman; it has become a metaphysical battle for eternal survival. The human learns what dying means as eternity takes over. "And all her heart broke stiff in leafy flame." The word "stiff" is the perfect adjective to evoke this permanence, this finality. The "leafy" flame is no longer mobile as was the tree into which she had fled for escape; now it "neither rose *nor* fell, but *stood* aghast." This last adjective's metrical and consonant power adds again to the terror. And she, "rooted," now transfixing in the eternal immobility, "stirred dully, hard-edged laurel." The sequence of the comma phrases and their pauses slows the line to literal immobility. The series of consonant changes also makes the abstraction of immobility more real for the reader: "Sti*rr*ed du*ll*y, ha*rd-edg*ed *l*aurel." She has already become, by the last phrase, a thing "in the past." And the god—now attracted in another direction with his fickle, inevitable godlike immortality—"like a cloud of silence or a name, / . . . .withdrew into Eternity." The similes are well chosen. Winters had known "clouds of silence" and "names that withdrew" which were never heard from again. He knew the struggle to be more than silent, more than just a name. For him, these are more than just physical metaphors. And the beautiful Daphne, now the *hard-edged* laurel, will never regain her initial softness. The god—in his inexorable quest—goes on into Eternity.

Particular words are perfectly chosen: "cellular and creeping pyre," "aetherial fire," "grasses' mesh," "time's slow agony," "cloud of silence."

The images are caught between the physical and the nonphysical in excellent Winters Post-Symbolist technique. He has adopted the strict limits of the sonnet and maintained with precision its iambic pentameter norm as he varies it to suit his narrative and philosophic purpose. The very first line and first word sound the struggling tone of the poem with "deep"—as an accented trochee *against* that norm. In the second line—"*sun*light, the *cell*u*lar* and *creep*ing pyre—the opening trochee is syncopated into the norm by means of the pause after it; and the elision of "light" with "the" affords the mathematic variation so important for this poet's freedom. The rhyme scheme is rigorously sonnet-bound; yet at the end of the sestet the poet manages a pristine reversal of the usual to show his finesse: *e, f, g*; then the reversal *f, e, g.* Within the most traditional form imaginable, within the most carefully controlled and contrived metrical circumstance, this poet shows his willingness to adopt the norm, yet display his brave independence within it. The poems that follow in the sonnet sequence all maintain this faith and this discipline.

. . . .

The Slow Pacific Swell

Far out of sight forever stands the sea,
Bounding the land with pale tranquility.
When a small child, I watched it from a hill
At thirty miles or more. The vision still
Lies in the eye, soft blue and far away:
The rain has washed the dust from April day;
Paint-brush and lupine lie against the ground;
The wind above the hill-top has the sound
Of distant water in unbroken sky;
Dark and precise the little steamers ply—
Firm in direction they seem not to stir.
That is illusion. The artificer
Of quiet, distance holds me in a vise
And holds the ocean steady to my eyes.

Once when I rounded Flattery, the sea
Hove its loose weight like sand to tangle me
Upon the washing deck, to crush the hull;
Subsiding, dragged flesh at the bone. The skull

Felt the retreating wash of dreaming hair.
Half drenched in dissolution, I lay bare.
I scarcely pulled myself erect; I came
Slowly, slowly knew myself the same.
That was the ocean. From the ship we saw
Gray whales for miles; the long sweep of jaw,
The blunt head plunging clean above the wave.
And one rose in a tent of sea and gave
A darkening shudder; water fell away;
The whale stood shining, and then sank in spray.

A landsman, I. The sea is but a sound.
I would be near it on a sandy mound.
And hear the steady rushing of the deep
While I lay stinging in the sand with sleep.
I have lived inland long. The land is numb.
It stands beneath the feet, and one may come
Walking securely, till the sea extends
Its limber margin, and precision ends.
By night a chaos of commingling power,
The whole Pacific hovers hour by hour.
The slow Pacific swell stirs on the sand,
Sleeping to sink away, withdrawing land,
Heaving and wrinkled in the moon, and blind;
Or gathers seaward, ebbing out of mind.

The poet-landsman stands in awe before the slow Pacific swell and tries to capture the reality, the omnipotence of this force for good or evil or nothingness. The poem is set in iambic pentameter with slow rhythm to match the seascape's swell; its rise and fall is reiterated in the regularity of the rhymed couplets that never fail to repeat themselves in monotonous pattern as expected. In fact, it is hard to end the poem, once set in motion; and only with the finale of "ebbing out of mind" can it seem to be cut off. This is a *tour de force* in making sound fit sense.

The theme of the poem is a typical Winters search for reality versus illusion. The metaphor of the sea with its rise and fall—its slow swell—becomes the subject of the poem as it connotes the swell of the poet's own mind between these two abstractions. There are three short declarative sentences in the poem, one for every stanza, as though the poet were trying to remind himself once a stanza of his own identity and his own rational mind's awareness of fact: "That is illusion"; "That was the ocean"; and "A landsman, I." These are climaxed with "The sea is but a sound." However, the poem does not end here; it ends as the mind drifts off into the sound many lines later, and the landsman listens to the hypnotic swelling of the sea and literally ebbs "out of mind" with it.

Structurally the poem is as regular as its meter and rhyme scheme; three stanzas of fourteen lines each. The first one describes the sea in the present moment as compared to the narrator's childhood vision of it. The second stanza reveals the sea as brute force, to be fought against physically in the realistic moment of the present. The third projects the future swell as it will remain with him throughout his memory, ebbing out of mind.

"*F*ar out of *s*ight *f*orever *s*tands the *s*ea"; the *f* and *s* sounds set the pattern for the recurrent sound-swell that re-echoes throughout the poem onomatopoetically. Its boundaries are pale, its limits uncertain; hence its attraction. (One is reminded of Robert Frost's "Neither out Far nor In Deep.") The image from childhood is recalled with the haze of the details of an April day long ago (the flowers, the hilltop, the rain, etc., are commingled) when the narrator watched the little steamers plying the ocean, yet seeming to stand still as though painted on a canvas. Their adjectives "dark" and "precise" bring back reality; "firm in direction," they are man's means of coping with the mysterious sea and being a part of it. Yet they *do* move, and the entranced narrator hastens to tell himself so: "That is illusion." Distance is an "artificer of quiet" in "moral" diction—which satisfies not only the metric necessity with its syllables and its accents, but also the appropriate sound-sense combination for the ear's and mind's imagination. The rational mind is still steady; it understands the vise in which the imagination holds it, it accepts its hypnosis and is not resentful so long as it is held steady only to "my *eyes*," not "my *mind*."

The spell is broken by the stanza's end, and the narrator approaches the sea from a new perspective, an experience from the reality of the present sharply etched in his mind. The narrator remembers with frightening clarity the physical details of a sailing accident that left him "tangled upon the washing deck." "The sea *hove* its *loose weight* like *sand* to *tangle* me." The sentence brings with it all the essence of the struggle in the very tone of the diction itself. Here is the theme of the poem evoked in its language: the descriptive elemental power of the sea versus the human determination to remain alive and cognizant. The final description of the human situation is a particularly fine synthesis of physical and mental reactions: "The *skull* / Felt the *retreating wash* of *dreaming hair.*" "Half *drenched* in *dissolution*"—but only *half* drenched! "I came back slowly, slowly knew myself the same." The line's enjambment with the metrical effect of the consciousness moving slowly from word to word, phrase to phrase, shows this master of form at his best. Then finally, "That was the ocean." The flatness of tone quickly returns the meandering senses to reality. The stanza ends with the majestic sight of the whales—their "long *sweep* of jaw," their "*blunt* heads *plunging clean* above the wave" are described in precise diction choice. And the best phrase of all is "in a *tent* of sea." The climax of line and stanza is reached simultaneously with the climax of image. The last line is actually as metrically poised on its caesura as is the whale on its wave. "The whale stood shining, and then sank in spray."

Reality returns in the last stanza; the narrator must reiterate his stance. "A landsman, I. The sea is but a sound." The landsman knows what is wrong with the land: it is "numb," unexciting to the senses. Yet his experience with the sea makes him wonder if this is wrong after all. "It stands beneath the feet, and one may come/ Walking securely. . ." This is indeed reassuring, but only so far . . . "till the sea extends / Its limber margin, and precision ends." It is at this point that the rational landsman must give over, lie down on the "stinging sand" and admit defeat. He will lie "stinging in the sand with sleep" many more times and hear this "*cha*os of *com*m*ing*ling p*ow*er." The words "roll" and "roar" reflect precision of choice of consonant and dipthong for sound quality here. Again "the *who*le Pacific *ho*vers *ho*ur by *hou*r." And as "the *sl*ow Pa*c*ific *s*well *s*tirs on the *s*and," it withdraws a bit of that sand with every tide and a bit of that landsman "*s*leeping to *s*ink away."

The final couplet is a masterpiece of rhythm, image, and idea combined. "Heaving and wrinkled in the moon"—the tide held within its control is yet "blind." The force is unharnessed, primitive, and the landsman is at its mercy. It is as old as its moon-mother; it is as inanimate and "blind." It gathers seaward "ebbing out of mind," and the future for all landsmen's minds looks small indeed as the slow Pacific swells beyond them into a tidal coda of monumental force. Where is the morality of absolutes against this absolute, inexorable in nature? Winters asks the question in most of his poems in one way or another, and he clings to whatever the mind can offer in the way of classical control. The use of abstract words in a descriptive context here combines the sensory vividness with the abstract meaning in such a way that they are not mere decoration or illustration but actual embodiment of the ideas. The "slow pacific swell" thus becomes by extension the threatening force of the subconscious that haunted Winters all of his life. It surges constantly against the constraints of his poetic form and becomes a part of his spiritual and artistic discipline.

Before Disaster

(Winter, 1932–33)

Evening traffic homeward burns
Swift and even on the turns,
Drifting weight in triple rows,
Fixed relation and repose.
This one edges out and by,
Inch by inch with steady eye.
But should error be increased,
Mass and moment are released;
Matter loosens, flooding blind,
Levels drivers to its kind.

Ranks of nations thus descend,
Watchful to a stormy end.
By a moment's calm beguiled,
I have got a wife and child.
Fool and scoundrel guide the State.
Peace is whore to Greed and Hate.
Nowhere may I turn to flee:
Action is security.
Treading change with savage heel,
We must live or die by steel.

This poem represents one of the genres for which Winters is famous: the satire. This does not mean that it is "satirical," but rather in the mode of the true Horatian satire: a short commentary on the state of the world. The world of this poem was the bleak winter of the thirties when the forces of Europe were about to collide, just "before disaster." Winters adopts the form of a short-lined, four-beat regular poem whose very jerky trochaic meter plays a counterpoint of anxiety against the smoothly established rhythmic pattern. The nervous driver—a single individual—feels himself at the mercy of the only security left in the madness, and that is action. He dares not stop in the traffic any more than the nations thus descending dare to stop in their precipitous, certain decline to war.

The poem opens with the first half of the metaphor described: "Evening traffic homeward *burns*, / *Swift* and *even* . . . *drifting weight . . . fixed* relation" . . . etc. These phases are reflected in high irony when the second stanza broadens the original single image into the mass traffic of nations vying for position on the freeways of international politics. "Inch by inch" with steady eye, they avoid the disaster that will assuredly happen if "error is increased" by any one falling out of the deadly rhythm. The combination of the words "mass" and "moment" and "matter" adds the gravity of sound as well as idea; and the eventual horror is contemplated by the narrator caught up in the rhythm of the road. Drivers will be levelled to matter, and human beings will become no more than their basic chemistry.

After the first-stanza focus on the haunted local driver, the poem widens into the second stage of the metaphor, always in the same inevitable rhythmic beat of Fate. The word "thus" rationally holds the stanzas together; but the ranks of men and nations are driven together by some irrational, mechanistic, historical doom. The narrator dares to jerk himself out of the hypnotic reverie to consider his individual position in all this: "By a moment's calm beguiled, I have got a wife and child." His responsibilities seem endless and hopeless to him in a stage where fools and scoundrels rule and where peace is purchased by greed and hate. The poem ends with the stoic conclusion of calm terror as the mass movement continues: "Nowhere may I turn to flee." The only security lies in the madness of precise action. "*Treading* change with *savage heel*" adds to the inexorability of man's failures and the brutishness of his nature. The final line projects the sad finale of contemporary man: "We must live or die by steel."

It could be argued that the poem might well have stopped before these last two lines to let the reader make the final resolution since the metaphors are complete. But Winters would never be satisfied with such an ambiguity. The tone of insensibility and complete futility is heightened as the author summarizes the irrationality of it all. The final couplet holds the poem in its trap of disaster. There is nothing left to say; and the focal line of three words in blatant cryptic brevity is recalled even after the end of the poem:

Action is security.

In a sense that is the end of the poem; the other two lines are overtones and afterthoughts; but they are most certainly Winters' necessity.

The Prince

The prince or statesman who would rise to power
Must rise through shallow trickery, and speak

The tongue of knavery, deceive the hour,
Use the corrupt, and still corrupt the weak.

And he who having power would serve the State,
Must now deceive corruption unto good,
By indirection strengthen love with hate,
Must love mankind with craft and hardihood:

Betray the witless unto wisdom, trick
Disaster to good luck, escape the gaze
Of all the pure at heart, each lunatic
Of innocence, who draws you to his daze:

And this frail balance to immortalize,
Stare publicly from death through marble eyes.

This is a modified sonnet, ending with the emphatic couplet which fixes the fate of all princes of state. The first stanza advises such a prince who would rise to power. The second builds on this achievement and advises one who, having so risen, would now serve the State. He must ironically reverse his direction and "deceive corruption unto good." The third stanza suggests that prince's final test—to be able to escape the gaze of the "lunatics of innocence" and thus preserve the frail balance that will bring him historical fame through death. The narrator's advice is spoken with typical Machiavellian tongue in cheek, yet with the utter sincerity of practicality. He could only wish that the lunatics of innocence and the pure in heart *could* capture the prince in their gaze and dazzle him with their honesty; yet the world does not work that way, and Winters had enough experience to know it and lament it. The poem could have evolved from some of his own frequent brushes with academic or civil power. Whether he was taking the Stanford English Department or the Santa Clara County officials to task is beside the point.

The first stanza lists the necessary steps along the way to power: shallow trickery, knavery, deception, corruption. The second stanza states the qualifications for the politician once he has found his way to office and must live with himself in his present administration. The last stanza projects his future as he approaches his final judgment. The final couplet suggests the necessary price of immortality for this "frail balance." So the sonnet's structure is carefully used to develop theme and subject matter. The choice of image and diction conveys a tone of brutal honesty in its candid advice and a realistic sense of the price to be paid. Yet the Machiavelli behind this prince is also aware that this is really *not* the way to a peaceful eternity; he presents these practical necessities without really believing in them except as they are expedient for a prince's life on earth. He reveals his own sentimental preference for the lunatics of innocence who have obviously influenced *him* with their gaze.

The "frail balance" is reflected over and over in the paired words: "corruption" versus "good"; "love" versus "hate"; "craft" versus "hardihood"; "witless" versus "wisdom." Winters had known this frail balance in his professional life as he had struggled to the top of the literary ladder. He had also experienced it in academic and civil circles. He recognized it as the general tragedy of his age, and many of his poems, like this one, dissect it and lament it. The balance is so "frail" because it is only *one* step between praise for the statesman who uses such corrupt methods for good ends and blame for the one who uses good methods for unfortunate ends. When and how can history really determine the difference? The continuing offenses against the moral order of the century in which Winters happened to live shocked him into poetry.

In this tragic sonnet Winters sees us so deeply bogged in our slough of despond and evil that only some prince of wisdom and good heart could truly extricate us from our fatal drift to self-destruction. Yet how can that prince be saintly and Machiavellian at once? How can he be both political alchemist to transmute baseness to perfection, and chivalric knight to defend us when he must be aware of the base human instincts with which he has to deal? If he *could* be both, he would truly deserve more from immortality than merely public gaze "through marble eyes." The sonnet ends with a dramatic yet stoical couplet that seems to clarify humanistic vision as it laments it. It is an excellent example of Winters' precise use of formal pattern, a highly civilized sonnet balancing terror and tact.

The California Oaks

Spreading and low, unwatered, concentrate
Of years of growth that thickens, not expands,
With leaves like mica and with roots that grate
Upon the deep foundations of these lands,
In your brown shadow, on your heavy loam
Leaves shrinking to the whisper of decay—
What feet have come to roam,
what eyes to stay?
Your motion has o'ertaken what calm hands?

Quick as a sunbean, when a bird divides
The lesser branches, on impassive ground,
Hwui-Shan, the ancient, for a moment glides,
Demure with wisdom, and without a sound;
Brown feet that come to meet him, quick and shy,
Move in the flesh, then, browner, dry to bone;
The brook-like shadows lie
where sun had shone;
Ceaseless, the dead leaves gather, mound on mound.

And where they gather, darkening the glade,
In hose and doublet, and with knotty beard,
Armed with the musket and the pirate's blade,
Stern as the silence by the savage feared,
Drake and his seamen pause to view the hills,
Measure the future with a steady gaze.
But when they go, naught fills
the patient days;
The bay lies empty where the vessels cleared.

The Spaniard, learning caution from the trees,
Building his dwelling from the native clay,
Took native concubines: the blood of these
Calming his blood, he made a longer stay.
Longer, but yet recessive, for the change
Came on his sons and their sons to the end;
For peace may yet derange
and earth may bend
The ambitious mind to an archaic way.

Then the invasion! and the soil was turned,
The hidden waters drained, the valleys dried;
And whether fire or purer sunlight burned,
No matter! one by one the old oaks died.
Died or are dying! The archaic race—
Black oak, live oak, and valley oak—ere long
Must crumble on the place
which they made strong
And in the calm they guarded now abide.

This poem's structure is set in five eight-lined stanzas with a very formal yet very unusual pattern of rhyme scheme: *a b a b c d (c d) b*. The seventh line is always divided, with the identical rhyme in the middle and at the end picking up the immediate rhymes before it; then the eighth line rhymes with the second and fourth in a dramatic finale of sound recapitulated. This is Winters at his most formal, and yet his most "free" in the unique variation that he has allowed himself within the discipline of the set pattern. The seventh line is also broken in the typographical spacing to point this shift from the usual. He maneuvers this with the long iambic pentameter line whose frequent enjambment adds dignity and weight to match his cosmic subject matter.

It is a cosmic theme that was one of Winters' favorites: the relationship of man to nature—his waste of the universe; waste of the natural resources of this planet; and more particularly, waste of his own geographical neighborhood, the coast of California. The poem is hung in the frame of praise for California oaks, but the oaks soon become the metaphoric image for all of the natural loss imposed by creeping civilization. The lament for the old, the archaic, the natural, the peaceful is here: the same lament that runs elegiacally through all of Winters' life and works. Yet the knowledge of passion, of the active, the sensitive, the ambitious, etc., is also here; and the poem develops as the two forces are held in balance of battle.

The first stanza describes these oldest of things, the California oaks: . . . "unwatered, concentrate / Of years of growth that thickens, not expands." The description is precise and minute: "leaves like mica," "roots that grate," "brown shadow," "heavy loam," etc. And yet these factual details are given in a poetic diction that adds an oral dimension in the onomatopoetic chorus of consonants, vowels, and dipthongs to serve the poet's purpose: "mi*c*a," "*g*rate," "thi*ck*ens," "l*oa*m," "*deep*," "*wh*i*sp*er," "r*oo*ts," "de*cay*." The "Ubi Sunt" theme is evoked with the rhetorical questions at the end of the first stanza, and the poem moves to an historical survey of the locale that continues to the poem's end.

Hwui-Shan, the ancient, is identified by Winters in the notes to *The Collected Poems* as "a Chinese Buddhist priest who may have come to California in 499 A.D." According to Winters' source—Charles E. Chapman's *History of California*—the story is found in the Great Chinese Encyclopedia and has long been known to Chinese scholars. Winters delighted in this sort of esoteric knowledge and doubtless took pleasure in tracing the California history back to Oriental influence with its "demure wisdom" and silent classicism. This stanza gives to the oaks all of these qualities as the sophisticated ancient Oriental meets the shy, quick native beneath them on the "impassive ground." The two influences commingle briefly there; then the "brook-like shadows" and the "dead leaves" gather "mound on mound," and time and history march on to another period.

The next stanza concerns the English exploration of Sir Francis Drake in "hose and doublet and with knotty beard." This time the foreigner is not a peaceful, wise philosopher, but rather a military force "armed with musket and the pirate's blade" of civilization. These visitors pause to view the hills, measure the future in a silence that the savage fears, and go away. "The bay lies empty where the vessels cleared," and yet there is the dark omen for an encroaching force to return.

Next came the Spaniard. He had more receptivity to the environment of the oaks than did the other invaders. He "learned caution from the trees," built his house of the native clay, and settled down to become a part of the local scene. The mingled blood of Spaniard and native Indian calmed him, yet it was somehow recessive, Winters observes. At the end of this stanza he allows himself the editorial remark that is really the whole point of the poem; it is spoken in the subjunctive, since Winters has no real conviction that it *will* happen, even though it *may*. ("Peace may yet derange . . . may bend," and therefore change the world. And indeed before peace had a chance, the forces of American evil did sweep down on California in their gold rush.) The exclamatory phrases pick up speed and rhythm and riot as the land is despoiled and the oaks begin to die. "And whether fire or purer sunlight burned, No matter!" Too late now to assess the cause and the blame. ". . . *o*ne b*y* *o*ne th*e* *o*ld *o*aks d*ie*d. / D*ie*d *o*r *a*re d*y*ing!" The long, flat vowel sounds of the monosyllables prolong the agony, but it is inevitable. The old civilizations die with the oaks. Who is to identify the sin and sinner? "No matter!" the poet says ironically. "The archaic race— / Black oak, live oak, and valley oak—ere long / Must crumble on the place which they made strong." In these lines the rhythm is ironically broken with an excellent "metaphysical" effect; the idea is also broken, and the poem becomes not only a physical death knell, but a philosophic one as well. The oaks "crumble" (Winters uses his favorite verb here), and the possibilities of this great landscape crumble with them. Man has again usurped nature beyond his earned limits. As they go down, so will he; but he isn't wise enough to know it yet.

The one frail hope is held in the last lines of the next to the last stanza; it is so placed by the poet because he sees it as a chance missed by fickle history to preserve this hallowed place of hallowed oaks. It "may" come again, but its position in this particular stanza seems to indicate that the poet hardly believes the possibility. The last stanza has already rolled inexorably into the future from the present.

> For peace may yet derange
>
> and earth may bend
>
> The ambitious mind to an archaic way.

This was the prayer of Winters throughout a lifetime of poetry. He acknowledges that it would be "derangement" of the natural impulses; but he would prefer it to the present arrangement of unnatural destruction developing all around him.

Sir Gawain and The Green Knight

Reptilian green the wrinkled throat,
Green as a bough of yew the beard;
He bent his head, and so I smote;
Then for a thought my vision cleared.

The head dropped clean; he rose and walked;
He fixed his fingers in the hair;
The head was unabashed and talked;
I understood what I must dare.

His flesh, cut down, arose and grew.
He bade me wait the season's round,
And then, when he had strength anew,
To meet him on his native ground.

The year declined; and in his keep
I passed in joy a thriving yule;
And whether waking or in sleep,
I lived in riot like a fool.

He beat the woods to bring me meat.
His lady, like a forest vine,
Grew in my arms; the growth was sweet;
And yet what thoughtless force was mine!

By practice and conviction formed,
With ancient stubbornness ingrained,
Although her body clung and swarmed,
My own identity remained.

Her beauty, lithe, unholy, pure,
Took shapes that I had never known;

And had I once been insecure,
Had grafted laurel in my bone.

And then, since I had kept the trust,
Had loved the lady, yet was true,
The knight withheld his giant thrust
And let me go with what I knew.

I left the green bark and the shade,
Where growth was rapid, thick, and still;
I found a road that men had made
And rested on a drying hill.

This poem is written in ballad verse with all the simple disarming effects of the old tale retold by its hero, Sir Gawain. It has all the ballad motifs: the four-line stanza; the skips from action peak to action peak without intervening description or meditation; the witch-lady of beautiful, sensual attraction; the tempting, heroic knight with the "green" mystery; the series of chivalric proofs; the trust and the tryst, etc. And yet the poem becomes much more than the old retelling for Yvor Winters, twentieth century citizen-poet.

He takes this opportunity to use the old legend, well known to medieval literature, and to translate it into a modern and even an autobiographical problem. The translation is never mentioned, but the effect is there. This is a poem in which Winters follows his own precepts of criticism: "to embody sensory experience in poetry rationally or logically constructed to express themes of universal significance." Winters uses the legend of Sir Gawain thus to supply the sensory experience for a rationally constructed poem that will express his favorite theme for *his* life and *his* poetry: the search for self-identity in the battle between reason and sensation. The theme, recurrent throughout the entire body of his poetry, involves the sensitive human being's temptation to immersion in sensation; a detailed description of particulars to the point of near disintegration; and finally the successful recovery to a life of rational order. "I found a road that men had made / And rested on a drying hill." This poem is in a sense the epitome of Winters' own career and life, both as poet, critic, and human being.

It opens with the highly sensory description of the moment of climax; in good ballad form it starts *in medias res.* "Reptilian Green, the wrinkled throat, / Green as a bough of yew the beard"; and all the mystery of the flourishing greenness of the knight is drawn along with the repulsion of wrinkled, reptilian—and therefore attractively evil—

appearance. Sir Gawain reacted entirely through impulse: "He bent his head; and *so* I smote"; then, *after* the action, after the vision, the thought came; and rationality as to its meaning developed.

The second stanza is also full of suggestive sensory detail: the beheaded knight picks up his head by the hair; it speaks to Sir Gawain and lays upon him the quest. It is the essence of evil directing him to temptation; and he takes the tryst to wait the season's round for another meeting. In the third stanza Winters uses exact "moral" diction to summarize the wonderful year between the tests: "The year *declined*"—toward its spiritual climax with inexorable downward sweep. However, "I passed in joy a thriving yule"—with the temporary rising effect of physical epicureanism. "And whether waking or in sleep / I lived in riot like a fool." And Sir Gawain's self-judgment after the fact shows his awareness during the fact. The attraction for the lady is supplemented by the physical hedonism of the knight's provision for love, food and shelter. "His lady, like a forest vine, / Grew in my arms; the growth was sweet; / And yet what thoughtless force was mine!" The simile "like a vine" represents the bewitched Gawain as utterly surrounded, choked, threatened by the fertility of the vine-woman's temptation; yet his once thoughtless force is recalled in his now thoughtful mind as he retells the story in retrospect. He comes to understand that which he had never known before: the power of practice and conviction that saved him again in this second moment of crisis. Winters makes his case for discipline in these lines as he blesses his "ancient stubbornness." Diction in this stanza is again chosen with expert "morality." The stanza is full of abstract language as far as the word "body." As the poet makes the transition from the abstract to the physical, he introduces it with "body" and then almost explodes it into pure physical sensation with "clung" and "swarmed." Her body "clung and swarmed," and his own passion almost overwhelms him. The diction of the passage is perfectly in keeping with the content. The stanza is projected out of its carefully abstract memory of the event into a flashback present of the passion through these two verbs. But the pure of heart and the disciplined of mind—Sir Gawain and Sir Yvor—surmount temptation and return to reason because of this practiced conviction and ancient stubbornness! The everpresent threat continues in its magnificent attraction. Even the threat of *ars-gratia-artis* is there: "her beauty, lithe, unholy, pure / Took shapes that I had never known"; Winters is proud that he did not falter at the brink. "Had I once been insecure. . ." It is difficult to see how the memory of things past which were so completely sensory can be recalled with the sweet calm of reason. How could they be concurrently so strong? But in this poet they were—whether in life or poetry. "Had I once been insecure" . . . he says, recalling his physical passion mixed with his rational control. And so the laurel graft was never made!

The knight let him go "with what I knew." That phrase is the subject of the poem. What he knew after the experience is what he has just recounted: the great threat to reason in the contemporary world of sensory attraction; the necessity for discipline and practice in lonely resistance; and the final purity of heart of those who keep the faith. The poem returns to its narrative end after that small but all-important transition into philosophy. "I left the green bark and the shade"; and by this time, "green," "bark" and "shade" have all taken on the metaphysical quality of the Post-Symbolist *dicta* ". . . Where growth was *rapid, thick*, and *still*." Sir Gawain realizes that evil has a natural, fast, and silent growth in the world of passion and sensory impression; and it is not to be endured for long without submission. Man must return to the world "men had made" and find rest for the next inevitable struggle on a "drying" hill. The high aridity of pure reason is here set against the low swamps of miasmic sensation as the poet's contemporary theme fades back into the pattern of the old medieval allegory.

Time and the Garden

The spring has darkened with activity,
The future gathers in vine, bush, and tree:
Persimmon, walnut, loquat, fig, and grape,
Degrees and kinds of color, taste, and shape.
These will advance in their due series, space
The season like a tranquil dwelling-place.
And yet excitement swells me, vein by vein:
I long to crowd the little garden, gain
Its sweetness in my hand and crush it small
And taste it in a moment, time and all!
These trees, whose slow growth measures off my years,
I would expand to greatness. No one hears,
And I am still retarded in duress!
And this is like that other restlessness
To seize the greatness not yet fairly earned,
One which the tougher poets have discerned—
Gascoigne, Ben Jonson, Greville, Raleigh, Donne,
Poets who wrote great poems, one by one,

And spaced by many years each line an act
Through which few labor, which no men retract.
This passion is the scholar's heritage,
The imposition of a busy age,
The passion to condense from book to book
Unbroken wisdom in a single look,
Though we know well that when this fix the head,
The mind's immortal, but the man is dead.

This is the poem used on the cover of Winters' last book of criticism; *Forms of Discovery*. The editors apparently felt that it was his credo poem, one which would describe him for his public audience. It is an excellent example of his philosophical use of physical image along with rational concept to arrive at some metaphysical truth: in this case, his own literary *raison d'etre*. The theme of the title statement shows the two polarities of the metaphor which he uses: *time* and the *garden*. The poem is shaped with a slow, meditative iambic pentameter rhythm and in the careful discipline of the heroic couplet to add to its precision. Its formal tone is heightened by elevated language and many closed couplets; though with typical skill he does introduce enjambment twice to hurry the tone and increase tension when appropriate. Thus the poem is an excellent synthesis of theme, content, image, diction, and tone.

It opens with the description of the garden: perhaps his own garden at Los Altos, where he had so carefully planned and planted through the years. The opening line presents the sense of fruition about to be completed: "The spring has *darkened* with activity"; and the word "darkened" involves not only ripeness, but also a sense of foreboding and finale. "The *future gathers* in vine, bush and tree." The fruits which he has chosen for it are those of the classical gardens of Greece and Rome: not apples, peaches, and cherries of American orchards—but ancient, esoteric fruits: "persimmon, walnut, loquat, fig, and grape." These are chosen not for their actual crop, but for their aesthetic qualities: "degrees and kinds of color, taste, and shape." With this precision of list the poet alerts the sensitive reader to the fact that there is more in the poem and the garden than mere horticulture. Each of the selected plantings represents a selected set of images to bring the poem—as well as the poet—to fruition.

After the listed statement of the garden's selectivity, the poet adds the next dimension: time. "These will *advance* in their *due series*, *space* / The *season* like a tranquil dwelling place." Time will not be pushed by anything the poet-gardener can do. It is a "due" season that develops the best fruits or poems. The season will be tranquil without the auspices of the human; time must take its course, and he can do nothing to hurry or impede it, no matter how much he may try. "Time" has been added to "garden," and "poem" progresses with equal selectivity and planning. The poet is actually preparing the ground, tilling it, and planting the seed for the reader to garner the final metaphysical crop.

In spite of the tranquil passage on inexorable time, the poet-gardener feels himself filled with the excitement of growth. He has worked over his lessons of discipline, and he would push time, if he could, to poetic fruition in his own growth. Here the rhythm shifts to a faster pace; enjambment pushes the line ends, and the narration breaks from slow declaration to hasty exclamation:

> I long to *c*rowd the li*tt*le garden, *g*ain
> Its sweetness in my han*d* and *c*rus*h* it *s*mall
> And *t*as*te* it in a momen*t*, *t*ime and all!

Fricative consonants rush the lines to the front of the reader's mouth. The artist's frenzy to "taste it in a moment, time and all," results from excited sensory perception demanding sudden fulfillment for his poetic garden, before the slow recollection of tranquility. It is every sensitive man's impatience with his career's frustrations; and it is especially Winters' own repressed effort rising to the surface in irritation. "Crush it small" and savor the essence; throw away the dross and seed; this was his desire throughout all of his critical life; yet he knew the ironic denial of time.

> I would expand to greatness. No one hears,
> And I am still retarded in duress!

This hopeful statement at the beginning of the first line shows his great bravado, his self-confidence. And the cryptic statement at the end of that line shows his realism, his objectivity. The second line records his personal sorrow and agitation. If there were any one line purely characteristic of Yvor Winters' poetry, it is surely this first one with its delicate balance of subjectivity and objectivity.

With the next lines the poet brings the conclusion into focus, and the images and ideas meet in the bridge passage: "And this is like that *other* restlessness / To seize the greatness not yet fairly earned / One which the tougher poets have discerned—." The subsequent list is the roster of Winters' "greats"—poets who made it or not in their historical moment, but poets who were all "great" for their sheer artistry in his eyes: Gascoigne, Ben Jonson, Greville, Raleigh, Donne. Their variety is evidence of Winters' catholic taste; their constant is their disciplined form. The naïve poet learns from his masters the facts of time, of fruition: "Poets who wrote great poems *one* by *one* / And *spaced* by many years, each line an act / Through which few labor, which no men retract." The balance of the rhyme and the phrase here is a fine example of making form fit idea. Winters' statement of the finality of poetry "which no men retract" shows again his total responsibility. The poem belongs to the poet so long as it is growing; once completed, it is irrevocable.

In the next lines the poet turns critic-scholar with his passion to condense, to transmit, to explicate, to paraphrase. "The imposition of a busy age"—is both the poet-scholar's life and death. He *must* wait for time in his garden. He sees the glory of his dream to be the Renaissance man: to know all, tell all, write all, shape all into "unbroken wisdom in a single look"—to be the poet-seer of his age. "Though we know well that when this fix the head, / The mind's immortal, but the man is dead." The vision will consume him; the garden will flourish or die without him after he is gone. It is Winters' last, best hope and dream of passion tempered with rational fact. "*Though we know well*" . . . and the monosyllabic spondees of actuality run through the entire emphatic next to the last line. Its feet are not iambic but heavily spondaic, the voice of Fate itself. It returns to the meditative iambic for the beautiful resolution of the last line. It is a hard line to accept, but a magnificent elegy to this poet whose "garden" took longer than he had to give it, though he nurtured it with a lifetime of care and devotion. Finally, he was himself as heir to the tougher poets of the past striving always against time to grasp "unbroken wisdom in a single look."

A Summer Commentary

When I was young, with sharper sense,
The farthest insect cry I heard
Could stay me; through the trees intense,
I watched the hunter and the bird.

Where is the meaning that I found?
Or was it but a state of mind,
Some old penumbra of the ground,
In which to be but not to find?

Now summer grasses, brown with heat,
Have crowded sweetness through the air;
The very roadside dust is sweet;
Even the unshadowed earth is fair.

The soft voice of the nesting dove,
And the dove in soft erratic flight
Like a rapid hand within the glove,
Caress the silence and the light.

Amid the rubble, the fallen fruit,
Fermenting in its rich decay,
Smears brandy on the trampling boot
And sends it sweeter on its way.

The theme of this poem is sensation; its subject is the exploration of sensory experience, and its meaning is the very quality of feeling. This topic was very important to Winters in the days of his Imagist free-verse, and he explores his interest in this poem with a fine blend of perception, emotion, and reason. The poem asks the question that he asked in "The Brink of Darkness"; and it is posed directly here: "Where is the meaning that I found? Or was it but a state of mind . . . In which to be but not to find?" It is reminiscent of Wallace Stevens' famous line from *The Emperor of Ice Cream*, "Let be be finale of seem." But unlike Stevens, Winters laments the limitation of the state of mind in which being is all; he does not think that he has yet "found" the answer, even with that stark actuality of image; and he is still questioning. Romance versus reality; reaction against action; perception before meditation? These are all suggested as questions which this provocative poem asks of a responsive reader.

The poet recounts the memory of his younger days' experience with sense impression. Youthful "sharper" senses attuned to the "farthest insect cry" were cause to stay him. The intensity of the images—audible, visual, or tactile—was sufficient to interrupt any action. The first stanza is full of sensory immersion which is evoked by the words and lines themselves. The three monosyllabic words that open line three, for instance, check the normal pattern of the iambic tetrameter with spondees to bring the run-on line to its halt at the semicolon. The thought closes; and the reader is jerked to attention at midline: "stay" rather than "stop" seems a voice from the past, not the present. The line resumes with this total sensory immersion of the narrator, now in a state of wonderment at his former nonintellectualized, purely "feeling" level.

The commas around the word "intense" stop him again as he resumes the self-analysis of his earlier sensitivity.

Stanza two opens with the direct question. What did the experience mean then; what does it mean now to the artist? Was it intellectualized meaning at all; has it changed to that now? The narrator muses, assuming that it was. Then the last three lines propose the directly contrary interpretation: "Or was it but a *state* of mind, / Some old *penumbra* of the ground, In which to *be* but *not* to *find*?" Not to find what? Meaning? The mature retrospective mind tries to recapture the original intense image and to analyze it. The "penumbra" image involves in its own meaning some partial shadow of blended dark and light: a proper "moral" choice of diction for the never-never land of the fantasy recreated.

Stanza three contrasts the manner in which the mature poet sees his present reactions as opposed to those of his youth. "Now" there are still sensory images to be recorded, but there is a difference. The "now" acts as a bridge through time, and the "now" mistrusts senses without reason, though indeed they are still tempting. The images now include "brown," "heat," "dust," "crowded sweetness," "unshadowed earth." There is a difference from the clarity of that first original freshness. "Even" and "very" are poised in their lines to add emphasis to the willing suspension of disbelief. Which age was more keen? Which vision more clear? Which more truly "moral"?

Stanza four allows the mature observer to return to his sensory immersion with a pure hedonism that does not even ask for meaning. It is as though he is trying to recapture what he once thought he had: pure aestheticism. Vowels and consonants together sing the sensuous song of perception and are joined by delicate connotation of diction: the unusual trochees of "The *soft voice* of the *nesting dove* / And the *dove* in *soft erratic flight*." The whole effect is nonreasoned, nondirected. Erratic flight of the senses is allowed in an almost feminine softness for its own sake. The mature narrator is testing his senses again, and their attraction is just as strong a "caress" now, as it was years ago. Even the elision of rhythmic syllables helps the rapid "erratic" flight into sense impression in such phrases as "of the" and "like a," where the line almost hypnotizes the reader as his own voice falls into the swift rush of the senses.

The final stanza reverses the effect with strong, masculine consonants, mature ideas, reasoned transitions. All bring the nostalgic narrator and reader back to reality: "rubble," "fallen fruit," "fermenting," "rich decay," "smears brandy," "trampling boot." The image is no longer worthwhile for its purely sensuous aspect; it has found meaning, interpretation, and reason. "Rubble," "fallen fruit," "fermenting decay" all indicate the maturity and the time span between this last stanza and the tentative youthful one. Life has been full of sensuous experiences since then; but the narrator concludes that only as they are transmuted to meaning are they valuable. "In defense of reason," Winters fills the last stanza with logical implication. The question is not answered as directly as it is asked. But the answer is contained in the more mature hedonism which includes a quality of judgment—of "morality" in it. Here is a new meaning for the image: the age old knowledge of death of pleasure and decay in nature. Here is the process of life being carried on in an indirect way by man himself as its unknowing agent. The boot of the strong male is "sent" (not "goes") on its way. The decay is rich, and the boot is sweeter for the experience once the meaning is found. Winters' "commentary" seems to be that this "man" has the possibility of direction if he will both sense *and* think simultaneously.

To a Military Rifle 1942

The times come round again;
The private life is small;
And individual men
Are counted not at all.
Now life is general,
And the bewildered Muse,
Thinking what she has done,
Confronts the daily news.

Blunt emblem, you have won:
With carven stock, unbroke,
With core of steel, with crash
Of mass, and fading smoke;
Your fire leaves little ash;
Your balance on the arm
Points whither you intend;
Your bolt is smooth with charm.
When other concepts end,
This concept, hard and pure,
Shapes every mind therefore.
The time is yours, be sure,
Old Hammerheel of War.

I cannot write your praise
When young men go to die;

Nor yet regret the ways
That ended with this hour.
The hour has come. And I
Who alter nothing, pray
That men, surviving you,
May learn to do and say
The difficult and true,
True shape of death and power.

This is an example of Winters' "occasional" verse, though the occasion is the entire Second World War. From it he selects a single symbol and proceeds to construct his philosophical satire around it. "Old Hammerheel of War" is addressed directly, and the rifle becomes the "blunt emblem" of the poet's lamentation. It is a quiet poem, for all its deadly meaning. The sound and the fury are far away; and the quiet poet muses on the larger nature of things far from the battlefield where Old Hammerheel is in action. It is more a poem of the future than of the present, and it is thoroughly "modern" in its connotations from the year 1942. (It was written ten years later than Winters' prediction in "Before Disaster," and the ranks of nations had now finally collided.) Its regular-irregular rhyme scheme and its direct address are reminiscent of the ode pattern; yet the celebration is ironic. The poet who predicted "Before Disaster" is still confused; he has a cool power to appraise evil, yet what could he have done to ward it off?—"the bewildered Muse, / Thinking what she has done, / Confronts the daily news." The cryptic, slender look of the poem with its short lines adds visually to the sense of fatalism and finality. The poet senses responsibility for the Muse who has not inspired the nations to peace; and now "individual men"—poets *or* soldiers—"Are counted not at all." In the "general" life of war, art seems not to count for much, and poetry has failed.

The second stanza speaks directly to the "blunt emblem." "Blunt" carries both denotation and connotation in its choice of diction; and the physical description of the weapon is developed at both levels: "carven stock unbroke," "core of steel," "crash of mass," "fading smoke" are all detailed as the blunt emblem explodes with its deathly intent. Consonants such as gutteral *c*'s are repeated here to add audible explosion to the lines themselves. One flat sentence of conclusion is all too ironic with its *double entendre*: "Your fire leaves little ash." The duplicity of ironic meaning is carried again through the irony: "Your *balance* on the arm / *Points* whither you intend; Your bolt is smooth with charm." These descriptive compliments to the sleek power of the physical machine are juxtaposed against its lethal purpose, and the stanza ends with a total summation: "When other concepts end, / This concept, hard and pure / Shapes every mind therefore. / *The time / is yours, be sure.*" This is the one "pure" totality of concept. War demands everything and everybody—it is all. "Blunt emblem, you have won. . ."

The structure of the poem depends on a particular philosophical progression from the general to the specific as the poem moves from stanza to stanza: the first, a statement of the present "general" world situation; the second, a physical and psychic description of the specific details of the gun and the war; and finally, the third, a personal apologia and recapitulation by one lonely artist lamenting his place and time. "I cannot write your praise / When young men go to die." How could any artist praise such terror? And yet with a kind of shock technique he adds: "Nor yet regret the way / That ended with this hour." There were necessities that needed to be fulfilled; wrongs to be righted; wars to be fought even now. "The hour has come." And the total terrible present absorbs him for whatever reason. The single artist—wondering if the pen is indeed mightier than the sword—feels his ineptitude. ". . . And I / Who alter nothing, pray / That men, surviving you, / May learn to do and say / The difficult and true." The poet-critic-teacher all speak together here in this final line. Winters-artist feels that his own art contributes little to peaceful solutions of world problems. Winters—critic of the world at large—feels incapable of solving his own personal problem; and Winters-teacher can only regret the brave young men who have gone from his classes to wield Old Hammerheel for power instead of their pens for poetry. His prayer is double for those young writers that they "May learn to do *and* say / The difficult *and* true." The poem ends with another stark direct address to the rifle: "True shape of death and power." The irony of the word "true" concludes the poem on a Platonic note: *its* current reality—its truth—is just that: death and power. This subtlety carries the poem's concept and the motive in the metaphoric image of the rifle; and the two are joined in a metaphysical balance that is Winters' ideal for artistic "morality."

To the Holy Spirit
(from a deserted graveyard in the Salinas Valley)

Immeasurable haze:
The desert valley spreads
Up golden river-beds
As if in other days.

Trees rise and thin away,
And past the trees, the hills,
Pure line and shade of dust,
Bear witness to our wills:
We see them, for we must;
Calm in deceit, they stay.

High noon returns the mind
Upon its local fact:
Dry grass and sand; we find
No vision to distract.
Low in the summer heat,
Naming old graves, are stones
Pushed here and there, the seat
Of nothing, and the bones
Beneath are similar:
Relics of lonely men,
Brutal and aimless, then,
As now, irregular.

These are thy fallen sons,
Thou whom I try to reach.
Thou whom the quick eye shuns,
Thou dost elude my speech.
Yet when I go from sense
And trace thee down in thought,
I meet thee, then, intense,
And know thee as I ought.
But thou art mind alone,
And I, alas, am bound
Pure mind to flesh and bone,
And flesh and bone to ground.

These had no thought: at most
Dark faith and blinding earth.
Where is the trammeled ghost?
Was there another birth?
Only one certainty
Beside thine unfleshed eye,
Beside the spectral tree,
Can I discern: these die.
All of this stir of age,

Though it elude my sense
Into what heritage
I know not, seems to fall,
Quiet beyond recall,
Into irrelevance.

The key line for this highly personal poem is the second line in the third stanza: "Thou whom I try to reach." Winters' search was lifelong for the mystery of the "holy" spirit. He tried through sense and through mind; through prose and through poems. This poem is precisely divided between two sections: the first two stanzas are descriptive and expository, written in a very factual, "prosy," public manner. The second half is written in a highly personal, private, spiritual manner. The shift to the familiar second person language of "thou" and "thy" signals the shift in tone and matter. Again the "Ubi Sunt" echo predominates as the narrator visits the deserted graveyard. It is also the poetic pilgrimage made by all poets in all times; how to find an identity for themselves and those who have gone before? How to seek the Holy Spirit whose fallen sons lie here? How to gain any communion with these long dead and thus transcend this little lifetime on earth? The theme here is again time versus timelessness.

This poem deals with the bare fact, the unapproachable mystery of death. The first two stanzas are charged with double meaning. The poem opens with a wide landscape through an "immeasurable haze." This haze introduces "immeasurable" timelessness; the desert, the valley, the trees thinning away—all give evidence of erosion in space and time. They "bear witness to our wills"—the small wills of man who would control them. "We see them, for we must; / Calm in deceit, they stay." Their deceit is their timelessness. The observer is forced to see them and yet to realize his own timeliness: his own transience. The pathetic fallacy is of no avail for this clear observer who knows himself to be *of* time and nature, yet *out of* them. "They stay"—a clear statement of fact; "we go"—as clear a fact evidenced by the author-narrator's very presence here and now.

The narrator is called back to "local fact" by high noon in the second stanza. He is localized in time and space, made specific: "Dry grass and sand", "no vision to distract." He comforts and fortifies himself—out of the vision back to the fact—with the available data of the here and now. "Old graves, old stones," etc., are something for the mind to think on. And yet the stones and the names are not enough to keep away the haunting spirit. For here is "the seat / Of nothing," and "the bones / Beneath are similar." The word "nothing" begins to ring through the poem at this point and tolls to its end. The irregularity of the stones reflects the irregularity and pointlessness of the lives of the men who lie beneath them. The first half builds to a climax in the grim double reference of the last word "irregular."

The local color ends with the second stanza, and the poem focuses from the general macrocosm to the most personal microcosm, "*These* fallen *sons*" carry over directly to "this fallen *son*" and his immediate problem: how to have a more *regular* life, how to count for more than these lost men, how to find immortality. The narrator-poet cries in his personal anguish of sense versus mind to the elusive Holy Spirit, long sought: "Thou whom the quick eye shuns. . . ." Sight and sound have not found Him: sense was not enough. "Yet when I go from sense/ And trace thee down in thought, / I meet thee then, intense, / And know thee as I ought." Yet how can a Holy *Spirit* be a thing of the mind . . . a *rational* concept? This is the problem that has always worried Winters (as it worried Francis Thompson and William Butler Yeats in *The Hound of Heaven* and *The Second Coming*!). If the two could meet at the level of pure reason, the union could be complete. "But thou art mind alone / And I, alas, am bound / Pure mind to flesh and bone / And flesh and bone to ground." Again the very word "ground" rings the knell of any such dream of union. "Thou—mind alone"; "I—pure mind" *plus* "flesh and bone." The humanity and mortality of all man moans for its potential spirituality and immortality to combine.

The narrator returns in the last stanza to the graveyard. The understanding mind accepts the reasonable, rational locale of the present; the vision is ended. He turns again to the men under the stones. "These had no thought"; and they were fortunate in their lack of cognizance—"at most / Dark faith and blinding earth." The adjectives "dark" and "blinding" are both physical. Added to the abstraction "faith" they make the exact "moral" choice of diction that carries the concept and the image of the poem to a complete totality here. The contemporary poet-narrator can see the old faith only as "dark" and "blinding" in the clear light of his new defense of reason. He asks the fatal question, "Was there another birth?" The agnostic can discern only one certainty. "Thine unfleshed eye" and "the spectral tree" all touch the senses and the spirit: but the mind also observes: "these die." The complexity of thought, sense, and heritage "seems to fall / Quiet beyond recall, / Into irrelevance." And the brave old Winters will not be deluded or tempted into the satiety of any other conclusion, however hungry he may be for it. The graveyard *is* deserted, and so is he. He has not found the Holy Spirit by faith *or* reason.

At the San Francisco Airport

(To my daughter, 1954)

This is the terminal: the light
Gives perfect vision, false and hard;
The metal glitters, deep and bright,
Great planes are waiting in the yard—
They are already in the night.

And you are here beside me, small,
Contained and fragile, and intent
On things that I but half recall-
Yet going whither you are bent.
I am the past, and that is all.

But you and I in part are one:
The frightened brain, the nervous will,
The knowledge of what must be done,
The passion to acquire the skill
To face that which you dare not shun.

The rain of matter upon sense
Destroys me momently. The score:
There comes what will come. The expense
Is what one thought, and something more—
One's being and intelligence.

This is the terminal, the break.
Beyond this point, on lines of air,
You take the way that you must take;
And I remain in light and stare—
In light, and nothing else, awake.

Winters has written many personal poems: "The Marriage," "A Prayer For My Son," "To My Infant Daughter," "For My Father's Grave," etc. This one grows from such a family association and seems to be the most organically "poetic" of any of them. Its subject and its imagery carry its theme: the familiar and heartbreaking nostalgia for the father-daughter relationship. "This is the terminal"—and it is the San Francisco local air terminal that here becomes the Winters' family terminal. The end has come, and the father realizes it as the daughter departs not only his city and his house, but his heart and mind as well. At the beginning, "The light gives perfect vision," and he is still caught, at the end of the poem, stark and bare and alone in that same bright factual light—"in light, and nothing else, awake"—awake in the realization that there can never again be the same relationship.

The light of the airport seems false and hard to him with its synthetic glitter of metal, noise, size, etc. The planes are ready to take her away: "They are already in the night." The contrast of light and darkness runs throughout the elegy. The night of his loneliness and the light of his reason are in constant tension. "And you are here beside me, small / Contained and fragile, and intent / On things that I but half recall." Age has separated their interests; their common ground is maintained only through this one inherited trait that he realizes only too sharply as they approach the departure gate: "*Yet* going whither you are bent." He too has gone his own "bent" direction with the same ferocity; and he admires her for it as he laments it. "I am the past, and that is all." Never one to sentimentalize—at least publicly—he maintains calm for the departure though it hurts and mocks him at the same time. He clings to whatever solace he can find in their common traits; "The frightened brain, the nervous will / The knowledge of what must be done, / The passion to acquire the skill / To face that which you dare not shun." All of these *are* his qualities too, transferred to her through paternal heritage, and he recognizes them and prizes their repetition in her character. His metrical excellence is shown here as the accents are made to fall precisely—"with moral choice"—on the *right* words: "must" and "dare." The iambic tetrameter serves him well, and he is master of it here with real virtuosity and freedom within his discipline.

The next stanza reverts from the inner to the outer world. The "rain of matter upon sense" evokes the sheer noise and confusion and light of the terminal as it beats against the soft privacy of the family moment. It "destroys me"—but only momentarily. The father-poet proceeds rationally to assess the moment for "the score"; and the assessment is stoic and resigned. "There comes what *will* come." Again he is in complete mastery of his accentual meter in the poetic line, just as he is in complete control of himself at the airport gates. He can do his fatal emotional accounting even as the plane approaches: The score versus the expense: ". . . what one thought and something more— / One's being and intelligence." He has given her these; they can never be taken from her, anymore than she took his away from him. These they have shared; and he is willing now to accept the terminal, knowing this Freudian fact.

"This is the terminal, the break / Beyond this point, on lines of air." The "break," the "point," the "lines of air" are all highly symbolic at this stage in the poem as is the terminal itself. And the moment has come: "You take the way that you must take." The spondaic syllables hammer out the reality and the truth of it all. The father remains at the gate, lost again in metrical reverie of self-analysis as the daughter goes off "on lines of air." Yet he remains "in light" and "awake"—even if it is "nothing else."

The poem's metrical pattern is perfectly adjusted to its meaning as the examples cited demonstrate. Enjambed lines and reversed trochees carry out the contradictory will of the father-poet who would send her away, yet hold her back at once. Spondees sound ominously in the father's mind to recall him to reality over and over, and he again reverts to the more graceful iambics for necessary relief. All in all, the "moral" choice of emotional meter for rational motive has been fulfilled. Sensory perceptions battle rational intelligence here for the climax of one of Winters' most touching personal poems. The high priority of what he has given her and what she must take with her is well earned: "One's being and intelligence."

Two Old-Fashioned Songs

(I "Danse Macabre" and II "A Dream Vision")

I Danse Macabre

Who was who and where were they
Scholars all and bound to go
Iambs without heel or toe
Something one would never say
Moving in a certain way

Students with an empty book
Poets neither here nor there
Critics without face or hair
Something had them on the hook
Here was neither king nor rook

This is something some one said
I was wrong and he was right
Indirection in the night
Every second move was dead
Though I came I went instead

The madness of nightmare is here; it is indeed a "danse macabre" with no punctuation and no rational sense; yet there is much that can be recognized from the life and times of Yvor Winters. As such, it is a kind of self-survey, a horrifying yet clear summing up. Coupled with the "Dream Vision" that follows, if seems to assess his past, present, and the future and be the logical conclusion. Winters added these two to his *Collected Poems* on the final pages when it was revised eight years after its original edition.

The muddled identity of his poet-peers and scholarly colleagues comes first to the frenzied mind of the participant in this "danse macabre." It whirls too fast for him to ascertain any definite outlines, and their enigmatic careers are identified only in the dervishlike activity of his literary century. "Who was who and where were they?" These "scholars all" do not know true iambs; they dance peculiarly in an antirhythm "without heel or toe," and there is no more regular order to their art than to the present nightmare in which this poet finds himself. Their verse is: "Something one would never say / Moving in a certain way"; the way Winters chose to move throughout his career. The poem goes wildly on as the dance veers—no punctuation, no transition, no syntax: a lively parody on "the way" of contemporary poetry as this poet had known it. He had sought order, but the rest danced about in their disorder. "Students with an empty book"—none of them taking education as seriously as he took it. "Poets neither here nor there"—none of them creating art with any order to it. "Critics without face or hair"—none of them able to be identified by any distinguishing features. All is mélange, sense impression, old-and-new phantom. Why? "Something had them on the hook / Here was neither king nor rook." There is a fatality to their dance macabre. They seem hung as puppets from a master's hook. Poets, scholars, critics have no direction: "Here was neither king nor rook"—no order, no hierarchy, no rationale. The chess board imagery is used without formality. The game of greatest order is suddenly, in this benighted poetic dance, without rule. There is no defense; and there is no attack. In fact, there is no game.

In chess the players play in turn after long study. Yet "This is something some one said / I was wrong and he was right." This "game" has moved into some historical accident by casual indirection rather than by direction, and "some one" has said that this poet-critic-teacher was wrong. He is a misfit in his own time; this idea haunts his dream-dance. "*In*direction in the *night*" reflects the sense of mystery that seems to surround him here. "Though I came, I went instead" and the poetic chess game does not allow him to progress when he goes-and-comes simultaneously. The stagnation, the terrifying quality of the dance going round and round and never really moving, the last sentence with no punctuation to end it—all of these sense impressions build to the rational *irr*ationality of grotesque confusion. Winters saw his own position at the end of his laborious career finally standing apart from it all. After the "Danse Macabre" of the past and present, he presents his "Dream Vision" of the future:

II Dream Vision

What was all the talk about?
This was something to decide.
It was not that I had died.
Though my plans were new, no doubt,
There was nothing to deride.

I had grown away from youth,
Shedding error where I could;
I was now essential wood,
Concentrating into truth;
What I did was small but good.

Orchard tree beside the road,
Bare to core, but living still!
Moving little was my skill.
I could hear the farting toad
Shifting to observe the kill,

Spotted sparrow, spawn of dung,
Mumbling on a horse's turd,
Bullfinch, wren, or mocking-bird
Screaming with a pointed tongue
Objurgation without word.

The poet here has long since ended the "danse macabre" and settled into some future eternity, into and from which the dream vision comes and goes. He is now "moving little." "All the talk" seems far, far away, and he tries to assess it objectively from this vantage point with its new perspective. Though a "vision," this poem has all the punctuation of rational reality. Winters is careful to end *this* poem with a period!

He still respects his plans that had been new; "There was nothing to deride." He still respects his original stance and his effort: "I had grown away from youth / Shedding error where I could;" And he has great respect for his current concentration in the image of "essential wood." The simple declarative statement comes as a finale in the last line of the second stanza.

The last two stanzas identify his present and future position. He sees himself as essential as the orchard tree, stripped "bare to core," "but living still"! The growth has been painful but essential. He has moved little from his original position; once set, he has held it.

The last seven lines throw a tone of stark realism over the end of the poem. It is a "dream vision," and the images are those from the dark, dim recesses of the primitive mind and body which Winters strove to escape in most of his poetry. It is as though he has decided to let his critics have one last sensual blast from him. They are represented in the debased animal imagery of the "farting toad," the "spotted sparrow," "the spawn of dung, mumbling on a horse's turd." Each "bullfinch, wren or mockingbird" objectifies some individual critic-offender, whose voice is now mere noise as Winters describes him—"Screaming with a pointed tongue / Objurgation without word." Whatever the criticism, it had come from inadequate bestial creatures who had no reasonable effect on this poet-critic "moving little."

It is one of the most bitter poems of the entire Winters canon; yet it represents a fair assessment of his position at the end of his poetic career. It also represents a candid awareness of his contribution to contemporary poetry and criticism. And it establishes for all time the quality of his "essential concentration into truth."

CONCLUSION

“Of Time and the Garden”

Conclusion

According to Winters' five directives in *The Anatomy of Nonsense*, the critic's ultimate task is "the final act of judgment, a *unique* act, the general nature of which can be indicated, but which cannot be communicated precisely since it consists in receiving from the poet *his* final and unique judgment of his matter and in judging that judgment."[3] When that poet is Yvor Winters himself, that final act of judgment is indeed a serious and formidable task—indeed unique! Knowing Winters' scorn for most critics' unstudied opinions and hesitating to bring down his posthumous wrath for less than learned judgments of judgments, one hesitates. However, the image of Winters himself on the occasion of that short midsummer visit a few months before his death keeps recurring. "How do you see me?" was his single and all-encompassing question. It was already too late then for amenities from him; it was too early for final considered judgment from me. But the tragic impending circumstances demanded that interview, and we both knew it. Now years later, the moral choice must be made; the judgment is demanded. Hints all through his life and writings indicate that he expected that it would be made, and he left as many guides and provided more organized assistance than most poets for his future critics: handbooks of criticism, a carefully organized canon of poetry, autobiographical essays to record his development. And last but not least, a characteristically direct, succinct statement in his very last poem, "A Dream Vision," to guide critics for all time lest they falter: "What I did was small but good." It is as though he had finally had the last word for himself.

Still the most naïve critic feels urged to identify, analyze, and assess—even with Mr. Winters' help—the very special addition that he has made to contemporary poetry within this cryptic quantitative and qualitative self-judgment. His poetic practices and his theories coincided; his style and his techniques of verse were—for the most part—meticulously "moral" for both his early experimental and his later traditional poetry;

above all, he took his responsibility for being this "moral" aesthetician with total seriousness. His unique contribution to twentieth century American poetry was his insistence on the artist's particular "morality." He expected it of all good poets; he demanded it of himself. It is the basis of his poetic and critical career—a philosophical *raison d'etre*. For him, the word "moral" had a very special meaning in its artistic context, and it stemmed from his basic humanistic faith. He believed that within quite large limits man is the unique being with choice; therefore the true poet will feel himself obligated to make those "moral" choices which are aesthetically proper for the complete artistic synthesis of the poem at hand. He saw no reason why poetry in a directionless period must be formless. The good poet's faculties will govern his choices within his range in accordance with his beliefs, emotional controls, intelligence, and perceptions. He will control the various technical aspects of poetry by his "moral" judgment, and thus create order out of chaos. It was a stringent judgment that he made for himself as an intelligent and "moral" human artist. He applied it to his own poetry and to that of others whom he criticized. In one passage in *Maule's Curse*, he used the term "human" as a parenthetical expression for "moral." For him it was a total, complete position involving every faculty of the dedicated poet-teacher-critic. It provided him in all of these capacities with an intelligent way of thinking about poetry, and it contained important directives for its creation and criticism.

As such, his small, carefully selected body of poetry represents a certain tragic force in the dissection of this age. He had faced the "brink of darkness" in his personal contemporary chaos, had known the menace of unreason as an invader to be confronted and subdued. In his one short story, the sane narrator remembered with bitter precision every stage of his delusion as he had suffered it, and he had come back to record it with the cool voice of restored reason. So in Winters' life and his poetry he records and accounts for each quiet terror that he faced in the development of his art, his teaching, and his criticism. He strove for clarity and form against critical tides of unreason and unconsciousness. His poetic odyssey ends with the power of unreason recognized and conquered. His personal life and public career ended after he was quite capable of definition and of measuring what had happened to him. His later poetry and his last book of criticism make that quite clear with their self-revelations. He was confident that his Post-Symbolist school would vindicate him in the future. Perhaps it is the case that his erudite efforts as critic somewhat limited his public production as poet, and that his

Collected Poems provides an overselective handbook for his students. But he would have it no other way.

In certain Winters essays and poems the reader senses his affinities for particular wrtiers with whom he felt great personal rapport. These passages help to clarify his own complex position in his twentieth century world. When writing of Hawthorne in *Maule's Curse*, he concludes:

> Only a few scattered individuals, at the end of inordinate labor have achieved the permeation of human experience by a consistent moral understanding, which results in wisdom and in great art. If art is to be measured by the greatness of the difficulties overcome—and the measure is not wholly unreasonable, for there can scarcely be virtue without a comprehension of sin, and the wider and more careful the comprehension the richer the virtue—then few writers are very great indeed. . . . Hawthorne strove to grope his way . . . and his groping was met wherever he moved by the smooth and impassive surface of the intense inane.[4]

Winters' self-analysis throughout his own development indicates that he saw himself the victim of the twentieth century's "intense inane"; certainly he faced his "difficulties to be overcome" with "inordinate labor."

If Hawthorne could represent for Winters his recreated public image, then Herman Melville must have certainly been his private image of himself. It was Melville's portrait that hung in Winters' study; it was Melville about whom he wrote two poems which he allowed to remain in *The Collected Poems.* He found in Melville's writings that symbolism for antithesis which he felt to be one of the great themes of his life and work: the known, the mastered, the rational experience against the half-known, the obscure, the irrational. Plagued as was Melville by the moral problems of the universal limbo, Winters must have read and reread him for hints about the great unknown. He wrote highly involved analyses of Melville's tortured novels in his criticism; and he concluded in one such essay from *Maule's* Curse:

> Man cannot remain simple and static. He cannot merely stay on land or he will perish of imperception, he must venture on the sea without losing his relationship to the land. In brief: the relationship of principle to perception: the problem of judgment. As a helmsman guides his ship: by perception of individual shifting and chaotic phenomena, but by perception trained in principle, in abstraction . . . to find its way amid the chaos of the particular.[5]

To find *his* way amid this chaos was Winters' goal in life and art. In his "Portrait of Melville" he wrote: "Wisdom and wilderness are here at poise . . . / But still I feel the presence of thy will." It is one of the most personal and revealing of all of Winters' poems; and his own battle to arrive at this tensely poised balance lasted all of his life.

He looked about in his own time and found this poise difficult to attain. He did not believe that our civilization was perfect—far from it. Yet the human capability for human individuals to improve it was the most exciting to him of all of its phenomena:

> We do not enjoy a high degree of civilization, and I believe that probably we never shall; the race is not capable of it. The philosophical problem, as I see it, is to define the various possible mysteries, and where choice is possible, to choose those which eliminate the greatest possible number of the remainder; and to keep as scientific, as Aristotelian, an eye as possible upon the conditions of our life as we actually find ourselves forced to live it, so that we may not make the mistake of choosing a mystery, which shall, in proportion as it influences our actions, violate those conditions and lead to disaster.[6]

He spent a lifetime criticizing those writers who he thought made the wrong "moral" choices for their art and so led themselves and others to literary and social disaster. He spent that same lifetime seeking the right "moral" choices for his own art. His ultimate hope was for a Post-Symbolist poetry motive, and feeling would be precisely and delicately balanced as a result of such "moral" choices. He did not believe that many poets found the way to these choices, nor that he always did. He once wrote wistfully of his friend Theodore Roethke: ". . . every poet, I suppose, has the right to his own kinds of failure; at least most poets find them. . . . It requires courage to deal with Platonic abstractions in a season of nominalists triumphant and untrammeled."[7] He too tried to deal with abstractions in a century of specifics and images; and few critics of his poetry understood his method of synthesis. He was willing to leave his work to the future for judgment of success, but he wanted it to be a reasonable, not an emotional judgment.

Present predictions of that success are impressive. Acknowledging his limited poetic production, his controversial critical attitudes, his unfortunate historical coincidence with a literary temper incompatible to his own, one still finds many optimistic indications for an even greater Winters impact on the future than in the present poetic generation. First of all, his criticism is now being studied as an accepted, standard part of the contemporary canon. His poetry is being anthologized by the most reputable publishers in the trade (especially since he was awarded the Bollingen Prize!). Young poets writing in the last half of this century are paying more attention to their own formal disciplines of writing than did those of the first half. They may not be following Winters' own classical metrical patterns, etc., but they are accepting his principle of freedom through variation *within* a discipline, whatever their chosen medium happens to be: syllabic, accentual, etc. They are more interested in the patterned, formal techniques of their craft than were the random free-versifiers of a half century ago; and they seem deadly serious about their right to make their own "moral" choices. Reputable poets and critics are seeing in Winters' poetry and criticism some of the guideposts for the future.

The introduction to the Lohf-Sheehy Bibliography of Yvor Winters, compiled in 1959, states the prognosis:

> In compiling a bibliography of a living author, one presumes a certain permanent value for his work and reputation. Either as poet or critic, or in the dual, and more common role as poet-critic, Yvor Winters promises such permanence. Perhaps because of the classical orientation of both his verse and critical studies, he has long been a controversial figure in modern letters; his critical theories have been the subject of frequent attack; his poetry subject to relative neglect. In presenting this bibliography, we hope to assist critics and scholars in making a complete assessment of Winters' contribution to American letters.[8]

Representative, highly qualified poets and critics have lately stated their unequivocal respect for Winters' contribution in both categories. Donald Justice: "We need him. . . . His volume will become a handbook for more than one poet of the future."[9] David Daiches: "A large number of his poems must be ranked with the finest of their kind to be written by modern American poets; criticism of the future will have to give more attention to the writings of Mr. Winters than it has so far afforded";[10] Howard Nemerov:

> His is the kind of lyric poetry that is relatively timeless and for long periods unaffected by fashion. . . . This ancient and continuing art belongs to life, serves it, and is in the most devoted sense occasional. . . . This lyric strain can be seen as continuous, a heartening connection with a long past which has more to do with much "modern" poetry than it is usually thought to do.[11]

Winters' devoted publisher Alan Swallow, wrote in the *Sequoia* tribute issue (1961):

> In typical fashion, his *Collected Poems* started slowly. But its career almost gives one hope that critical intelligence *does* have effect, that time can right some wrongs. For the volume not only persists; it looms ever larger in the consciousness of all those concerned with important poetry. . . . We shall gradually learn to acclaim the great poet who has long been with us and whom we have neglected.[12]

Behind all the critical controversies concerning his poetry and poetic theories in the present or the future, there remains the vision of the aging, ailing man in his garden: impassive, strong, stony; sure of himself and his convictions; worshipped by his students and certain other poets; ignored by the general lay public; hated by his professional enemies. His last poem suggests his resignation and his quietly bemused retrospection:

> What was all the talk about?
>
> . . . .
>
> moving little was my skill.

Robert Lowell calls this poem "a magnificently defiant and meek confession of his life and practice."[13] Having moved little from his original conception and perception of poetry's potential, this poet had written early in his career: "Perfection in its nature is unchanging; it is desirable, and presumably we labor to come closer to it; and in that labor is the narrative of the spiritual life and its drama, and in the disastrous failure or frustration of the labor is tragedy. But perfection is an unchanging abstract ideal."[14] To its service he literally devoted a lifetime; "tragic" or otherwise—it is too early to decide; but certainly "laborious" in the most spiritual sense of the word.

Two of his colleagues at Stanford pay him the highest tribute as they assess his career. The younger, Don Stanford, praises his combined success in both poetry and criticism:

> According to Sainte-Beuve, the good critic should be able to recognize and evaluate at first glance new poetry by unestablished writers, and according to Baudelaire the best critic is the poet who has, as a result of a spiritual crisis, felt the need to discover the obscure laws underlying the art of poetry. These statements are exactly applicable to the poetry and criticism of Yvor Winters.[15]

The elder, Albert Guerard, estimates the organic totality of Winters' career through his analysis of this poet's significant autobiographical short story:

> For the narrator of 'The Brink of Darkness' is a man who is . . . sane and who is capable of definition. He is capable of measuring what has happened to him.[16]

In Winters' own eyes, this would be success, for such a mature, objective self-analysis is what he sought and prized most highly for himself and other poets.

He knew that the future of poetry—his own and that of others—lay in the young writers of the next generation. He trusted them more than any older critics or scholars, and he was willing to leave his legacy with them. Three whom he had carefully nurtured at Stanford have paid tribute in prose and poetry to his genius. Thom Gunn's poem in *Sequoia* and his remarks at the recent Winters Memorial Reading at the Guggenheim Museum are typical:

To Yvor Winters, 1955
I leave you in your garden

. . . . .

All is relative
For mind as for the sense, we have to live
In a half-world, not ours nor history's,
And learn the false from half-true premises.
But sitting in the dusk—though shapes combine,
Vague mass replacing edge and flickering line,
You keep both Rule and Energy in view.
Much power in each, most in the balanced two:
Ferocity existing in the fence
Built by an exercised intelligence.
Though night is always close, complete negation
Ready to drop on wisdom and emotion,
Night from the air or carnivorous breath,
Still it is right to know the force of death,
And as you do, persistent, touch in will,
Raise from the excellent, the better still.[17]

When Winters' final book came out Gunn reviewed it using one of Winters' own quotations. It was more than praise for the single volume; it is a tribute to an entire life of service to his "goddess of poetry." "The book is an extended definition of what poetry *can* be: 'the finest medium that we have for explanation and understanding of the complete human experience.' "

After Winters' death in 1968, another of his student poets, Wesley

Trimpi, sent to Mrs. Winters an unpublished quatrain which he had written. It was based on a quotation from the early Winters poem entitled "The Bitter Moon." In it the young Winters had vowed his lifelong allegiance and sacrifice to the high tradition of "the living dead" poets who had gone before him: Trimpi, in replying to his dead "Maestro," wrote a moving verse entitled "For the Dead Living":

> To know that someone dead still lives
> Is his bequest: for we the living
> Live by the knowledge of his giving,
> And we, the dead, forget he gives.[18]

Winters' proud preference to be numbered among the "living dead" rather than the "dead living" is thus achieved in the minds and memories and poems of his students. This would doubtless be his greatest satisfaction.

Yvor Winters cannot—indeed, need not—be "placed" in the history of poetry. Granted that he was an enigma in his era, he represents the totality of the classical tradition set down in modern times. He has remained above the storms of contemporary "schools" in his calm, if somewhat haughty tradition of dignified reason and resultant form. His iconoclastic critical views have often seemed prejudiced and at times even savage; his stance, patronizing and pedagogical. But his *poetry* remains clearly serene, refined, and reflective. Near the end of his career, he was asked to join five other eminent poets (Robert Frost, e.e. cummings, Marianne Moore, Archibald MacLeish, and John Crowe Ransom) at the Johns Hopkins University Poetry Seminars of 1962. Each poet was asked to epitomize his poetic theory in prose and to offer one poem that might elucidate it. Winters summarized his theory with a typical metaphoric equation, characteristic of his balanced poetry:

> If it is correct to say that poetry is well-directed motion, then it is also right to add that poetry is motion to and fro. 'The Wind bloweth where it listeth. . .'

It is this balanced motion that seems to summarize his full span of career from earliest Imagist verse to final "Post-Symbolist" poetry. Few contemporary poets have managed such a complete virtuosity in their sequential development. He does not need any special literary category because he has been through *all* categories and brought them to fruition in the historical present of the newly collected *Poetry of Yvor Winters*, 1980. One of the poems from that volume speaks an elegy to one of his friends and colleagues ("To Herbert Dean Merritt") and "forms" an explanation of Winters' own *cause célèbre:* "With cool persistent tact / You form what men would say."

Donald Davie, at the end of his introduction to *The Poetry of Yvor Winters*, remarks: "Winters . . . is not 'dated.' On the contrary, his achievement is, through his style, to have enforced the . . . paradox that the more rootedly particular poems are . . . the more universal their significance."

So he exists simultaneously in the tradition of the best classical poets of the past, in the constant present of his own carefully *Collected Poems*, and in the future of his students' poetry. It would undoubtedly please him to have the last tribute spoken by that student of his whom he called "the most consistently distinguished poet writing in English today . . . whose work in prose and verse alike has been more valuable to me than that of any other writer of our time—J. V. Cunningham."[19] His lines from *The Critiad* identify Winters and defend him against his enemies.

> Yet I will publish still, and if I must
> Share with the great obscurity and dust.
> They left me richer, having kept the trust.
> And if the faint worm try his lips on me,
> Such are the hazards of mortality.[20]

Out of the quiet of that little study in his classical California garden rise the ghosts of those from the past who wrote the lines "through which few labor, which no men retract:" who knew "the passion to condense from book to book / Unbroken wisdom in a single look." It is his own candid and characteristic self-analysis that places him here among those whom he called "the tougher poets," who saw the *right* "moral" choices and made them:

> My faithful reader may as well face bare facts, no matter how painful the experience: namely that I know a great deal about poetry, theoretically, historically, and practically.[21]

Yvor Winters—"poet, professor, critic"—has taught not only a way of writing but a way of living. As Jean Paul Sartre said of Bach: "He taught us how to find originality within an established discipline; actually—how to live." The final "moral" metaphor for him seems to be his own image: dying in the fatal passage "Of Time," yet living in the growing art of "The Garden." It was there that he asked his goddess the last fatal question.

To the Moon

Goddess of poetry,
Maiden of icy stone
With no anatomy,
Between us two alone
Your light falls thin and sure
On all that I propound.

Your service I have found
To be no sinecure;
For I must still inure
My words to what I find,
Though it should leave me blind
Ere I discover how.

What brings me here? Old age.
Here is the written page.
What is your pleasure now?

Notes

Preface and Part One

1. Yvor Winters, *The Brink of Darkness* (Denver: Alan Swallow, [Swallow Pamphlets Number 15]), p. 1.
2. Yvor Winters, *The Function of Criticism* (Denver: Alan Swallow), p. 6.
3. Guy Cardwell, "Review of Forms of Discovery," *Phi Beta Kappa Reporter* 33 (Summer 1968): p. 5.
4. Denis Donoghue, "The Black Ox," *New York Review of Books* 10 (Feb. 29, 1968): p. 23.
5. Howard Nemerov, *Poetry and Fiction* (New Brunswick: Rutgers), p. 252.
6. Allen Tate, "Clarity, Elegance, and Power," *The New Republic* 128 (March 2, 1953): p. 17.
7. Donald Justice, "A Great Master Obscured by History. . . ," *Western Review* 18 (Winter 1954): p. 167.
8. Harriet Monroe, "Youth and the Desert," *Poetry* 18 (September 21, 1921): p. 340.
9. Yvor Winters, *The Early Poems of Yvor Winters* (Denver: Alan Swallow), p. 71.
10. Yvor Winters, "Agnes Lee," *Poetry* 54 (February 1940): 336.
11. Monroe, "Youth and the Desert," p. 340.
12. Yvor Winters, *Forms of Discovery* (Denver: Alan Swallow), p. 330.
13. Winters, *The Early Poems*, p. 15.
14. Yvor Winters, *In Defense of Reason* (Denver: Alan Swallow), p. vii.
15. Yvor Winters, *Poets of the Pacific* (Stanford: Stanford University Press), p. v.
16. Judith Roscoe, "Winters at Stanford," *Sequoia* 6 (Winter 1961): p. 15.
17. Winters, *Forms of Discovery*, p. 347.
18. *Ibid*, p. 344.
19. Winters, *The Function of Criticism*, p. 199.
20. *Ibid.*, p. 13.
21. *Ibid.* p. 27.
22. Winters, *Poets of The Pacific*, p. 11.

23. Winters, he Function of Criticism, p. 22.
24. *Ibid.*, p. 34.
25. *Ibid.*, p. 6.
26. Alan Swallow, "A Publisher's Comment," *Sequoia* 6 (Winter 1961): p. 7.
27. Winters, *Forms of Discovery*, p. 360.
28. Thomas Moser, "Famed Poet, Critic Dies," *San Jose Mercury*, February 26, 1968.
29. Tate, "Clarity, Elegance, and Power," p. 18.
30. Winters, *Forms of Discovery*, p. 359.
31. Alan Swallow, *An Editor's Essays of Two Decades* (Denver: Alan Swallow), p. 204.
32. Winters, *The Function of Criticism*, p. 73.
33. Winters, *Forms of Discovery*, p. 317.
34. Winters, *In Defense of Reason*, p. 225.
35. *Ibid.* p. 229.
36. Yvor Winters, *E. A. Robinson*: Makers of Modern Literature (Norfolk: New Directions), p. 45.
37. Winters, *In Defense of Reason*, p. 562.
38. Winters, *Forms of Discovery*, p. 175.
39. Winters, *In Defense of Reason*, p. 317.
40. Winters, *Forms of Discovery*, p. 346.
41. Winters, *The Function of Criticism*, p. 84.
42. Winters, *Forms of Discovery*, p. 29.
43. Winters, *In Defense of Reason*, p. 153.
44. Edward Honig, "The Mind's Immortal," *Poetry* 65 (October 1944): p. 45.
45. Winters, *Forms of Discovery*, p. 359.
46. *Ibid.*, p. 277.
47. Winters, *In Defense of Reason*, p. 69.
48. Winters, *Twelve Poets of The Pacific*, p. 10.
49. Allen Tate, "Homage to Yvor Winters," *Sequoia* 6 (Winter 1961): p. 5.
50. Winters, *Forms of Discovery*, p. xxi.
51. Donald Justice, "A Great Master Obscured by History," *Western Review* 18 (Winter 1954): p. 169.

Part Two

1. Pearl Andelson, "One Poet Speaks for Himself," *Poetry* 20 (September 1922): p. 342.
2. Winters, *In Defense of Reason*, p. 14.
3. Stanley Edgar Hyman, "Yvor Winters and Evaluation in Criticism," in *The Armed Vision* (New York: Alfred Knoph, 1948) pp. 49–72.
4. Winters, *Forms of Discovery*, p. xxi.
5. Winters, *The Function of Criticism*, p. 27.
6. *Ibid.*, p. 199.
7. Winters, "To the Laodiceans," in *The Function of Criticism*, p. 167.
8. Winters, *The Function of Criticism*, p. 199.
9. Winters, *In Defense of Reason*, p. 10.
10. *Ibid.*, p. 11.
11. *Ibid.*, p. 372.

12. Robert Lowell, "A Tribute to Yvor Winters," *Poetry* 98 (April 1961): p. 41.
13. Tate, "Clarity, Elegance, and Power," p. 18.
14. Winters, *The Function of Criticism*, p. 26.
15. John Crowe Ransom, *The New Criticism* (Norfolk: New Directions), p. 212.
16. Allen Tate, "Homage to Yvor Winters," *Sequoia* 6 (Winter 1961): p. 3.
17. Yvor Winters, "A Cool Master," *Poetry* 19 (February 1922): p. 280.
18. Winters, *Forms of Discovery*, p. 338.
19. *Ibid.*, p. 1.
20. Yvor Winters, "Holiday and Day of Wrath," *Poetry* 26 (April 1925): p. 40.
21. Winters, *In Defense of Reason*, p. 355.
22. *Ibid.*, p. 462.
23. Winters, *Forms of Discovery*, p. 253.
24. Winters, "A Cool Master," p. 16.
25. Winters, *Forms of Discovery*, p. 2.
26. Yvor Winters, "Poetry, Morality, and Criticism," in *The Critique of Humanism* (New York: Brewer and Warren), p. 306.
27. Winters, *In Defense of Reason*, p. 246.
28. Yvor Winters, "The Progress of Hart Crane," *Poetry* 36 (June 1930): p. 164.
29. Yvor Winters, "Three Poets, *Hudson Review* 1 (Autumn 1948): p. 403.
30. Yvor Winters, "The Poetry of Louise Bogan," *New Republic* (October 16, 1929): p. 247.
31. Yvor Winters, *The Poetry of J. V. Cunningham* (Denver: Alan Swallow), p. 39.
32. Winters, "The Poetry of Louise Bogan," p. 248.
33. Winters, "Three Poets," p. 402.
34. Yvor Winters, *The Poetry of W. B. Yeats* (Denver: Alan Swallow), p. 8.
35. Yvor Winters, "Foster Damon's Second Book," *Poetry* 35 (March 1930): p. 341.
36. Winters, *The Poetry of J. V. Cunningham*, p. 5.
37. Winters, *The Function of Criticism*, p. 5.
38. Yvor Winters, "Fugitives; An Anthology of Verse," *Poetry* 32 (May 1928): p. 106.
39. Winters, "Poetry, Morality, and Criticism," p. 310.
40. Winters, *In Defense of Reason*, pp. 365–67.
41. Winters, *The Poetry of J. V. Cunningham*, p. 4.
42. Winters, "The Progress of Hart Crane," p. 155.
43. Winters, "Three Poets," p. 402.
44. Yvor Winters, "The Poetry of Edgar Bowers," *Sewanee Review* 64 (Autumn 1956): p. 660.
45. Winters, *The Function of Criticism*, p. 103.
46. Winters, *Forms of Discovery*, pp. 331–33.
47. Yvor Winters, "A Protest," *American Scholar* 19 (April 1950): p. 229.
48. Winters, *E. A. Robinson*, p. 69.
49. Winters, "To the Laodiceans," p. 169.
50. Winters, *Forms of Discovery*, pp. 2–9.

51. William Barrett, "The Temptations of St. Yvor," *Kenyon Review* 9 (Autumn 1947): p. 547.
52. Stephan Stepanchev, "The Unreasonable Reason," *New Leader* (December 4, 1967).
53. Louise Bogan, "Review of the Giant Weapon," *New Yorker* 20 (July 22, 1944): p. 58.
54. Howard Kaye, "Yvor Winters: 1900–1968", *New Republic* (October 1929): p. 33.
55. Tate, "Homage to Yvor Winters," p. 4.
56. Alan Swallow, "Yvor Winters; A Publisher's Comment," *Sequoia* 6 (Winter 1961): p. 10.
57. Yvor Winters, "Reply with Rejoinder," *Poetry* 63 (February 1944): p. 293.
58. Winters, *In Defense of Reason*, p. 15.
59. Winters, *The Function of Criticism*, p. 27.
60. Winters, *Forms of Discovery*, p. 346.

Part Three

1. Winters, *The Function of Criticism*, p. 22.
2. Tate, "Homage to Yvor Winters," p. 2.
3. David Daiches, "Six Poets," *Yale Review* 42 (Summer 1953): p. 628.
4. Richard Elman, "A Word for Yvor Winters," *Commonweal* 74 (July 14, 1961): p. 402.
5. Rolph Humphries, "Forward with Poems," *Poetry* 45 (February 1935): p. 291.
6. Robert Lowell, "Yvor Winters; A Tribute," *Poetry* 98 (April 1961): p. 43.
7. Alan Swallow, *Yvor Winters: A Special Issue*, *Sequoia* 6 (Winter 1961): p. 10.
8. Richard Ellman, "Review of Early Poems" *Commonweal* 87 (October 20, 1967): p. 87.
9. Winters, *The Function of Criticism*, p. 255.
10. Winters, *Forms of Discovery*, p. 255.
11. Winters, *The Function of Criticism*, p. 58.
12. Lowell, "Yvor Winters; A Tribute," p. 40.
13. Monroe, "Youth and the Desert," p. 339.
14. Yvor Winters, "Merrill Moore's Poetry," oetry 36 (May 1930): p. 105.
15. Winters, *In Defense of Reason*, p. 288.
16. J. V. Cunningham, "The Gyroscope Group," *Bookman* 75 (November 1932): p. 703.
17. Yvor Winters, *The Collected Poems of Yvor Winters*, Introduction by Donald Davie (Athens: Ohio University Press/Swallow Press, 1980 [c. 1978]).
18. Agnes Freer, "A Poet-Philosopher," *Poetry* 32 (April 1928): p. 43.
19. Yvor Winters, "The Poetry of Theodore Roethke," *Kenyon Review* 3 (Autumn 1941): p. 515.
20. Winters, *Poetry, Morality, and Criticism*, p. 303.
21. Winters, *In Defense of Reason*, p. 129.
22. Ransom, "Yvor Winters, The Logical Critic," p. 150.

23. Cunningham, "The Gyroscope Group," p. 192.
24. Yvor Winters, "Mr. Winters' Metrics," *Saturday Review* 7 (Oct. 4, 1930): p. 188.
25. Justice, "A Great Master," p. 161.
26. J. V. Cunningham, "Obscurity and Dust," *Poetry* 40 (June 1932): p. 163.
27. Winters, *The Early Poems*, pp. 13–14.
28. Winters, *The Function of Criticism*, pp. 58–62.
29. Yvor Winters, "The Audible Reading of Poetry," *Hudson Review* 4 (Autumn 1951): p. 433.
30. Winters, "The Poetry of Louise Bogan," p. 348.
31. Winters, *Forms of Discovery*, p. xiii.
32. Winters, *In Defense of Reason*, p. 119.
33. Winters, "Mr. Winters' Metrics," p. 188.
34. Winters, *In Defense of Reason*, pp. 141–49.
35. Lowell, "Yvor Winters, A Tribute," p. 41.
36. Winters, "Poetry, Morality, and Criticism," p. 319.
37. Lowell, "Yvor Winters, A Tribute," p. 31.
38. Keith McKean, *The Moral Measure of Literature* (Denver: Alan Swallow, 1961), p. 109.
39. F. O. Matthiessen, "Four American Poets," in *The Responsibilities of The Critic*, (New York, Oxford Press, 1952), p. 45.
40. Winters, *In Defense of Reason*, p. 64.
41. Babette Deutsch, "Poets and Some Others," *Bookman* 67 (June 1928): p. 441.
42. Tate, "Clarity, Elegance, and Power," p. 17.
43. Yvor Winters, "Carlos Williams' New Book," *Poetry* 20 (June 1922): p. 218.
44. Winters, "Holiday and Day of Wrath," p. 43.
45. Yvor Winters, "The Poetry of Edgar Bowers," *Sewanee Review* 64 (Autumn 1956): p. 660.
46. Winters, "The Progress of Hart Crane," pp. 18–19.
47. John Ciardi, "Review of Winters' *Collected Poems*," *New York Times*, February 15, 1953, p. 241.
48. Winters, *In Defense of Reason*, p. 10.
49. Winters, *Forms of Discovery*, p. 362.
50. Howard Nemerov, "On Shapiro, Roethke, and Winters," p. 305.
51. Yvor Winters, "The Poetry of Robert Bridges," in Zabel, *Literary Opinions in America*, New York, Harper Brothers, p. 238.
52. Yvor Winters in Conrad Aiken, *Yvor Winters: A Reviewer's ABC*, Meridian Books, p. 389.
53. Donoghue, "The Black Ox," p. 23.
54. Kaye, "Yvor Winters: 1900–1968," p. 32.
55. Howard Baker, "Yvor Winters' Stoicism," *New Republic* 70 (May 4, 1932): p. 332.
56. Hayden Carruth, "Write Little; Do It Well," *Poetry* 82 (June 1953): p. 155.
57. Deutsch, "Poets and Some Others," p. 441.
58. Ellman, "A Word for Yvor Winters," p. 403.
59. Edward Honig, "The Mind's Immortal," p. 45.

60. Humphries, "Review of *Collected Poems*," *Nation* 176 (February 1953): p. 89.
61. Martin D. Zabel, "A Poetry of Ideas," Poetry 37 (January 1931): p. 229.
62. Justice, "A Great Master," p. 170.
63. Lowell, "Yvor Winters, A Tribute," p. 40.
64. Tate, "Clarity, Elegance, and Power," p. 18.
65. Kenneth Fields, "The Free Verse of Yvor Winters," *Southern Review* 3 (Summer 1967): p. 772.
66. Winters, *In Defense of Reason*, p. 237.

Part Four and Conclusion

1. Winters, *In Defense of Reason*, p. 372.
2. Fields, "The Free Verse of Yvor Winters," p. 773.
3. Winters, *In Defense of Reason*, pp. 372–73.
4. Winters, *In Defense of Reason*, p. 174.
5. *Ibid.*, p. 229.
6. *Ibid.*, pp. 411–17.
7. Yvor Winters, "The Poems of Theodore Roethke," p. 515.
8. Lohf & Sheehy, *Yvor Winters, A Bibliography* (Denver: Alan Swallow, 1959), preface.
9. Justice, "A Great Master," p. 172.
10. David Daiches, "Six Poets," p. 302.
11. Howard Nemerov, "On Shapiro, Roethke, and Winters," p. 226.
12. Alan Swallow, "Yvor Winters: A Publisher's Comment," *Sequoia*: p. 10.
13. Lowell, "A Tribute to Yvor Winters," p. 44.
14. Winters, *E. A. Robinson*, p. 69.
15. Don Stanford, "The language and the Truth," *Sequoia* 6 (Winter 1961): p. 20.
16. Albert Guerard, "The Brink of Darkness," *Sequoia* 6 (Winter 1961): p. 28.
17. Thom Gunn, "To Yvor Winters," *Sequoia* 6 (Winter 1961): p. 4.
18. Wesley Trimpi, "For the Dead Living," unpublished poem, courtesy of Janet Winters.
19. Winters, "The Poetry of J. V. Cunningham," p. 3.
20. Winters, "The Poetry of J. V. Cunningham," p. 3.
20. Cunningham, "Obscurity and Dust," p. 165.
21. Winters, *Forms of Discovery*, p. 346.

Selected Bibliography

Primary Sources

Winters, Yvor. "Agnes Lee." *Poetry Magazine* 54 (February 1940): 335–38.

______. "The Audible Reading of Poetry." *Hudson Review* 4 (Autumn 1951): 433–47.

______. *The Bare Hills*. Boston: The Four Seas Company, 1927.

______. *The Brink of Darkness*. Denver: Alan Swallow, 1947.

______. "Carol Williams' New Book." *Poetry Magazine* 20 (June 1922): 216–20.

______. *The Collected Poems*. Denver: Alan Swallow, 1952 and 1960.

______. *The Collected Poems of Yvor Winters*. Introduction by Donald Davie. (Athens: Ohio University Press/Swallow Press, 1980 [c. 1978]).

______. "A Cool Master." *Poetry Magazine* 19 (February 1922): pp. 278–88.

______. "A Discovery (F. G. Tuckerman's "The Cricket")." *Hudson Review* 3 (Autumn 1950): pp. 453–58.

______. *The Early Poems of Yvor Winters, 1920–1928*. Denver: Alan Swallow, 1966.

______. *E. A. Robinson; Makers of Modern Literature*. Norfolk, Connecticut: New Directions, 1946.

______. *Forms of Discovery*. Denver: Alan Swallow, 1967.

______. "Foster Damon's Second Book." *Poetry* 35 (March 1930): pp. 340–42.

______. "Four Poems." *Poetry* 51 (March 1938): pp. 320–23.

______. "Fugitives: An Anthology of Verse." *Poetry* 32 (May 1928): pp. 102–107.

______. *The Function of Criticism*. Denver: Alan Swallow, 1957.

———. *The Giant Weapon.* Norfolk, Connecticut: New Directions, 1943.
———. "Hart Crane's *White Buildings.*" *Poetry* 30 (April 1927): pp. 47–51.
———. "Holiday and Day of Wrath." *Poetry* 26 (April 1925): pp. 39–44.
———. *In Defense of Reason.* Denver: Alan Swallow, 1947.
———. *The Magpie's Shadow.* Chicago: Musterbookhouse, 1922.
———. "Mr. Winters' Metrics." *Saturday Review* 7 (October 4, 1930): p. 188.
———. "Merrill Moore's Poems." *Poetry* 36 (May 1930): pp. 104–6.
———. "Mina Loy." *Dial* 80 (June 1926): pp. 496–99.
———. "Monodies." *Poetry* 14 (June 1919): pp. 301–05.
———. "More Santa Clara Justice." *New Republic* 80 (October 10, 1934): pp. 239–41.
———. "Poems of Theodore Roethke." *Kenyon Review* 3 (Autumn 1941): pp. 514–16.
———. "The Poet and the University." *Poetry* 75 (December 1949): pp. 170–78.
———. "Poetry, Morality, and Criticism." in Grattan, C. H., *Critique of Humanism,* New York, Brewer & Warren, 1930.
———. "The Poetry of Charles Churchill." *Poetry* 98 (April 1961): pp. 70–79 and (May 1961) pp. 104–17.
———. "The Poetry of Edgar Bowers." *Sewanee Review* 64 (Autumn 1956): pp. 657–62.
———. *The Poetry of J. V. Cunningham.* Denver: Alan Swallow, Swallow Pamphlets, 11, 1961.
———. "The Progress of Hart Crane." *Poetry* 36 (June 1930): pp. 153–65.
———. "The Poetry of Louise Bogan." *New Republic* 60 (October 16, 1929): pp. 247–48.
———. *The Poetry of W. B. Yeats.* Denver: Alan Swallow, Swallow Pamphlets, no. 10, 1960.
———. *Poets of the Pacific.* Stanford: Stanford University Press, 1949.
Winters, Yvor. "Problems for the Modern Critic of Literature." *Hudson Review* 9 (Autumn 1956): pp. 325–86.
———. "A Protest." *American Scholar* 19 (April 1950): pp. 227–30.
———. "Reply with Rejoinder." *Poetry* 63 (February 1944): pp. 291–93.
———. "Robinson Jeffers: *Dear Judas.*" *Poetry* 35 (February 1930): pp. 279–86.

———. "Streets in the Moon." *Poetry* 29 (February 1927): pp. 278–81.
———. "Three Poems." *Poetry* 69 (December 1946): pp. 138–41.
———. "Three Poets." *Hudson Review* 1 (Autumn 1948): pp. 402–6.
———. *Twelve Poets of the Pacific.* Stanford: Stanford University Press, 1937.
———. *Uncollected Essays and Reviews.* Edited by Francis Murphy. Chicago: Swallow Press, 1973.
———. "Under the Tree." *Poetry* 22 (May 1923): pp. 45–48.
———. "A White Spiritual." *Nation* 185 (October 5, 1957): p. 225.
———. "A Woman with a Hammer." *Poetry* 20 (April 1922): pp. 93–95.

Secondary Sources

Aiken, Conrad. '*Yvor Winters' A Reviewer's A.B.C.*, Meridian Books, pp. 387–89.
Alvarez, A. "The Professional Critic." *New Statesman and Nation* (September 24, 1960): pp. 438–39.
Andelson, "One Poet Speaks for Himself." *Poetry* 20 (September 1922): pp. 342–44.
Baker, Howard. "Yvor Winters' Stoicism." *New Republic* 70 (May 4, 1932): pp. 331–32.
Barrett, William. "The Temptations of St. Yvor." *Kenyon Review* 9 (Autumn 1947): pp. 532–51.
Blackmur, R. P. "A Note on Yvor Winters." *Poetry* 57 (November 1940): pp. 144–52.
Bogan, Louise, "Review of *The Giant Weapon.*" *New Yorker* 20 (July 22, 1944): pp. 57–58.
Cardwell, Guy. "Review of *Forms of Discovery.*" *Phi Beta Kappa Reporter* 33 (Summer 1968): p. 85.
Carruth, Hayden, "Write Little: Do It Well," *Poetry* 82 (June 1953): pp. 151–57.
Ciardi, John. "Review of Winters' *Collected Poems.*" *New York Times*, February 15, 1953, p. 24.
Collins, Seward. "Criticism in America." *Bookman* 72 (October 1930): p. 225.
Cunningham, J. V. "The Gyroscope Group." *Bookman* 75 (November 1932): pp. 703–7.
Cunningham, J. V. "Obscurity and Dust." *Poetry* 40 (June 1932): pp. 163–65.
Daiches, David. "Six Poets." *Yale Review* 42 (Summer 1953): p. 628.

Davis, Robert Graham. "A Reply to Yvor Winters." *American Scholar* 19 (Winter): pp. 49–50.

Deutsch, Babbette. "Poets and Some Others." *Bookman* 67 (June 1928): pp. 441–43.

Donoghue, Charles. "Philosophy versus Literature." *Commonweal* 20 (February 10, 1939): p. 442.

Donoghue, Dennis. "The Black Ox." *New York Review of Books* 10 (February 29, 1968): pp. 22–24.

Ellman, Richard H. "Review of *Early Poems* of Yvor Winters." *Commonweal* 87 (October 20, 1967): pp. 87–90.

Ellman, Richard H. "A Word for Yvor Winters." *Commonweal* 74 (July 14, 1961): pp. 401–403.

Fields, Kenneth. "The Free Verse of Yvor Winters and William Carlos Williams." *Southern Review* 3 (Summer 1967): pp. 764–75.

Fitzell, Lincoln. "The Sword and the Dragon." *South Atlantic Quarterly* 50 (April 1951): pp. 214–32.

Fitzell, Lincoln. "Western Letter." *Sewanee Review* 55 (Summer 1947): pp. 530–535.

Fitzgerald, Robert. "Against the Grain." *Poetry* 50 (June 1937): pp. 173–77.

Flint, F. Cedworth. "A Critique of Experimental Poetry." *Virginia Quarterly Review* 13 (Summer 1937): pp. 453–57.

Fraser, John. "Letter to the Editor." *Times Literary Supplement*, March 14, 1968.

Fraser, John. "Winters' *Summa*," *Southern Review* 5 (Winter 1969): pp. 184–202.

Freer, Agnes Lee. "A Poet-Philosopher." *Poetry* 32 (April 1928): pp. 41–47.

Glicksberg, Charles I. "Yvor Winters: Preliminary Problems" in *American Literary Criticism; 1900–1950*. New York: Hendricks House, 1951, pp. 533–36.

Gregory, Horace. "Of Vitality, Regionalism, and Satire." *Sewanee Review* 52 (Autumn 1944): pp. 572–95.

Gunn, Thom. "This World." *San Francisco Sunday Examiner and Chronicler*, March 17, 1968.

Honig, Edward. "The Mind's Immortal, but the Man Is Dead." *Poetry* 65 (October 1944): pp. 43–46.

Horton, Phillip. "The California Classicism." *Poetry* 51 (October 1937): pp. 48–52.

Hough, Graham. "Review of *Forms of Discovery*." *New Statesman* 75 (January 5, 1968): p. 15.

Howells, Thomas. "Yvor Winters: Anatomist of Nonsense," *Poetry* 63 (November 1943): pp. 86–96.
Humphries, Rolf. "Forward with Poems." *Poetry* 45 (February 1935): pp. 288–91.
Humphries, Rolf. "Review of *Collected Poems." Nation* 176 (February 14, 1953): p. 176.
Hyman, Stanley Edgar. "Yvor Winters and Evaluation in Criticism," in *The Armed Vision.* New York: Alfred Knopf, 1948, pp. 49–72.
Justice, Donald. "A Great Master Obscured by History." *Western Review* 18 (Winter 1954): pp. 167–72.
Kaye, Howard. "Yvor Winters: 1900–1968." *New Republic* 158 (March 2, 1968): pp. 31–33.
Kellams, Dan. "Yvor Winters: Forms and Techniques for Contemporary Poetry." Master's thesis, Cornell College Library, 1958.
Lohf and Sheehy. *Yvor Winters, A Bibliography.* Denver: Alan Swallow, 1959.
Lowell, Robert. "Yvor Winters: A Tribute." *Poetry* 98 (April 1961): pp. 40–43.
Lewis, Janet. "Two Poems." in *Twelve Poets of the Pacific.* Stanford: Gyroscope Press.
McDonald, G. D. "Review of *Collected Poems.*" *Library Journal* 78 (March 15, 1953): p. 525.
McKean, Keith F. *The Moral Measure of Literature.* Denver: Alan Swallow, 1961, pp. 98–134.
McWilliams, Carey. "The Writers of California." *Bookman* 72 (December 1930): pp. 355–56.
Matthiessen, F. O. "Four American Poets, 1944." in *The Responsibilities of the Critic.* New York: Oxford Press, 1952.
Merwin, W. S. "Review of *The Function of Criticism.*" *New York Times*, July 21, 1957, p. 10.
Mizener, Arthur. "The Anatomy of Nonsense in Three Critics." *Sewanee Review* 52 (Autumn 1944): pp. 597–604.
Monroe, Harriet. "Youth and the Desert." *Poetry* 18 (September 21, 1921): pp. 339–43.
Nemerov, Howard. "On Shapiro, Roethke, and Winters" in *Poetry and Fiction: Essays.* New Brunswick, New Jersey: Rutgers, 1963.
Nyren, Dorothy. *A Library of Literary Criticism.* New York: Frederick Unger, 1960, pp. 542–45.
Pritchard, John Paul. "Yvor Winters" in *Criticism in America*, Norman, Oklahoma: University Press, 1936, pp. 261–65.
Ransom, John Crowe. "Yvor Winters, the Logical Critic" in *The New*

Criticism. Norfolk, Connecticut: New Directions, 1941, pp. 211–75.

Roberts, Daniel. "The Discontent of Our Winters." *Sewanee Review* 51 (Autumn 1943): pp. 602–06.

Robinson, Fred C. "Forms of Discovery." *Comparative Literature Studies* 5 (December 1968): pp. 489–92.

Sexton, R. J. *The Complex of Yvor Winters' Criticism.* The Hague: Mouton, 1973.

Stanford, Don. "Review of *The Function of Criticism.*" *Poetry* 91 (March 1958): p. 393.

Stapanchev, Stephen. "The Unreasonable Reason." *New Leader* (December 4 1967).

Swallow, Alan. *An Editor's Essays of Two Decades.* Denver: Alan Swallow, 1962.

Tate, Allen. "Clarity, Elegance, and Power." *New Republic* 53 (March 2, 1953): pp. 17–18.

______. "Review of *The Collected Poems of Yvor Winters.*" *New Republic* 128 (March 2, 1953): pp. 17–18.

______. "Review of *The Early Poems of Yvor Winters.*" *Times Literary Supplement*, February 9, 1967, p. 108.

Thomas, F. P. *Hart Crane and Yvor Winters*, University of California Press, 1978.

"Yeats in Winters' Grip." *London Times Literary Supplement*, 3286 February 18, 1965.

"Yvor Winters, *Forms of Discovery.*" *London Times Literary Supplement*, 3440 February 1, 1968, p. 106.

Yvor Winters: A Special Issue. Sequoia (Winter 1961).

"Yvor Winters," *Who's Who In America*, 1962–63.

Zabel, M.D. *Literary Opinion in America.* New York: Harper and Brothers, 1937, pp. 636–37.

Zabel, M.D. "A Poetry of Ideas." *Poetry* 37 (January 1931): pp. 225–30.